BY ALL
MEANS
NECESSARY

BY ALL
MEANS
NECESSARY

*HOW CHINA'S RESOURCE QUEST IS
CHANGING THE WORLD*

BY

ELIZABETH C. ECONOMY

AND

MICHAEL LEVI

A Council on Foreign Relations Book

OXFORD
UNIVERSITY PRESS

OXFORD
UNIVERSITY PRESS

Oxford University Press is a department of the University of Oxford.
It furthers the University's objective of excellence in research, scholarship,
and education by publishing worldwide.

Oxford   New York
Auckland   Cape Town   Dar es Salaam   Hong Kong   Karachi
Kuala Lumpur   Madrid   Melbourne   Mexico City   Nairobi
New Delhi   Shanghai   Taipei   Toronto

With offices in
Argentina   Austria   Brazil   Chile   Czech Republic   France   Greece
Guatemala   Hungary   Italy   Japan   Poland   Portugal   Singapore
South Korea   Switzerland   Thailand   Turkey   Ukraine   Vietnam

Oxford is a registered trade mark of Oxford University Press
in the UK and certain other countries.

Published in the United States of America by
Oxford University Press
198 Madison Avenue, New York, NY 10016

Library of Congress Cataloging-in-Publication Data
Economy, Elizabeth, 1962–
By all means necessary : how China's resource quest is changing the world / by Elizabeth C. Economy and
Michael Levi.
pages cm
Summary: "In the past thirty years, China has transformed from an impoverished country where peasants
comprised the largest portion of the populace, to an economic power with an expanding middle class and
more megacities than anywhere else on earth. Like every other major power in modern history, China is
looking outward to find the massive quantities of resources needed to maintain its economic expansion; it
is now engaged in a far flung quest around the world for fuel, ores, water, and land for farming. Chinese
traders and investors buy commodities, with consequences for economies, people, and the environment
around the world. Meanwhile the Chinese military aspires to secures sea lanes, and Chinese diplomats
struggle to protect the country's interests abroad. In By All Means Necessary, Elizabeth Economy and
Michael Levi explore the unrivaled expansion of the Chinese economy and what has been required to
sustain this meteoric growth. Clear, authoritative, and provocative, By All Means Necessary is a sweeping
account of where China's pursuit of raw materials may take the country in the coming years and what the
consequences will be—not just for China, but for the whole world"— Provided by publisher.
ISBN 978–0–19–992178–2 (hardback); 978–0–19–022922–1 (paperback)
1. Natural resources—Government policy—China.   2. China—Foreign economic relations.
3. China—Economic conditions—2000-   4. China—Economic policy.
5. National security—China.   I. Levi, Michael A.   II. Title.
HC427.5.E36 2014
333.70951—dc23
2013029331

1 3 5 7 9 8 6 4 2

Printed in the United States of America
on acid-free paper

CONTENTS

PREFACE

THIS IS A WIDE-RANGING book, necessitated by its subject matter: China's resource quest extends from energy to minerals to land to water and is pursued to varying degrees through trade, investment, political maneuvering, and military means. Hence the title *By All Means Necessary*. Despite the broad nature of this book, though, it is not all encompassing. We do not dive into every one of the minerals China pursues or the countries with which it engages; instead we focus on representative examples. In addition, we do not investigate domestic Chinese resource consumption or production unless it directly affects resource availability beyond China's borders. This ultimately leads us, in particular, to exclude a host of domestic Chinese activities that have important global environmental consequences, most notably the burning of coal and its impact on climate change. In contrast, efforts to secure water within Chinese borders (which can affect the flow and availability of water in downstream countries) often fit our definition of a "resource quest" and hence are included.

In researching and writing this book, we relied on intensive use of the existing scholarly and business literature (along with our own analysis of both) and of statistical data. We also conducted research on the ground in many of the countries affected by China's resource quest, including Canada, China, Kenya, Mozambique, Zambia, Kuwait, Qatar, the United Arab Emirates, and Brazil, and we interviewed officials, scholars, and businesspeople from other countries such as Mongolia, Vietnam, and Peru. A book like this is only possible with such a mix of primary and secondary resources, and we are indebted to all those from whose knowledge this book has benefited.

ACKNOWLEDGMENTS

———

WE BENEFITED FROM THE help of many people. We thank Council on Foreign Relations President Richard Haass and Director of Studies James Lindsay for their steady support and for providing us with the time and freedom to research and write this book. We were privileged as well to have colleagues who provided an enjoyable and stimulating place to work. We were also fortunate over the past several years to have the assistance of a very talented set of research associates—Jaeah Lee, Alexandra Mahler-Haug, Jared Mondschein, William Piekos, and Charles Warren—as well as interns, including Amy Burns, Edward Delman, Dagny Dukach, Jeffrey Golladay, Mark Jia, and Sarah McGrath. Without their assistance, this book would not have been possible. We benefited greatly from the advice of Deborah Brautigam, Erica Downs, and Robert Kapp, all of whom took time from their own scholarly research to review particular chapters. Two anonymous reviewers, as well as Richard Haass and James Lindsay, also made excellent suggestions that helped improve the soundness and clarity of our arguments. We are thankful to David McBride for his patience and wisdom in shepherding us through the publication process. We are deeply grateful to the Henry Luce Foundation, Starr Foundation, and Alfred P. Sloan Foundation for providing the financial wherewithal to undertake the research for this book, and to the Starr Foundation and David M. Rubinstein for their generosity to the Council on Foreign Relations in support of the endowed chairs held by Elizabeth Economy and Michael Levi, respectively. Our greatest appreciation goes to our families and significant others for all their support during the long days and nights of research and writing. Liz thanks her husband David Wah and children Alexander, Nicholas, and Eleni; Michael thanks Megan Bradley.

I

Introduction

ON JANUARY 2, 2008, an Omaha-based commodities trader instructed
a colleague in New York to bid $100 for a barrel of Oklahoma oil.
"This is the big one," he declared. It was: the transaction pushed
the price of crude to the $100 mark for the first time.[1] Prices for
resources ranging from natural gas to copper to wheat, traded in
London, Chicago, New York, and beyond, had already set records
in the preceding months and years.

The apparent source of the surge was halfway around the world.
Double-digit Chinese economic growth was driving unprecedented
demand for resources. As Chinese people moved into the middle class,
they consumed more, rapidly outstripping China's own ability to produce the resources needed to fuel its economy. The trend was turbo-
charged in the mid-2000s as China built up cities, industry, power plants,
roads, and railways, boosting demand for everything from steel to coal.

Alarm bells sounded throughout much of the world, as fears grew
that Chinese demand was leading to resource scarcity and ever-higher
commodity prices. With what often appeared to be the full weight
of the Chinese government behind them, Chinese firms seemed to
be scouring the world for resources, striking deals at terms no other
competitor could equal. Resource-rich economies were the beneficiaries of China's wide-ranging trade, aid, and investment deals,
but worries about consequences for the environment and labor, and
about corruption, plagued Chinese investments. Meanwhile, warnings of rising Chinese influence spread well beyond commerce: scholars, pundits, and politicians raised the prospect of resource wars, and

defense planners began to worry that China would seek to control the seas through which the resource trade flowed.

Natural resources have always been a flashpoint between emerging and established powers. Big countries can generate most of the essential elements of national power and prosperity from within their own borders. But even great powers are stuck with the natural resources they have. To be certain, for a time, they can turn to technology and exploration to boost domestic production as demand for resources outstrips their homegrown supply. Eventually, though, emerging powers inexorably turn outward in search of the natural resources they need, with widespread consequences.

This is not a new phenomenon. Ancient Athens disdained international commerce but found itself seeking timber in Macedonia and corn in Egypt. England and Spain built colonies in the New World partly to sate demand for gold, silver, wood, and furs. In the first half of the twentieth century, as European powers fought over Africa and the Middle East, they were driven in part by competition for natural resources that they lacked at home; Japan sought control over much of East Asia at the same time for similar reasons. After World War II, the United States extended its influence over distant resource-producing lands and spent large sums to protect seaborne commerce, in part to assure itself of reliable access to the resources lacking at home.[2]

The Last Time Around

China is thus hardly the first power whose quest for resources promised far-reaching consequences. It is not even the first emerging power to generate alarm in the last fifty years. That distinction belongs to Japan.

In the 1950s and 1960s, as Japan emerged from World War II, the country consistently posted growth rates similar to those seen more recently in China.[3] In the 1960s, Japan also turned heavily to resource-intensive investment to drive economic growth. The consequences were most prominent for oil and iron ore. Between 1965 and 1973, Japanese oil use rose from 1.7 to 5.3 million barrels a day.

(The latter figure was 9 percent of global consumption.) Japanese oil imports accounted for a considerably larger part of the world market than Chinese imports do today. Japan boosted its share of world steel production, the main source of demand for iron ore, from 6 percent in 1960 to 17 percent by 1973, nearly passing the United States, and spurring demand for iron ore imports that greatly exceeded U.S. demand.[4]

Just as rising Chinese commodities consumption in the 2000s coincided with growing popular fears that the world was running out of natural resources, so too did growing Japanese demand collide with worries about "limits to growth" rooted in resource scarcity.[5] Surging Japanese oil demand also appeared to usher in a new world of geopolitics when, in 1973, growing world oil use shifted the balance of power toward the Organization of Petroleum Exporting Countries (OPEC), which used the opportunity to hike prices and inflict economic turmoil on the West.

Rising Japanese resource demand also manifested itself in overseas Japanese investment in resource development, from Australia to Africa.[6] And, as is the case today with China, there was widespread concern about the methods and goals that the Japanese pursued. Among U.S. analysts, much of it could be chalked up to how fundamentally different the Japanese approach was from that of the United States. U.S. resource producers typically operated independently of government and of each other. Americans were inclined to believe in the reliability and inevitability of markets, which they turned to in order to ensure secure supplies. Japan appeared to operate differently. Its island geography and lack of domestic resources meant the country had a longer history of import dependence. The structure of Japanese industry, its relationship with government, and the attitudes of both industry and government toward markets were also different. Industry, through powerful business organizations, worked far more closely with government than U.S. companies did. Government could also direct industry to make moves for national, rather than corporate reasons, as when it required the Japanese conglomerate Mitsui to stay in the Iranian petrochemicals market "long after the firm was eager to withdraw."[7]

Japanese firms entered competition for overseas resources with some of the same controversial trappings that Chinese companies bring today. They availed themselves of government financing at relatively low rates in order to facilitate overseas investment. Starting in 1967, the government-owned Petroleum Development Corporation subsidized overseas exploration and production by Japanese firms. Together with private efforts, this led to a tenfold rise in exploration and production expenditures between 1968 and 1973. In 1973, in the wake of the first oil crisis, corporate Japan came together to create the Japan Cooperation Center on the Middle East, which aimed to facilitate better relationships between Japanese firms and oil-rich Middle Eastern countries. This was followed the next year by a government effort to use diplomacy and government coordination to open doors for Japanese firms; the effort was also boosted by support from the country's Export-Import Bank and Overseas Economic Cooperation Fund. In terms of sheer scale, Japan's oil strategy was remarkably successful, and by 1980, 45 percent of Japanese imports came from resources owned or otherwise controlled (through long-term purchase contracts) by Japanese firms.[8]

The Metal Mining Agency of Japan, created in 1963, matched these efforts when it came to raw metallic ores. In addition to taking ownership stakes abroad, Japanese buyers entered into long-term purchase contracts that could help mine owners obtain financing for development and production. They also organized themselves into consortia in order to leverage their market power in price negotiations with potential suppliers. Japan came to be a dominant player in many critical markets; by the late 1970s, it was the main buyer of iron ore from Australia and India, the top purchaser of Australian copper ore, and a major buyer of Brazilian iron ore.[9] At first, Japanese efforts were, in many ways, less oriented toward "locking up" resources than were the efforts of many Western firms; American firms "were relying heavily on vertical integration for the security of their foreign supplies of bauxite, copper ore, and iron ore."[10] Eventually, as Japanese firms built up capital, this shifted, and the companies increasingly took ownership ("equity") stakes in overseas mines.

Yet for all the portent of change and disruption, three decades later no one would claim that Japan fundamentally altered how global oil and mineral markets function. This is not because the United States and others mobilized a forceful response to the rise of Japan. The latter's economy never became the overwhelming force analysts had anticipated; instead, it stagnated, and as the rest of the world grew, Japan's share declined. At the same time, as resource prices rose and geopolitical worries intensified, consumers cut back and production grew, leading to plunging prices across a range of commodities. Australia did not become a Japanese mine, and not because Canberra blocked Japanese access; instead, other parts of the Australian economy inevitably grew. Meanwhile the United States remained the dominant power in the Middle East, despite the fact that an ever-larger fraction of the region's oil exports was destined for Asia and not for Europe and the United States.

Enter China

The rise of Japan came at a time when China was a tiny player in world markets. The Chinese economy was relatively isolated during the 1960s and 1970s. In the 1980s, as Japan first surged and then sputtered, China's economy began to take off. But it was starting from a long way behind and was able to avoid becoming dependent on foreign natural resources for a time. Ultimately, sustained economic growth through the 1990s and 2000s, which spurred ever-higher demand for natural resources, made isolation impossible. Today Chinese demand for natural resources appears to be changing the world even more so than people once predicted for Japan.

Indeed, many observers have given credit (or assigned blame) to China's quest for natural resources for an extraordinary host of transformations around the world. In this telling, Chinese demand for imported resources is the root of record price rises for everything from oil and ores to wheat and soy, impoverishing consumers and making small resource-endowed countries rich.[11] Chinese investment in overseas resources is transforming the commodities world from one governed mainly by free markets to one in which China locks up reserves and creates its own mercantilist system for trade.[12] Western companies, previously used to competing with each other on commercial terms, now face Chinese state-owned behemoths that secure resource deals by using every lever of the Chinese government—and availing themselves of ultra-cheap loans—to beat the competition, shifting the balance of economic power from free markets to state capitalism in the process.[13] When the Chinese companies arrive, they variously enrich despots, despoil the environment, exploit labor, and intensify corruption.[14]

Meanwhile, China's resource quest appears to color the country's foreign policy too. China seemingly clashes with its coastal neighbors over the oil and gas riches of the South and East China Seas, uses its muscle to divert rivers to the detriment of other countries downstream, and strikes bargains with former Soviet republics and others to its west to secure new supplies of fuel and new routes to transport them.[15] Chinese diplomats skew their votes in the United Nations Security Council (UNSC) on everything from the Iranian nuclear program to the Sudanese civil war, hoping to ensure reliable resource flows and harming international peace and security in the process.[16] And, in the background, the People's Liberation Army Navy (PLAN) steadily builds strength and scouts overseas bases, preparing for a day when it, not the United States, will police the distant lands and narrow sea lanes through which much of China's and the world's critical resources trade flows.

Yet for nearly every contention that China's resource quest is transformational, there is a ready counterpoint on offer. Forces beyond China—scarce supplies, strong demand from other countries, nefarious speculators—are driving resource prices up.[17] (And besides, the prices for many resources aren't that high by historical standards.)[18] Far from locking up global resources and steering the world away from free markets, China is dependent on—and being drawn ever deeper into—the market arrangements that preceded its rise.[19] Chinese companies are no different from Japanese and U.S. companies before them in investing in overseas supplies.[20] Their performance on environment, labor, and corruption, many claim, is entirely within the mainstream, particularly when it is measured against that of firms from other developing countries.[21] And even though local populations often recoil at large Chinese investments, they have similarly hostile reactions to many non-Chinese incursions, including from Western multinationals, massive Middle Eastern sovereign wealth funds, and opaque global investment funds.[22] Indeed, as China gains experience abroad, some contend, it is changing its own initially weak practices to meet high world standards, rather than the other way around.[23]

What about international security? To many eyes, Chinese disagreements with Japan, Vietnam, and other neighbors about resources in the South and East China Seas are much ado about nothing and unlikely to provoke significant conflict.[24] India and others may raise a hue and cry about Beijing's efforts to dam international rivers, but in practice the threat posed by Chinese water diversion schemes is grossly overstated, particularly as China adjusts its plans in the face of downstream concerns.[25] As for supposed Chinese intransigence at the Security Council, as China sees the downside to instability in a world where it depends on resources from around the world, some see it becoming more invested in the tools that the West has used to promote international stability.[26] And despite U.S. worries, the PLAN has not built a single overseas base, and it possesses just one (secondhand) aircraft carrier.[27] China appears to have accepted a world where the United States patrols the seas; if that eventually changes, perhaps the two countries will cooperatively share the burden of sea-lane security, rather than fight over control.[28]

Which vision is right? Is China's quest for energy, minerals, land, and water—pursued through a mix of trade, investment, political, and military means—fundamentally changing the world, whether for good or for ill? Or, as China seeks resources, is the quest in fact changing China, bringing it into the fold of existing international rules, practices, and institutions?

We argue in this book that the truth does not lie cleanly at either pole, or even in some neat place in between. Instead, as we will show by examining the many dimensions of China's resource quest, it is found in a host of places that depend on the aspect of China's resource quest that one is looking at. Pundits, scholars, and policy makers have too often blown China's resource quest and its consequences out of proportion with reality: their warnings of intolerable rises in commodity prices, unprecedented social and environmental damage to countries where China invests, a competitive playing field ever more tilted against Western companies, and inevitable resource-related conflict—perhaps even wars—between China and other powers are not supported by the facts on the ground. Part of this is because China's resource quest occurs against a well-established global economic, political, and security backdrop that has considerable inertia of its own. Much of it, though, is because China is not simply pursuing its resource quest with reckless abandon; instead, it is adjusting its strategy and tactics as it learns from experience, moderating its global impact in the process.

This is not to say that China is not special, or that its quest for resources is entirely benign. Its behavior abroad is often distinctly shaped by long and dense roots at home: Chinese companies bring their domestic practices to the places where they invest, Chinese policy makers bring assumptions about markets forged through decades of domestic experience to their practice of international strategy, and Chinese security planners are spurred by nationalist pressures and domestic bureaucracies as much as by calculations of what will strengthen Chinese resource security abroad. These forces—along with China's sheer size—can create important frictions as China ventures abroad. Moreover, some observers have been too quick to extrapolate modest impacts from past Chinese efforts to secure natural resources into the future, thus blinding themselves to possible challenges down the road. For example, China's military could take on a far more prominent role in resource security in the coming decades than it did in the last two, as China's capability to project force far from its shores grows. Similarly, as the scale of Chinese overseas resource investment rises, its consequences for governance could become substantially larger, too. Still, not all future trends will be more disruptive than those seen thus far: for example, rising Chinese demand for oil is unlikely to lead to anywhere close to the same sorts of staggering price increases over the next decade as it did arguably over the last one.

Despite the fact that alarming claims are frequently unsupported by reality, then, China's resource quest still poses important challenges. Sorting through the varied and rich territory of China's resource quest—the task of this book—is essential to responding intelligently to these challenges, whether as an individual, business, or government. But indiscriminate hype about Chinese activities, far from sounding a useful alarm, only distracts from those problems that are genuinely important. Were all the claims about China's resource quest true, it would be so overwhelming as to be all but impossible to formulate an effective response. And if none of it were true, no response would be necessary. Distinguishing the real consequences of Chinese behavior from the mass of imagined possibilities is thus essential if people and countries around the world are to adapt and respond effectively to China's ever-changing—and sure to continue—quest for natural resources.

2

From Tribute to Treaty Port to Global Trade

THE STORY OF CHINA'S resource quest begins not with China's emergence in the 1980s and 1990s, or even with the founding of modern Communist China in 1949, but rather centuries ago when China was last a global power. Indeed, even as Chinese strategists craft novel paths forward today, many facets of modern Chinese efforts to secure resource supplies have roots in centuries of traditional Chinese statecraft and economic practice.

Chinese emperors during the Ming (1368–1644) and Qing (1644–1911) dynasties and successive Chinese leaders in the twentieth century often looked beyond China's borders to secure resources for their people, yet were ambivalent about relying too greatly on the outside world. Rules and regulations governing resource trade thus changed frequently and sharply depending on the preferences of individual Chinese rulers. In addition, the link between resource shortages (particularly of grain) and social unrest shaped Chinese resource policy, contributing to Chinese rulers' fear of the market and desire to control resource access and allocation. The Chinese resource trade was also tightly bound into a set of broader political and diplomatic understandings and objectives; decisions regarding trade were often driven less by Chinese economic strategy than by China's broader view of the world and its place within it. Finally, the Chinese state traditionally sought to capture significant economic benefits from the resource trade and to prevent local officials and businesspeople from profiting too much. This produced ongoing political battles between the center and periphery, and it contributed to corruption as local officials and businesspeople sought (often together) to seize as much profit as they could.

The Search Beyond China's Borders

Chinese imperial management of the resource trade from the Ming dynasty through the Qing reflected deep ambivalence with regard to China's relations with the world outside. The country's willingness to engage with the outside world and economy—to welcome outsiders in and send those inside out—waxed and waned through the centuries. The benefits of engagement were balanced by a fear that the country could become overly dependent on unreliable foreign partners, as well as a fear that too much foreign knowledge, technology, and integration would undermine the essence of what it meant to be Chinese.

During the Ming dynasty, for example, various emperors adopted radically different approaches to the outside world. Emperor Zhu Di (the Yongle Emperor) gained fame for the seafaring exploits of his eunuch, Admiral Zheng He. Sailing on ships that were among the largest and most sophisticated in the world, Zheng traveled through the South China Sea and the Indian Ocean as far as the Maldives and coastal East Africa, demonstrating the emperor's power and wealth and collecting treasures in the process.[1] Zhu Di's motivations for this outward orientation have been described by China scholar Wang Gungwu as a combination of "treasure hunting, tribute seeking, court rivalries, and personal imperial vanity," but official Ming history states that the emperor was driven by a desire that "none of the ten thousand countries in distant lands should not be his subject."[2] Yet Zhu Di's successors closed the door to such expeditions, banning further explorations and destroying his world-class ships. More restrictions were placed on Chinese merchants, first preventing them from engaging in overseas trade in particular goods, and then banning overseas trade entirely. Trade became acceptable only in the form of tribute.[3] Later Ming rulers argued that the sea "represented problems, not opportunities."[4]

With the fall of the Ming dynasty in 1644 and the ascension to power of the Qing, China once again looked outward to grow its resource base, but it still retained a deep-seated unease over Chinese interaction with foreigners. The Kangxi Emperor, whose reign from 1661 to 1722 made him the longest-reigning emperor in Chinese history, expanded China's resource base by launching military expeditions to the south and west, incorporating Xinjiang, Taiwan, and the Miao territory (in modern-day Guizhou Province). Taiwan, in particular, became an important source of rice and other resources. Chinese settlers moved in to claim large tracts of land for rice cultivation that had been used as aborigines' traditional hunting grounds. Fierce battles ensued in which the Chinese established aborigine battalions, which they designated as "cooked" (tame), and sent them to attack the "raw" (wild) aborigines who refused to submit to imperial authority. The settlers developed rice plantations in the newly acquired territories and exported the rice to shortage-prone areas on the mainland, particularly Fujian, which was only eighty miles from Taiwan.[5]

By the mid-1700s, trade flows between China and Southeast Asian countries included substantial Chinese imports of raw materials and food, particularly rice. China imported rice, wood, and raw materials for medicine from Siam, for example. Silver also became an important import; China's silver mines supplied only one-third of the country's stocks, and the rest was imported from Japan, Mexico, Peru, and India.[6] China was so prosperous during the first half of the Qing dynasty that the American Charles Thomson proposed in 1768 that America look to China as a model of successful development.[7]

Strong Hand of the State

As China's rulers expanded the reach of their resource trade, they also attempted to keep a tight rein on the overall management of those resources, controlling in some cases where merchants and businesspeople traded and invested, the prices they charged, and how resources were distributed.[8] Chinese rulers maintained monopolies (or near monopolies) over valuable resources to ensure not only that any economic activity benefited the state before enriching private players but also that resources were sufficiently available to maintain political stability.

Foreign trade was subjected to a wide array of regulations to ensure that central government coffers were the primary beneficiaries. During the early years of the Ming dynasty, officials financed overseas trade and then took 70 percent of the profit. Eventually, however, they made the state the only legal entity engaged in foreign trade and forbade their citizens from going overseas. By 1394, ordinary Chinese were not permitted to use foreign goods.[9] Despite its best efforts, however, even during this most restrictive period, Ming rulers never fully monopolized the resource trade.

Qing rulers also sought to prevent local officials from gaining too much wealth and power. For example, the Qing set up only four maritime customs offices to handle foreign trade and established steep tariffs on foreign goods.[10] During much of the Qing's reign, local officials managed trade, sharing in the merchants' profit and sending a portion to the emperor as maritime customs revenue.

In all these efforts, the most important resource was grain. Grain shortages, or even just the fear that grain prices might rise, could lead to riots in Chinese cities.[11] To stave off unrest, imperial and local officials issued directives aimed at ensuring adequate grain supplies. Soon after the establishment of the Ming dynasty, Emperor Hongwu declared "Agriculture is the foundation of the nation" and embarked on an effort to achieve economic self-sufficiency.[12] Despite such intentions, as the Ming population expanded from 103 million to 308 million, Ming farmers began growing specialized crops such as silk and thus needed to import rice from surrounding areas to sustain the food supply.[13] Later, when tobacco production began to rise during the Qing, the emperor attempted to limit its development, declaring "Tobacco is not healthy for the people, and because cultivating tobacco requires using rich land, its cultivation is harmful for growing grain."[14]

Despite officials' best efforts, grain shortages persisted. Guangdong, for example, became a "chronic food-deficit region," producing only one-half of the rice needed to meet its people's needs because the farmers there continued to plant more profitable commercial crops such as sugarcane, tobacco, and indigo. As a result, it needed to import the rest from within China and from other regions in Southeast Asia.[15]

As part of its efforts to acquire resources, the Ming also embarked on an aggressive acquisition campaign in the border states of Guangxi and the southwestern part of China. Soldiers and settlers expropriated land from ethnic minorities, and farmers were ordered to relocate to take advantage of newly acquired territory.[16] Although some reports at the time portray a positive picture of ethnic Chinese commerce in the newly acquired regions, historians of the period also decry the Ming farmers and other settlers' "displacing aborigines and local people, ruining upland areas, and reducing forest lands."[17]

The Great Wall Comes Crumbling Down

Throughout history, Chinese rulers have embedded their trade and economic relations in a much larger context of Chinese diplomacy and a sense of their place in the world. China's diplomacy reflected the belief that China, as the Middle Kingdom (*Zhongguo*), would shape the less-civilized world through its interaction. At the same time, rulers controlled interactions with foreigners, a reflection of fear on their part. The movements of the foreign emissaries were highly circumscribed from the moment they arrived. They were not, for example, permitted to travel within the country. Some Chinese rulers, such as those during the Qing dynasty, believed that trade could be used by outside forces to learn about the state of the empire's defenses. Chinese citizens were not permitted to go overseas in a private capacity, except if engaged in the copper trade with Japan, and shortly thereafter not permitted to live overseas.[18]

China's ability to manage its diplomatic and economic relations with the outside world diminished dramatically, though, as a result of the Opium Wars (1839–1842 and 1856–1860). Although estimates vary widely, by the mid-1800s between four and twelve million Chinese were addicted to British-produced opium.[19] The Opium Wars pitted Great Britain, which sought to maintain its lucrative opium trade, against China, which wanted to ban the trade. Opium was devastating to the Chinese people, particularly young men in the coastal regions, and it drained silver from government coffers. The military battles that ensued revealed the weakened state of the Chinese forces and the superiority of the British.

In the wake of military losses, China was forced to sign a series of treaties, which became known in the nation as the "unequal treaties" and led to greater integration with the world economy. The first of them, the 1842 Treaty of Nanking, was signed with Great Britain. It opened additional Chinese ports to foreign trade, ceded Hong Kong to Britain, and granted extra-territorial rights to British citizens in China. China then signed similar treaties in rapid succession with the United States and France. The 1858 Treaty of Tientsin further broke down Qing protection against foreign involvement in China's economy. It gave foreigners the right to travel in the interior provinces of the country, allowed foreign ships access to the Yangtze River, and opened up ten new ports, including Taiwan, to foreign trade. Several trade restrictions, however, remained. For example, the major southern port city of Canton was open for trade only from October to January, and ships sailing to Canton were required to undergo numerous inspections and pay fees and extra tariffs.[20] In addition, all trade items had to be approved a year in advance, and prices of goods were fixed by Chinese merchant guilds, eliminating any room for open competition or bidding.

Just as the Qing grappled with the loss of its monopoly on foreign trade, the empire also gradually lost control of its natural resource monopolies at home as a result of both political and economic forces. As overpopulation spurred a rise in poverty and famine, China became the perfect breeding ground for social unrest. In 1850, a charismatic young man, Hong Xiuquan, claiming he was the younger brother of Jesus Christ, led a rebellion against the Qing and threw southern China into a brutal civil war. At least twenty million died before the Taiping Rebellion was finally quelled in 1864 with the help of foreign forces from England and France.[21] And by 1900, the nativist Boxer Uprising had resulted in the death of more than two hundred foreign diplomats, businessmen, and missionaries in several areas of northern China.[22]

At the same time, China's economy and relationship with the outside world was transformed. Resource-based economies within China, such as that of Taiwan (incorporated into China just a century earlier), became far more profitable. Taiwan transitioned from an agricultural economy that produced primarily rice and sugarcane for the mainland into a commercial agricultural economy, creating new and important sources of production for tea and camphor. By the 1890s, Taiwan boasted two-thirds of the world's camphor supply.[23] Through its forceful acquisition of Taiwan, the Qing thus turned the island from a potential source of costly resource imports into a vital source of export revenue for Peking, which desperately needed money to pay the indemnities resulting from the various unequal treaties. By the start of World War I, ninety-two Chinese cities were formally open to foreign trade, with many hosting foreign banks, manufacturers, insurance firms, and more. Trade flourished as rice from Siam, opium from India, and silver from Mexico poured into the country. At the same time, silk, tea, and porcelain went out.

Yet at its political core China was weak. The emperor's inability to defend Nanjing against the Taiping Rebellion spurred provincial rulers to take a larger role in creating their own infrastructure and weapons industries to aid in the Qing's fight against the rebels. These regional rulers became a new generation of powerful provincial governors with their own militaries, economies, tax systems, and devoted followers. Eventually, this fragmentation contributed to the "Warlord Era" that followed the Qing's downfall in 1911, resulting in a period of disarray and division in China.

After the Emperors

Efforts made by competing political forces to establish a united government in the immediate aftermath of the collapse of the Qing dynasty foundered, and from 1916 to 1927 the country descended into a dark and violent period of competition for control by military warlords. The country was fragmented, with little central government control outside the capital of Beijing.[24] Eventually the

Nationalist Party (Kuomintang, or KMT), which had been established in 1912 but failed to unite the country, joined forces with the newly emergent Chinese Communist Party (CCP) in the 1920s to undermine the warlords and unify the country. But in April 1927, the leader of the Nationalist Party, General Chiang Kai-shek, and his supporters turned on their Communist collaborators, killing as many as twenty thousand and forcing the rest underground.[25]

Chiang Kai-shek established the Republic of China and began to regain control over important government functions such as setting trade tariffs and operating the Maritime Customs Service. The government also reduced the number of foreign concessions in China from thirty-three to nineteen. The war with Japan prompted the government, in 1935, to expand the mission of its defense planning effort through the National Defense Planning Commission to include resource acquisition; it renamed the organization the National Resources Commission (NRC).[26] The NRC's mission was to develop and manage all the nation's basic industries, mines, and other enterprises.[27] Between 1937 and 1944, it grew from twenty-three industrial and mining units and fewer than two thousand staff members to more than one hundred manufacturing, mining, and electrical enterprises and twelve thousand staff members.[28] By 1944, nearly 70 percent of the total capital of public and private enterprises belonged to state-run operations, with three-quarters of the capital going to NRC operations.[29]

The NRC, along with other entities, also began to brainstorm postwar economic strategies to promote industry and state control.[30] In 1946, the NRC released its First Five-Year Program for China's Postwar Economic Reconstruction; it included plans for agriculture and water conservation, and it divided the nation into nine economic regions. But the plan, along with others established during this time, was based on the faulty assumption that postwar China would enjoy peace and significant capital investment from the United States and Japan. It was only partly implemented as a result.[31]

Despite the KMT's efforts to unify the country economically, serious political challenges remained. Rampant corruption within the KMT and the KMT's failure to undertake significant land and other reforms allowed the CCP to broaden its underground base throughout rural China and establish party cells in urban areas. Throughout the late 1930s and early 1940s, the KMT was thus forced to fight a two-front war, against the Chinese Communist Party on the one hand and the Japanese on the other. At the conclusion of World War II, compared to the CCP, the KMT possessed greater military and manpower, as well as the support of the United States. However, its troops were demoralized and riven by corruption; over the course of the following four years, the CCP amassed a string of victories, ultimately resulting in the establishment of the People's Republic of China (PRC) under CCP rule in 1949.

For both the KMT and its successor, the CCP, the postwar experience reinforced not only the value of state planning but also the need for China to rely on itself to develop its basic industrial and economic needs, including a coordinated strategy for oil, steel, electricity, machinery industries, and military arsenals. After the establishment of the People's Republic of China, the economy was tied largely to that of the Soviet Union: the PRC imported 50 percent of its oil from the Soviets and used Soviet coal-processing technology to exploit its own reserves.[32] As relations with the Soviet Union deteriorated in the 1950s, however, Mao Zedong, the first chairman of the CCP, began to extol the virtues of self-reliance or *zili gengsheng*, a policy that had originated within the Communist Party during the revolutionary Yenan period (1935–1947) but claimed deep roots in Imperial China as well.[33]

China also adopted the Soviet strategy of five-year plans to manage economic development with quotas, targets, and timetables for all aspects of the economy, virtually eliminating the role of the market in the process. The first official five-year plan extended from 1953 to 1957 and focused primarily on increasing heavy industry and agricultural yield; in 1957 Beijing launched the Great Leap Forward, which was designed to increase production dramatically by decentralizing industry with the creation of thousands of small-scale industrial operations throughout the countryside and by moving people into large agricultural communes.[34] By 1962, an estimated twenty to forty million people had died from starvation as a result of this ill-designed and poorly executed plan.

Throughout Mao's era, Chinese rulers continued to attempt to promote their political values globally. Mao put China forward as a leader of the nonaligned movement and the developing world more broadly, competing directly with the Soviet Union. In 1954, Premier Zhou Enlai enunciated the Five Principles of Peaceful Coexistence—mutual respect for territorial integrity and sovereignty, nonaggression, noninterference in the internal affairs of others, equality, and mutual benefit—as a means of establishing China's peaceful international intentions. And even though it was desperately poor itself, the nation reached out to the developing world as a provider of assistance. With its 1964 eight principles of foreign aid, China promised to train locals to use any technology the PRC exported, provide high-quality equipment and materials, and ensure that Chinese aid helped countries become self-reliant.[35]

In the middle to late 1960s, however, China transformed its foreign policy, abandoning developing-country regimes that it had formerly supported in favor of abetting national liberation movements in these same countries. China provided military and financial support to revolutionary movements throughout Asia and Africa, in places such as Angola, Indonesia, and Mozambique, with the result that the governments of many of these countries broke off their relations with China.

Nonetheless, trade between China and the developing world overall boomed. Between 1955 and 1965, Sino-African trade increased nearly sevenfold, and China entered into relations with fourteen newly established African states.[36] But the most significant trading partners were in its backyard; throughout the late 1960s and 1970s, trade with Japan, countries in Southeast Asia, and Hong Kong increased on average 25 percent annually. Chinese exports shifted from primary commodities to manufactured goods, and imports were dominated by producer goods, such as petroleum refinery installations, production plants, and—portentously—raw materials.[37]

After the PRC was admitted to the United Nations in 1971—which led to the establishment of official relations with many more countries than before—it began to trade with the United States and more broadly within the global economy. Chinese foreign trade over-all grew at an average annual rate of more than 20 percent; by 1979, Chinese foreign trade had increased nearly ten times over that of 1950, and the gross domestic product (GDP) growth rate had jumped from close to 0 percent to 7 percent annually (although many believe this figure to be exaggerated).[38]

Reform and Opening

Despite the rapid growth in foreign trade through the 1960s and 1970s, it was not until the 1976 death of Mao Zedong and the consolidation of power by Deng Xiaoping in 1978 that China began to transform into a modern economy. The Four Modernizations (agriculture, industry, national defense, and science and technology)—proposed as early as 1963 but never realized—became the development platform for China's leaders to bring the country's economic, military, and technological capabilities up to world standards. To accomplish this economic modernization, Deng adopted a series of reforms, including welcoming foreign investment (capital, technology, and managerial skills) through a system of special economic zones (SEZs) in selected coastal provinces; gradually introducing market forces into the state-run economy by allowing enterprises—once they had met their state-set quotas—to sell their surplus on the market; opening the door to small-scale private entrepreneurs; and dismantling the system of communes in favor of a household responsibility system that allowed farmers to plant their own side crops, primarily fruits and vegetables, and sell their produce on the open market once they had met their government quota. These reforms ushered in more than a quarter-century of double-digit Chinese economic growth.

Yet as we will see, even as these changes transformed China's resource predicament, long-held traditions have continued to influence Chinese resource strategy. The state continues to play a dominant role in guiding resource investment and pricing. And concern over resource security remains a central focus of Chinese decision makers.

3

China Emerges

IN THE 1980S, DENG XIAOPING'S reforms quickly led to rapid economic growth, and with that, surging demand for natural resources. Chinese leaders attempted to boost domestic natural resource production, in order to forestall the need to rely on imports. Their most heroic efforts, which betrayed an intense desire to avoid imports, centered on grain.

Grain security, a core concern of Chinese leaders through the centuries, gained special salience in the mid-1990s with the publication of the American environmentalist Lester Brown's 1994 article "Who Will Feed China?"[1] Chinese leaders were already primed to worry about food prices: many blamed the Tiananmen Square protests in 1989 in part on the rising cost of food the year before.[2] Brown took things a step further, arguing that declining grain production and rising demand for food in China would produce not only soaring grain imports into China but also dramatic increases in the price of food worldwide. Brown's argument appeared to be partly validated when Chinese grain consumption did, in fact, rise steeply. The article ignited a political firestorm in China, underscoring deeply ingrained concerns about the country's ability to feed itself. In early 1995, Xie Zhenhua, then director of the National Environmental Protection Agency, responded. "Who will feed China?" he asked rhetorically. "The Chinese people will feed themselves."[3]

It was not to be. In the years that followed, Chinese food consumption rose steadily, and diets shifted to include more meat, boosting demand not just for foodstuffs but also for animal feed. In response, the Chinese government issued White Papers, adjusted regulations, and pushed new technology onto farmers. It even succeeded in avoiding large-scale grain imports. But China was increasingly trapped in a zero-sum game: as it steered land toward grain, it was forced to cut back on other basic food production. The inevitable result was increasing reliance on imported food and feed.

Agriculture was far from an isolated case: for resource after resource, Chinese consumption boomed, and imports rose. Between 1980 and 2010, oil and coal consumption both doubled roughly every dozen years.[4] Natural gas use took longer to accelerate, but between 1995 and 2010 it doubled roughly every five years.[5] From 2000 to 2010, copper use more than tripled; steel production quintupled, driving demand for its main ingredient, iron ore; and aluminum production rose even more rapidly, spurring surging demand for bauxite and alumina (the raw and semiprocessed materials, respectively, from which aluminum is made) in the process.[6] Meanwhile, between 1980 and 2010, electricity use doubled roughly every eight years, with hydroelectricity and coal both contributing strongly.

In the face of growing demand for resources, Chinese leaders attempted to boost domestic resource production across the board. It quickly became clear, though, that this would be insufficient to meet domestic demand. The old China might have put self-sufficiency ahead of growth and avoided imports even to the detriment of domestic economic development. But the surge in economic growth was itself the product of an increasingly liberal and open approach to economic management. Chinese leaders were pragmatic. In its 2003 White Paper on mineral resources (the leadership often uses White Papers to set and communicate major policy thrusts), Beijing claimed that "China will depend mainly on the exploitation of its own mineral resources to guarantee the needs of its modernization program." But it had to admit this wasn't enough: "At the same time," the White Paper declared, "it is an important government policy to...make use of foreign

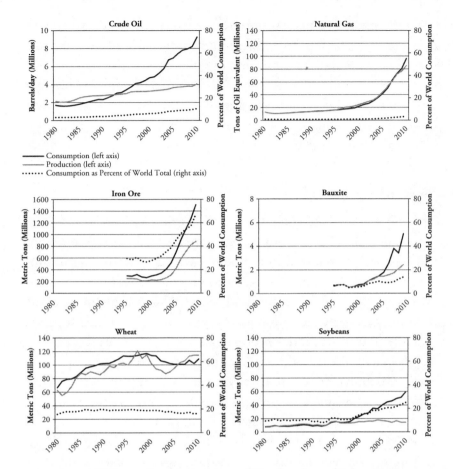

FIGURE 3.1 Chinese Consumption and Production of Select Resources.
Sources: U.S Geological Survey, "Iron Ore," Mineral Commodities Summaries (1996–2011). Annual Publication; BP, BP Statistical Review of World Energy June 2012 (London: BP, 2012); U.S. Department of Agriculture, "Production, Supply, and Distribution Online," Foreign Agriculture Service. Accessible at http://www.fas. usda.gov/psdonline/psdHome.aspx. Accessed August 2012; World Steel Association data (accessed August 8, 2013 via Bloomberg); World Bureau of Metal Statistics data (accessed August 8, 2013 via Bloomberg); China General Administration of Customs data (accessed August 8, 2013 via Bloomberg); authors calculations. Data series for iron ore and bauxite are truncated at 1995 due to lack of reliable data.

markets and foreign mineral resources."[7] The Chinese leadership was blunt: "There is a fairly large gap between the supply and demand in oil, high-grade iron, high-grade copper, fine-quality bauxite.... We shall open still wider to the outside world."[8]

China became a net oil importer in 1993 and a net natural gas importer in 2007.[9] It moved from depending on iron ore imports for only 3 percent of consumption in 1981 to more than half by 2003, while similar trends prevailed for other mineral resources.[10] Beijing ultimately had no choice—and neither did the rest of the world. China is a central part of global markets for a host of resources, and its impacts are being widely felt.

Pumping Up Prices

The most immediate consequence of growing Chinese demand for natural resources has been rising prices for a host of critical commodities. The widely followed Commodity Research Bureau (CRB) Index comprises nineteen publicly traded commodities, including oil, natural gas, copper, nickel, sugar, and wheat, and is a useful, if crude, indicator of worldwide commodity prices. Between January 30, 2002, and July 2, 2008, the index nearly quadrupled.[11] Crude oil prices rose eightfold over the period.[12] Copper prices began their steep ascent in 2003 and ultimately rose to twenty times their original level.[13] Wheat prices stayed relatively steady through 2007, but by the middle of 2008 they too had risen by a factor of four or more.[14]

Many people quickly pointed to China as the culprit behind these and other commodity price increases. Resource demand in developed countries had been relatively stagnant. Emerging economies such as India and Brazil still consumed too few natural resources to make such a big impact on world markets. Chinese demand—first for energy, then for minerals, and finally for food—was thus a natural place to turn for an explanation. By 2010, China accounted for 38 percent of global copper demand, 42 percent of aluminum use, and similar fractions of world consumption for other metals.[15] It also consumed 23 percent of world soybeans along with more than 10 percent of world oil.[16] Observers projected the trends into the future and warned of ever-rising resource prices for years to come.[17]

But assigning blame to China for high and rising prices requires more than merely observing that Chinese demand and world prices rose at the same time. High and growing demand does not automatically imply high prices; world oil prices, for example, were lower in

1970 than at any time in the preceding hundred years, despite the emergence in the interim of the automobile and oil-powered industry and a resulting explosion of oil demand.[18] High prices require a second critical factor: supplies must be so scarce that prices end up rising strongly in order to boost production and curb consumption until supply matches demand. Moreover, prices are affected by a host of factors other than how much a single consumer uses, including broader economic growth, technology, and resource availability, any of which can in principle overwhelm changes attributable to China. As a result, not all natural resources have been (or will be) affected in the same way by rising Chinese demand. Understanding how various resource prices respond can give a valuable clue as to how China might affect resource prices in the future.

Energy Explodes

Start with oil. At the turn of the twenty-first century, most forecasters predicted inexpensive oil for decades to come.[19] A barrel of crude would cost $20, perhaps $30 in the extreme. Few foresaw the rise to nearly $150 a barrel that ultimately occurred, and many pointed to Chinese growth as the cause of the higher prices that materialized over the course of the 2000s.

Indeed, Chinese demand for oil has grown faster than many expected. But the discrepancy is not nearly as large as most assume, and it alone is not enough to explain what happened to prices. In particular, if oil markets had worked the way most analysts assumed they did fifteen years ago, they would have accommodated the Chinese rise. Then, the dominant assumption was that big oil producers in the Middle East (perhaps along with other members of OPEC) would expand production to accommodate growing world demand without allowing prices to rise much. This would have kept prices from rising strongly even with surging Chinese demand.

But OPEC countries didn't react this way to the emergence of China. World oil production didn't jump; instead, it was actually far smaller by 2010 than most had projected a decade before. It is the combination of greater Chinese demand and smaller-than-expected world supplies that explains why prices have risen so much.

But this isn't the end of the puzzle: why did supplies fall short? Some experts contend that the shortfall was due to strong limits on how much affordable oil lies underground. But that is a minority position; most experts believe world oil resources remain vast.[20] Instead the low amount of oil production is usually chalked up to decisions by oil producers (and occasionally to wars) that put oil off-limits or otherwise deter developers from producing it.

Indeed, it turns out there is good reason to conclude that Chinese growth helped spur many oil producers to hold supplies back. Many governments put development of their natural resources in the hands of state-owned companies or otherwise control them tightly. Many of these companies aim to meet set revenue targets rather than maximize profits. Thus they have little incentive to expand production in the face of rising prices. Indeed, since higher prices can allow them to meet their goals even with less production, high prices can actually prompt them to curb production, or at least reduce incentives to boost output, leading prices to climb.[21]

What does this have to do with China? These dynamics require a spark, something that initially pushes prices higher and begins the cycle of production restraints and higher prices that result. Strong (and to some extent unanticipated) Chinese demand does the job. More important, absent strong growth in world oil demand, stagnant production from state-controlled oil producers would have led to declining oil prices and falling revenues, creating incentives for those producers to expand. Rapidly rising Chinese demand allowed oil producers to grow their revenues without increasing their production. The side effect was higher prices for everyone.

This dynamic helps explain what happened over the past decade. It is also likely to prevail for the foreseeable future, so long as China continues to demand more imported oil. As its demand continues to rise, many state oil producers will find themselves with little incentive to boost supplies, allowing prices to remain high. Absent a significant downshift in oil demand—a possibility we will return to later—the only way out is if oil production elsewhere in the world comes on strong, squeezing state-owned oil producers' profits and encouraging them to pump more. Indeed, in recent years oil production in the United States and Canada has surged, leading some to speculate that high prices may soon come to an end.[22] Those production gains may help moderate the high prices brought on in part by Chinese growth. But they are subject to two important limits. Chinese oil demand growth will continue to be high, and it will be difficult for gains in U.S. oil output (and production from other free-market economies where U.S. technology is employed) to meet it fully. Moreover, oil prices must be relatively high in order for strong U.S. oil supply growth to be profitable, which rules out low prices like those that prevailed fifteen years ago.

In contrast with oil, it is difficult to pin rising natural gas prices directly on Chinese demand. Natural gas markets are often more balkanized than oil markets. Transporting natural gas across long distances is expensive; as of early 2013, for example, the cost of liquefying natural gas, shipping it from the United States to Japan, and turning it back into gas at the destination was several times the price of the gas itself.[23] The alternative to seaborne transport is pipelines, which are more cost-effective over modest distances but create rigid relationships between suppliers and customers, making buyers vulnerable to the political whims of sellers on the other end. For these reasons, growth of the global natural gas trade has been relatively weak, with most large countries, China included, preferring to source most of their natural gas at home. China also has the option of using oil or coal (depending on the use) instead of natural gas. The result so far has been a relatively low import level and, as a result, limited immediate impact on natural gas prices beyond China.

Yet China has still influenced natural gas prices indirectly through its impact on oil markets. World markets for oil and gas have long been closely connected. Most natural gas has historically been produced as a byproduct of oil extraction, keeping the costs of oil supply and gas supply closely tied. Oil and gas have also long been important substitutes for each other in power generation, industry, and home heating. This has kept the prices for the two commodities from getting too far away from each other. And since much of the world's natural gas is sold at prices determined through formulas that are based on oil, rising oil prices—partly due to growing demand from China—have further driven up the price of natural gas.

The Many Faces of Mining

Metallic ores present another story; indeed, the impact of Chinese demand on world metals prices is as diverse as the metals themselves. Copper and bauxite—two of the most significant commodities traded by China—tell two very different stories.

Chinese demand for both metallic ores has grown strongly and now constitutes a large fraction of world demand. But the consequences differ. Spot prices for copper rose fourfold between 2000 and 2011 in the wake of surging Chinese demand.[24] ("Spot prices" are prices at which commodities are traded on "spot markets," which are characterized by one-off exchanges among buyers and sellers, in contrast with sales under "term" contracts that set pricing rules for trade over periods ranging from weeks to decades.) The initial reason for escalating prices was slow response from miners, who faced long lead times for new projects; high prices were therefore required to restrain demand. After crashing during the financial crisis, copper prices rose again, still reflecting slowness in expanding supply but also the increasing cost of producing new copper.[25] Countries that host mines have also pushed for higher wages and greater government shares in profits, raising operating costs further.[26] In addition, iron ore has seen strong price gains akin to copper, and for similar reasons: rapidly rising demand and slow-to-catch-up supply.

Bauxite, though, has responded differently. Despite increases in both Chinese and global demand similar to those seen for other base metals, bauxite prices have not risen as much.[27] What explains this difference? One theoretical possibility is that other consumers easily cut back on their use of aluminum (for which bauxite is a raw input) in the face of rising Chinese demand. This sort of "flexible" demand would prevent total world consumption from rising much and thereby keep prices restrained. But it turns out that demand for aluminum is highly unresponsive to prices (even more so than demand for copper), so this theory doesn't work.[28] Moreover, bauxite mining involves lead times similar to what is seen in other base metal mining, and it is fairly concentrated in a small number of countries, so neither slow supply response nor concentration is a good explanation.

Three other factors likely explain why bauxite prices did not rise much. First, even before the emergence of China, industry was expecting strong growth in bauxite demand (particularly for the replacement of steel with aluminum in cars as well as other uses) and had put in place plans to meet it.[29] (This suggests that producers of other minerals, now conditioned to expect rising demand, may be able to meet Chinese growth in the future with far smaller price rises than were experienced between 2000 and 2010.) Second, China has a large amount of relatively high-cost bauxite production capacity that comes online to keep rising prices in check and then shuts down when prices fall.[30] (This, however, may become a smaller factor over time, as growth in Chinese bauxite demand—and more fundamentally aluminum demand—greatly outpaces domestic supply.) Third, not only are world bauxite resources massive, they are also well understood. This reduces risk for those who seek to increase bauxite production, which in turn makes it less likely that the costs of developing bauxite mines will turn out to be surprisingly high, sending prices upward.

Bauxite thus offers an important lesson: surging Chinese resource demand does not always lead to the sorts of massive price rises that are typically assumed. Industry-level details—particularly on the supply side of the equation—matter. So does the predictability of demand.

Feeding China

Despite the coincidence of strong growth in prices for energy, minerals, and food, China's actual impact on food markets has been considerably smaller than its influence on other commodities. Researchers commissioned by the UK government capture the prevailing view among experts well: "It has been suggested that the rapid rise in incomes in China and India is the main cause of the [2007–08] food price spikes," they write, "but this direct effect is unlikely."[31] Demand for agricultural commodities, they observe, actually rose more slowly in the 2000s than in the 1990s, a decade when global food prices were stable. High food prices in recent years are better explained by a mix of broadly rising demand, volatile weather, demand for crops and cropland to produce automobile fuels, and moves by major food producers (notably Russia and India) to throttle back food exports in the face of these events, further intensifying the resulting price rises.

Growth in Chinese demand for raw agricultural commodities has been relatively small in the global context. Between 2001 and 2007, China accounted for considerably more than half of global growth in base metals demand and for roughly a fifth of global oil demand growth. In contrast, it contributed barely 10 percent of growth in demand for raw agricultural commodities (corn, rice, soybeans, and wheat).[32] Looking ahead, mainstream projections foresee China continuing to play a relatively modest role in growth of global agricultural demand. A 2012 joint study from the United Nations Food and Agriculture Organization (FAO) and the Organization for Economic Cooperation and Development (OECD), for example, foresees China accounting for 4 percent of global growth in rice demand through 2021 (its final projection year) and for slightly more than 10 percent of global growth in wheat consumption. Indeed, mainstream projections foresee the relative role of China in many agricultural commodities markets declining in the coming years (with soybeans the most notable exception) as demand from other countries rises.[33]

Pressures on global food prices are also moderated by the powerful Chinese desire to be self-sufficient in most raw agricultural materials. This creates an incentive for the Chinese government to take steps that help domestic supplies rise in order to match growth in domestic demand. Such efforts stretch back centuries. More recently, in 1996, in the wake of the controversy following Lester Brown's "Who Will Feed China?" Beijing published a White Paper on the issue of grain. "[T]he small quantity of grain imported by China will not imperil the stability of the international grain market," it asserted. "There is no basis to the international clamor about a 'China threat in food supply.'" But it also observed delicately that "the balance between the supply of and demand for grain in the country will have to be further enhanced, and the tense situation between supply and demand will continue to exist for a long time to come," an oblique way of saying that China would pull out all the stops to avoid becoming dependent on imported grain.[34] Not until the end of the document did Beijing acknowledge the role of international trade, noting that "China will not refuse to use international resources as a necessary complement," but reinforcing that this would "only play the role of regulation in varieties, in case of crop failures and to support poor regions."[35]

Little changed over the decade that followed. In 2007, Premier Wen Jiabao noted that when it comes to food, "even a one yuan increase in prices will affect people's lives."[36] Still today, Chinese officials reinforce the importance of grain independence for China's security. Minister of Agriculture Han Changfu proclaimed in 2011, "To ensure national grain security, it is important that China adheres to the principle of self-sufficiency. The livelihood of the Chinese people cannot end up in the hands of others. Depending on international trade to ensure food security is unreliable."[37] Or as he put it more succinctly the following year, "Chinese people's rice bowl should only be filled by themselves."[38]

But grain is a special case even among agricultural commodities. China's economic reform and opening up increased agricultural efficiency and output, yet the combination of a paucity of arable land and the breakneck pace of industrialization strained the system. Today China has less arable land per person than it did a decade ago. Beijing once declared 120 million hectares of arable land—an area about the size of South Africa—to be its minimum for food security, but by the end of 2011 it reportedly had only about 121.9 million hectares of arable land.[39] Direct impediments to efficient farming are exacerbated by the fact that the price of food continues to be politically charged, and hence subjected to controls that weaken producers' incentives. Consumption of food today accounts for more than a third of household expenditures, compared to less than 15 percent in most developed nations and less than 10 percent in the United States.[40] This tension is compounded by the trade-offs in making land available to agriculture, industry, and continuing urbanization, as well as by domestic environmental degradation.

Were Chinese demand not growing, the government would likely steer increasingly scarce land to uses other than agriculture. The result would be lower total world food supply. This Chinese tendency to seek self-sufficiency in food—greater Chinese consumption and production go hand in hand—ultimately means that the impact of increased food demand on world markets is lower than it would be otherwise.

Even with Chinese efforts to expand domestic supplies, though, the country has become dependent on food imports in important areas. Faced with limits to the ability to expand domestic farming, and a desire to produce its own grain, China has been forced to depend heavily on imports for its soybean supply.[41] The world should not expect, however, considerably larger gains in soybean prices than in the prices of other raw agricultural commodities as a result, since prices of many agricultural commodities tend to move together over the long haul.[42]

To be certain, as world food demand grows, it is possible that prices will rise strongly, particularly if productivity gains do not remove pressure on the availability of land.[43] But high prices would not primarily be a product of Chinese food demand; the source would be growth in global food demand far more broadly.

Looking Forward

The future impact of Chinese resource demand on world resource prices depends on three big factors: the ability and willingness of suppliers around the world (including those in China itself) to respond to higher resource demand through greater resource production, the composition of economic growth, and the efficiency with which the country uses resources in the future. We have already taken a look at the first factor. But the other two are significant unknowns.

Perhaps the biggest question mark looming over the future is the course that the Chinese economy will take. Economic activity can be broken down into investment, consumption, and exports. The typical large country gets the bulk of its economic activity from consumption, with smaller fractions coming from investment and exports. For example, almost 70 percent of the U.S. economy is personal consumption, and an even higher fraction is attributable to consumption once consumption by government is factored in.[44] Private investment makes up another 15 percent of the economy. Net exports for the United States have, for many years, been negative.

Chinese economic activity looks very different. It has long been heavily weighted toward investment, a trend that has only intensified in recent years. Between 2001 and 2010, roughly half of the economy was directed toward investment, with that figure spiking even higher in 2009 on the back of a massive stimulus effort.[45] Fixed investment requires a lot of energy and minerals. Factories, buildings, trains, and automobiles require steel and aluminum; power plants need coal, oil, and gas to run; all of these use electrical wiring that depends on copper. Exports also occupy an unusually large role in the Chinese economy, ranging between 10 and 20 percent of the economy in the decade ending in 2012.[46] Much of what China exports is both energy- and minerals-intensive; steel, for example, draws on coal for energy and iron for materials, and aluminum uses energy as well as bauxite.[47] High investment and exports have been accompanied by low personal consumption, which remains stuck at around 35 percent of the economy.[48]

China's leadership has long expressed determination to rebalance the country's economy away from investment and exports and toward consumption. If it succeeds, the patterns of resource demand will change too. In particular, personal consumption is far less minerals-intensive than industrial activity. Its impact on energy is more ambiguous; industry uses energy intensely, but so do consumers, whether to power their cars or heat and light their homes.

But China has struggled to effect a decisive shift. In 2006, reflecting on the previous five years, a senior official warned: "During the 10th Five-Year Plan period, the [investment] rate increased from 36 percent to 44.8 percent. . . . If such kind of growth continues, though successful in short-term fast expansion, it will lead to a more extensive growth mode and instability of the economy."[49] The country's Eleventh Five-Year Plan, which covered the years 2006–2010, thus aimed to "adjust the relationship between investment and consumption." It also set a series of goals for economic rebalancing, with a particular focus on the resource-light services sector, aiming to increase that sector's share of the economy. In addition, it aimed to make more use of people (and less of machines) in service activities, a step designed to boost individual income and hence spur personal consumption.[50]

Yet by the end of the Eleventh Five-Year Plan, China failed to meet its major goals. Investment had actually increased as a share of the economy.[51] Chinese leaders thus declared with the Twelfth Five-Year Plan (2011–2015) that they would finally begin to steer the economy in a new direction, boosting the role of personal consumption in economic growth through a larger service sector, higher wages, and a stronger social safety net.[52]

But the challenges in accomplishing this are daunting: Beijing will have to rein in powerful industrial and local interests whose political and personal economic fortunes have been made on the back of the investment-led growth of the past two decades. The process of urbanizing an additional 300 million people by 2030, as the government has outlined, will also encourage investment-led growth. Moving China from a manufacturing economy to a service and technology-driven economy, moreover, requires diminishing the power of the central government by reducing capital controls to enable the private sector to flourish, something leaders have resisted for fear of losing their ability to direct financial flows to meet economic policy goals. And although building up the social welfare net to help boost consumer spending has nominally been a top priority for a decade, the imperative of continued rapid economic development continues to crowd out initiatives to improve the country's health, education, and social security systems.

If China fails to shift its economic priorities, one of two things will happen: the economy will continue to grow apace, driving energy and minerals demand upward in a similar way to the past decade; or, at the opposite extreme and perhaps more likely over time, the economy will falter, gutting demand across the board, including for minerals and energy imports.

What if China succeeds in rebalancing the economy? There is broad agreement that greater consumption-led growth would have limited impact, one way or the other, on food demand, particularly within the context of much broader growth in global food demand. There is less agreement for minerals and energy. Some experts argue that China is on the verge of a significant rebalancing, with large consequences for energy and particularly minerals markets. A team at the U.S. bank Citigroup, for example, has estimated that annual growth in global copper demand will be 14 percent lower in the coming years if China shifts to a consumption-driven model; it also projects slower growth for aluminum and iron ore demand—roughly 6 and 4 percent lower, respectively.[53]

Other experts argue that any rebalancing will be slow, if only for political reasons, since attempting to effect a rapid shift would risk a sharp slowdown in economic growth.[54] They also warn that even if investment decreases as a share of Chinese economic growth, it will remain substantial, and with it so will growth in minerals demand, at least for the next several years. Much of the country, particularly away from China's coastal region, remains only poorly developed; moreover, with roughly half of Chinese people still living outside cities, considerably more urban infrastructure remains to be developed.[55] But even analysts who are skeptical of a large near-term shift foresee a major turn over time: as one analyst who is skeptical of an immediate shift wrote in 2011, "After 2015, China's demand for major mining commodities will begin to fall gradually with the expected slowdown in investment and infrastructure activities."[56] On the energy front, a shift from investment to consumption is likely to be neutral, with industrial energy demand replaced by individual use of electricity (ultimately coal or gas) for homes and oil products for cars. The upshot will be still-growing demand for energy and minerals.

The second big factor that will shape future resource demand is the efficiency with which China uses resources. A team at the consultancy McKinsey and Company has analyzed global opportunities to reduce resource demand cost-effectively.[57] They find opportunities to reduce Chinese energy demand through 2030 by an amount equivalent to nearly half of present U.S. energy consumption. Moreover, they find opportunities to cut steel consumption by

120 million tons—roughly 10 percent of current global demand—through such steps as more efficient building construction. Other studies show similar opportunities in these and other mineral and energy areas.[58]

The barriers to realizing these opportunities, though, are often substantial. Greater efficiency, for example, typically requires larger up-front investment in return for savings later, an opportunity that may not be pursued if capital is scarce, or if long-term ownership is not clear. Similarly, because the Chinese economy still contains many nonmarket features, it may not be possible for those who invest up front to reap the rewards from increased resource productivity down the road. All of this makes it unwise to assume that China will become radically more efficient in its resource use in the coming years, in the process removing pressure from world prices.

The Changing Shape of Resource Markets

Growing Chinese demand for resources is not just influencing prices; it is also affecting how underlying markets work. A lot of ink has been spilled on worries that China is "locking up" resource supplies, eroding the role of global markets in governing resource trade. The real impact on global markets, however, is different, more varied, and often more broadly beneficial than this caricature suggests.

China Transforms the Iron Ore Market

Among the three biggest mineral markets—for copper, bauxite, and iron ore—only the copper market comes close to resembling the flexible and transparent market for oil. From the end of World War II through mid-1978, the copper market was characterized by a mix of long-term contracts and spot market sales.[59] Contract sales were based on a "producer price," which reflected supply costs plus a premium, while spot sales were based on prices determined through the London Metals Exchange (LME); large differences between the two prices could persist. In the late 1970s, following the nationalization of copper production in Chile, Peru, Zaire, and Zambia (the four top copper exporters), long-term contracts were broadly broken, and producers shifted to selling on a spot basis through the LME. Today, copper is sold through a mix of spot and long-term contracts, but the latter differ from their past structures: instead of setting prices on the basis of producers' costs, they typically price according to New York or London exchange prices, essentially in the same way that markets work with oil.

The iron ore market has long been different from both those of copper and oil. The emergence of China, though, has changed things radically. The story of how this happened sheds light on the surprising ways in which China can influence the structure of global markets.

Much of the world's iron ore has historically been produced in "captive" mines owned by steel producers and priced at levels designed for internal corporate convenience rather than to reflect its market value. Since steel making requires large up-front capital investments, securing a stable supply of the material (in order to make sure steel plants are put to full use) has been more important to many companies than realizing the lowest possible price. Most other trade between merchant iron ore producers (those that do not own their own steel plants) and steel makers without captive mines was conducted on long-term contracts with prices set through specially structured annual auctions.

Here's how those worked. Three companies, Vale, Rio Tinto, and BHP Billiton, together control more than 70 percent of seaborne iron ore trade.[60] A handful of large companies—primarily from Japan, South Korea, and Taiwan—similarly dominated the demand side of the picture until recently. Early every year, the largest iron ore producer would enter price negotiations with the largest consumer. Once they came to an agreement, their price would be used for all companies' iron ore deals for the year. Spot trade has long been tiny in comparison.

Beginning in the early 2000s, Chinese steel makers assumed an ever greater role in global iron ore markets. Until 2005, though, Japan-based Nippon Steel still dominated negotiations on the side of the steel makers, but beginning that year the Chinese firm Baosteel took the lead in annual negotiations, as China moved to become the biggest steel-producing country in the world.[61] Baosteel was followed in 2006 by a consortium, now organized by the Chinese government but still represented by Baosteel, which aimed to gain more power in price negotiations. In principle, this shifted China into a stronger role in the iron ore market.

At the same time, though, a host of smaller Chinese steel makers chose to procure their iron ore through spot market sales.[62] The domestic industry was highly fragmented—far more so than the steel industries in other major steel making countries. (China had three thousand companies, Japan had five, and Taiwan and South Korea each had one.)[63] This contributed to growth in spot markets. By 2005, nearly half of Chinese iron ore imports were made through spot markets.[64]

As this trend emerged, the Chinese government did not embrace it. Instead, over the next several years, the government focused on reducing competition among iron ore importers, hoping to reduce prices as a result. Between 2006 and 2009, it repeatedly took steps to limit the number of companies able to import iron ore, restricting licenses, raising capital requirements, and limiting each company's allowed imports.[65]

Meanwhile, though the big Chinese steel companies continued to use long-term contracts, they competed among themselves, reducing their market power. In 2006, Baosteel, attempting to represent the broader Chinese industry, failed to come to timely agreement with the major iron ore producers. Producers thus shifted to talks with the major Japanese, Korean, and European buyers. Chinese contract buyers were ultimately forced to accept the price agreed to in those talks—substantially higher than what they sought.[66]

The big shift came in 2009. Chinese buyers failed for months to come to agreement with the major iron ore suppliers. Korean, Japanese, and Taiwanese steel makers all ultimately agreed with the big three producers to prices (the same for all three) for their 2009–10 contracts. But the big Chinese firms, with their growing collective market power, continued to demand a lower price. On July 4, amid this conflict, China arrested four Shanghai-based Rio Tinto executives, accusing them of stealing secret Chinese information of value to the iron ore negotiations.[67] China's state-run news service *Xinhua* reported that a "new Chinese report said Rio's spying meant Chinese steel makers paid more than 700 billion yuan ($102.46 billion) more for imported iron ore than they otherwise would have."[68] China eventually walked back some of its accusations, but tensions remained.[69]

The iron ore price negotiations were ultimately inconclusive. Both the iron ore producers and the big Chinese buyers—the latter eager to take advantage of falling spot market prices spurred by the global financial crisis—turned to spot market trade, which had already grown on the back of demand from small Chinese mills. The spot market ultimately accounted for 60 percent of global iron ore trade in 2009.[70] From there, the entire iron ore trade moved strongly toward shorter-term pricing. Long-term contracts with non-Chinese buyers began to shift away from the old, pitched annual negotiations over prices, ending the forty-year-old approach to iron ore trade. Instead, prices were increasingly determined by reference to spot markets.[71] "This is a momentous occasion," one analyst told the *Financial Times*. "The industry is revolutionizing the way iron ore is priced."[72] The period in some ways resembles what happened in the 1970s and 1980s as the world oil market underwent a similarly radical transformation.

The ensuing years have brought growing conflict over the new system.[73] Within China, smaller steel mills, previously disadvantaged relative to their larger competitors, have welcomed the change; larger producers, now with even greater potential market power, have regularly suggested that a return to annual contract talks would make sense.[74] Similar sentiments have come from outside China; Posco, the Korean leader, has called for a return to annual contract prices, without success thus far.[75]

Meanwhile volatile prices have increased the appeal to Chinese buyers of owning their own supplies; this sort of vertical integration, common in North America, is the most obvious way to hedge against iron ore price volatility absent deep financial markets. Together with the broader government interest in owning overseas resource deposits, this helps explain growing Chinese efforts to take equity stakes in overseas iron ore mines.

The broader story of iron ore carries an important lesson: the emergence of China has changed the system radically—but not at all in the way Chinese policy makers or industry wanted. (Something similar has happened with bauxite markets, which have become more flexible in recent years, following iron ore's lead.)[76] Large Chinese steel makers, aided by the government in attempting to negotiate collectively, hoped to use the old structure of price negotiations to exercise market power and get lower prices. But a combination of two other Chinese-driven factors—the emergence of large numbers of smaller producers, and a volatile price environment that complicated negotiations—ultimately helped push the system in precisely the opposite direction.

Natural Gas: What Does China Want?

Unlike oil and copper, which have long been traded in deep and flexible markets, and unlike iron ore and bauxite, which are moving that way, natural gas remains traded in relatively inflexible and opaque markets, making the natural gas trade more vulnerable to political machinations. The biggest future prospect for Chinese influence may be the possibility of changing this situation and helping usher in a more transparent market-based approach to trading Asian natural gas.

In North America, natural gas is priced transparently and openly, both through exchange-traded contracts and extensive physical trade. The continent is well integrated through a dense network of pipelines, making it relatively straightforward to translate prices from one place to another. Asia, though, is strikingly different. The main Asian consumers of natural gas are Japan, China, Thailand, South Korea, India, Malaysia, Indonesia, and Pakistan. These markets are balkanized. Japan and Indonesia are islands; South Korea is effectively an island too, cut off from other markets by oceans and by North Korea. India and Pakistan have warred with each other and proven unable to build pipelines across their border; and the border between China and India, meanwhile, is too rugged and mountainous to accommodate an effective pipeline system. This all thwarts efforts to create a single transparently determined price for Asian natural gas, since there is no reason natural gas should sell for the same price in, say, both Japan and India. Instead, Asian natural gas buyers typically enter long-term contracts with sellers in which the price they pay for natural gas is set by a formula that itself is based on the price of oil.

Moving to a more open and transparent system would take a willful act by a powerful consumer to create a trading hub. That consumer would need to put in place the physical and institutional infrastructure (pipelines, storage equipment, transparent and reliable contracts, and so on) that allows prices to be determined through open markets. It would need to require foreign suppliers, which typically prefer the lucrative "oil-linked" contracts that are still the norm, to use it—and the market in question would also need to be important enough that those suppliers couldn't say no.

China might seem a prime candidate to play this role, thanks to its large and growing market for natural gas and the potential to secure lower natural gas prices through a market-based trading system. But to do this, the Chinese government would need to develop a physical hub where natural gas prices could be determined, and a pipeline network that connected the hub to much larger markets within the country. It would also need to liberalize its own internal natural gas market, so prices could be transparently determined; it might also need to open its financial markets enough to allow the creation of derivative financial products so traders could hedge against price changes. And it would need to invest enough in gas-using infrastructure (probably power plants) to make its import market too big for suppliers to ignore.

In early 2013, a team at the International Energy Agency assessed the potential of several Asian countries to become liquefied natural gas (LNG) trading hubs. It found that China failed to meet several requirements the team deemed necessary: deregulated gas prices, sufficient pipeline capacity, competitive markets (three companies dominate LNG trading in China), and relatively free access to capital markets, which would enable the participation of international financial institutions in trading and in creating derivative contracts.[77]

Most fundamentally, then, Chinese leaders would need to decide they were ready for significant economic changes before they could effectively create a natural gas trading hub. If Chinese leaders prefer to keep pricing opaque and to use their leverage as a big consumer to negotiate low prices, then they will not take the steps needed to transform the Asian LNG market. One way or the other, though, China's rise as a consumer means it will play a larger role in determining how commerce in natural gas, especially in Asia, develops.

The Political World of Food Trading

What about the structure of global markets for raw agricultural materials? In many ways, these are even more politically distorted than markets in energy and minerals. Large numbers of developing countries strictly control food prices, which are near-universally matters of political sensitivity, particularly where they make up a large part of household budgets. Many more countries—developed and developing—subsidize food production. Food markets are, moreover, particularly prone to interference with trade. Food-exporting countries have frequently erected export bans or quotas in the face of global price spikes in order to lower domestic prices. It is not entirely unreasonable, in this context, for China to desire some control over its food supply.

It is not clear, though, that the emergence of China will change very much the way food markets work. To the extent that the country pursues domestic self-sufficiency while retaining some controls on prices, its activities will largely be isolated from global markets. Chinese overseas food production, meanwhile, is unlikely to be exempted from emergency export restrictions imposed by food-producing countries. Limits to Chinese acquisition of land will also be constrained by other countries' own concerns (whether or not well founded) over food security and their unwillingness, therefore, to let large tracts of land fall into the hands of other countries. It is far too early to conclude from this that the quest for productive overseas land will fundamentally change the distribution of food production worldwide, particularly as the Chinese role in world food markets remains limited.

Oil Markets Hold Up

But the biggest popular focus of attention on how China might transform the structure of world markets hasn't been on minerals, natural gas, or food. It has emphasized oil, and it warns of drastic changes. These are severely overwrought.

Some have argued that Chinese investment (which we explore in more detail beginning in the next chapter) is "locking up" oil supplies and removing them from the global market.[78] If that were indeed happening it would be disturbing; it could raise prices for others, inhibit market flexibility, and thus increase the vulnerability of other oil consumers. Yet there is no evidence that China is regularly removing large volumes of oil from world markets. Most overseas Chinese oil production, perhaps the target of greatest concern, is actually sold onto world markets rather than shipped back home.[79] Moreover, even if it insisted instead on sending all the oil that its companies produced back to domestic refineries, the net impact on world supply and demand wouldn't change. Resulting world prices would also remain the same.

There is one more possibility, though, that could allow ventures abroad to affect the global price of resources, particularly the price of oil. China has historically controlled consumer prices for refined oil products (gasoline, diesel) in order to shield citizens from high and often volatile costs. Doing this was far easier when China controlled its own sources of supply. (The same was true for the United States when it relied only on domestic and captive overseas production.) As China has become reliant on oil imports, this approach has become untenable, creating intolerable financial burdens on state-owned oil companies having to procure expensive oil abroad only to sell the resulting products at a loss back home. As a result, beginning in the mid-2000s, China began to remove controls on prices for oil products. The consequence has been higher domestic prices, less demand for oil than would otherwise be the case, and therefore lower world prices as the ultimate result.

Were Chinese firms at some point in the future to control enough overseas oil to supply fully the country's needs, it would become possible for the Chinese government to reimpose strong price controls without creating large and explicit fiscal burdens on companies at the same time. (Under these conditions, Chinese firms would not need to "buy" oil; they would simply transfer oil internally. Fiscal burdens could, however, still arise from costs associated with acquiring control of overseas fields and producing oil from them.) In this way, control of overseas oil could effectively create a separate world of "Chinese oil" and raise prices for everyone else. But the possibility is remote and distant at most; China shows no prospect of buying up as much oil as it expects to consume and has not shown a desire to use overseas oil ownership to return to the price controls of the past.

Many Resource Stories

Chinese economic growth has led to demand for resource imports with far-reaching consequences for resource prices—though with distinct dynamics for each resource, and big price increases for some resources and much smaller impacts for others. The biggest impact so far has been on the prices of a host of critical commodities, most notably oil, but also several essential industrial minerals. That in turn has affected producers and consumers around the world, regardless of their direct relationships with China. The country has also been changed by its own resource quest—high resource prices resulting from strong domestic demand have been a prime motive for efforts to curb resource consumption and rebalance the domestic economy—yet these impacts on China have thus far been dwarfed by its impact on the world. Meanwhile, those who predicted that China would alter the basic structure of world markets have largely been proven wrong: oil, in particular, is still traded on open markets, contrary to what some foresaw. In some places where China actively sought to use its power to transform markets—most notably in iron ore—the ultimate impact has indeed been transformational, but not in the way its leaders foresaw.

What about the future? Many believe that past price increases are a mere taste of things to come—that past will indeed be prologue for world commodity prices. Underlying market dynamics, however, suggest that the biggest price impacts driven by Chinese demand may well have largely run their course; it is considerably more likely than not that the price gains of the last decade will not be repeated again. Indeed, depending on how the Chinese economy evolves— partly in response to high prices themselves—those price rises could reverse in part. In the coming years, the bigger impacts of Chinese demand may be seen through transformations in the very structure of critical markets, particularly for natural gas. Ironically, given the popular fixation of China as a mercantilist and anti-market power, these changes are more often likely to point in the direction of more flexible and transparent markets rather than opaque and politically charged ones: China is slowly acquiring the ability to change the structure of global markets, though only if it pushes in a direction others also support.

But trade is only the start of how China's resource quest is affecting the world at large. This resource quest is far more likely to transform commercial relationships through the interactions between China and the countries in which its companies are increasingly investing than through its trade relationships. The dynamics on display there are fundamentally different from those we've encountered thus far.

4

China Goes Out

MARCH 14, 2013, BROUGHT important news: state-owned China National Petroleum Corporation (CNPC)—the largest integrated energy company in China—planned to acquire 20 percent of a massive Mozambican natural gas field in a deal worth $4.21 billion.[1] It would not be the first Chinese resource investment in the East African nation. Chinese companies were involved in coal, timber, agriculture, and more. Indeed, at first blush the fit seemed natural. Chinese companies had gained a reputation in recent years for availing themselves of every lever of national power to gain access to investments in the world's resources, and rarely were Beijing's relationships as strong as in the former Portuguese colony. China had supported the Mozambican rebels through their decades-long, and ultimately successful, fight for independence. All it took to confirm the still-solid relationship was a glance at the Foreign Ministry in the capital, Maputo, its pagoda-style roof a nod to the Chinese developers who had built it—and the Chinese government that had paid the bill.

Yet beneath this seemingly simple surface lay much more complex terrain. State-owned Wuhan Iron and Steel had indeed attempted to develop Mozambican coal but, as of 2013, had failed.[2] The Chinese agricultural investments that were scattered throughout the country were then due mostly to small private farmers, not big state-owned behemoths. And CNPC's natural gas buy didn't come courtesy of crooked politicians and bureaucrats in Maputo. Instead, the company struck a deal with Eni, the Italian oil company that had discovered natural gas off the Mozambican coast more than a year before.[3]

One thing about China's resource quest is decidedly conventional: as demand for resource imports has grown, it has followed a path well trodden by other countries, including the United States and Japan before it, by increasingly focusing on owning overseas resources outright. But the strategies driving the details of Chinese investment—and the tactics through which China and its companies have pursued their goals—remain opaque and puzzling to many observers. Is China merely doing what other countries have done before? Or is how it approaches investments in foreign natural resources fundamentally different?

Investing Abroad

The roots of Chinese resource investment abroad were established well before China became a major resource importer. Deng Xiaoping, who led the early efforts to open up China, believed that the future of China's economy rested in engagement with the outside world. In a scheme reminiscent of the imperial port system, Deng identified a number of cities and provinces (primarily along China's coast) as special economic zones. These areas were allowed to receive foreign investment, establish joint ventures, and export. As economic reform expanded domestically, Beijing loosened the reins on overseas investment as well. By the late 1980s and early 1990s, the range of players involved in overseas investment expanded rapidly. Beijing began to maintain control over large and nationally important state-owned enterprises (SOEs), in the process boosting their stature, while relinquishing its grip on less essential enterprises. This meant that SOEs in key industries, such as chemicals, minerals, energy, and heavy machinery, retained monopolies in the domestic economy and were permitted to operate internationally. Overseas investment was primarily a means to square a desire by these firms to expand with limited opportunities to do so at home. It also provided opportunities for officials and others to use overseas investment to transfer state property into their own names.[4]

Yet engagement with the outside world did not come easily. Chinese overseas investment grew slowly and was the source of fierce debate within top political circles. Some Communist Party officials believed that overseas direct investment was detrimental to the country because it would encourage corruption, capital flight, and capitalist influence.[5] The early overseas projects were experimental, primarily small-scale efforts by cities and provinces to establish joint ventures with other developing nations. Between 1979 and 1985, only 189 such ventures were approved, totaling $197 million in government expenditures, and in all these early ventures the government held controlling equity.[6]

The reemergence of Deng Xiaoping to public life in 1991 after his formal retirement in 1989 put to rest any debate over the wisdom of China more deeply engaging in the global economy. During a well-publicized visit to Shanghai in 1991, Deng stated, "Reform and opening up includes taking over the useful things of capitalism."[7] He soon followed his time in Shanghai with his famous 1992 "southern tour," during which he criticized those who opposed further economic reform and urged the people: "We should be bolder than previously in the past in carrying out reform and our opening-up policies. We must not act like women with bound feet."[8]

The next critical transition came under President Jiang Zemin, who served as general secretary of the Communist Party from 1989 to 2002 and president of China from 1993 to 2003. Jiang followed Deng's lead in pushing ahead with economic reform and opening. He became well known outside China for his ability to recite the Gettysburg Address, willingness to break out into song, and a positive disposition toward foreign businessmen. But one of his greatest legacies, along with that of then Premier Zhu Rongji, was the development and implementation of China's multipronged and integrated "going out" strategy.

Soon after assuming power, Jiang confirmed that economic liberalization was a core priority: "If we fail to develop our economy rapidly, it will be very difficult for us to consolidate the socialist system and maintain long-term social stability."[9] In 2001, under the leadership of Jiang and Zhu, China joined the World Trade

Organization (WTO). Jiang positioned international expansion as critical to development: "Foreign funds, resources, technology and skilled personnel, along with privately owned enterprises that are a useful supplement to our economy, can and should be put to use for the benefit of socialism." Therefore Beijing should "grant to enterprises and to science and technology research institutes the power to engage in foreign trade, and . . . encourage enterprises to expand their investments abroad and their transnational operations."[10]

Premier Zhu—perhaps China's most powerful economic reformer to date—formally invoked the term "going out" (*zou chuqu*) in a 1999 speech on the country's economic future. He asserted a connection between the paucity of resources (particularly oil) and a need to go abroad, claiming, "Domestic development and production of oil can no longer keep pace with the needs of the country's economic and social development, resulting in an increasing imbalance between oil supply and demand."[11] Zhu recommended that China implement a going-out strategy, encouraging enterprises with comparative advantages to make investments abroad, contract for international engineering projects, and increase the export of labor. To encourage enterprises to make investments, he urged Beijing to "provide a supportive policy framework to create favorable conditions for enterprises to establish overseas operations."[12] Beijing and provincial governments offered companies incentives including tax breaks, cheap land at home, and low-interest funding from state-owned banks. The government also established a special export credit insurance corporation (Sinosure) to advance international investment.

Zhu's push to promote Chinese firms investing abroad was not entirely new, but the political support Beijing provided to help ensure their success raised the effort to a new level. As part of the Tenth Five-Year Plan, announced in 2001, Beijing adopted new measures to encourage outward investment under state direction. The State Development Planning Commission (renamed the National Development and Reform Commission, or NDRC, in 2003) compiled a list of overseas opportunities for investment in those resources of which China was in short supply, such as oil, gas, and timber. The government encouraged overseas investment and set out to develop fifty multinationals that would be part of the top 500 firms globally by 2015.

Today the government has a formal and well-articulated going-out strategy that nominally involves a wide range of players, among them state entities at every level of the political system and private actors as well. From the outside looking in, then, it often appears that China's going-out strategy is a well-orchestrated dance.

Although many state actors are involved in the going-out effort, five in particular play central roles. The State-owned Assets Supervision and Administration Commission (SASAC), established in 2003, either outright owns or has a controlling share of 112 powerful SOEs (as of December 2013), some of which are the biggest resource companies in China. (Increasingly, private Chinese actors—including smaller mining companies, farmers, traders, manufacturers, and even independent workers—are also investing abroad in natural resources.) As the primary shareholder in each SOE, SASAC is largely concerned with growth and profit, which is often the spur for overseas investment.

The Ministry of Commerce (MOFCOM) is another powerful bureaucracy tasked with aiding outward-bound investment. It contains the Department of Outward Investment and Economic Cooperation, which regulates all Chinese companies engaged in international business with large investments. MOFCOM also plays a central role in foreign aid, distributing money to United Nations organizations and canceling foreign aid debt. Its Department of Foreign Aid also approves corporations' bids on aid projects—these projects are often proposed by the NDRC as part of a broader package of resource and infrastructure development projects—and is responsible for a project's overall management.[13] In recent years, MOFCOM also has assumed significant responsibility for ensuring good relations between Chinese firms and the countries in which they invest, publishing an annual guide to the laws, challenges, and overall state of relations with China for each country in which these firms invest.

The Ministry of Foreign Affairs (MOFA) plays a critical role in diplomatic engagement and in calibrating China's foreign policy.

MOFA provides consular and diplomatic services for the hundreds of thousands of Chinese workers abroad, and increasingly it is asked to organize noncombatant evacuations and defend Chinese investments and property abroad.

Financing for Chinese projects is provided by state-owned banks. Two in particular stand out. The Export-Import Bank of China (EXIM Bank) oversees all the country's concessional loans and provides export credits for commercial undertakings overseas, primarily in infrastructure development. (A loan or other financial instrument is concessional if it is provided with terms that are more generous than those available on commercial markets; concessional loans are typically marked by lower-than-commercial interest rates in particular.) China Development Bank (CDB) provides inexpensive loans, notably to state-owned companies seeking to make large natural resource investments overseas. The country's sovereign wealth fund, the Chinese Investment Corporation, has also taken a role in buying stakes in foreign resource companies.

These formal contributions are bolstered by the Communist Party itself. The Party directly engages in the activity of the SOEs by appointing the top officials in the fifty most powerful ones through the Party's Organization Department. The department's influence is extensive; there is even a specialized school under its auspices that is charged with training top management from SOEs and financial enterprises. Top SOE officials may also be appointed to top party posts; for instance, Su Shulin, former chairman of the oil company China Petroleum and Chemical Corporation (Sinopec), was named the governor of Fujian province.[14] The heads of these large SOEs, therefore, command a political role themselves, often enjoying minister or vice minister status. In this way, they help to shape China's resource acquisition strategy.

Even though there is more coherence to resource acquisitions than one finds in a country such as the United States, which does not attempt to coordinate its diplomatic, security, and economic policy nearly as tightly as China does, there is a strong current of independent action as well. Chinese SOEs often compete with each other for overseas contracts; for example, CNPC and Sinopec battled for control over oil projects in Sudan in 2004.[15] And some high-level efforts at coordination are less than meets the eye: NDRC may propose a sweeping investment plan encompassing an array of natural resource and infrastructure projects, but it cannot compel Chinese companies to participate.[16] Moreover, despite nominal ownership of SOEs, SASAC often has difficulty forcing them to follow its orders.[17] Conflict among the various parts of the bureaucracy is also not uncommon. In some instances, what appears to be a massive investment and trade and aid deal structured from on high may in fact be constructed largely from a bottom-up amalgam of various interests. Rather than being directed by the central government to acquire particular resources, SOEs are usually motivated by the possibility of profit; encouragement from the government typically comes more in the form of advantageous financing and a helping hand from MOFCOM and MOFA officials when needed rather than specific instructions to pursue particular projects. Leaders of SOEs may also, more subtly, integrate their perception of the national interest into their decisions, since success for them may well be promotion to higher political office.

Chinese companies' efforts to go out are therefore bolstered by supportive policy even while overseas investment is not necessarily centrally coordinated. This supportive environment appears poised to continue. The fourth-generation leaders were staunch supporters of the country's going-out policy, repeatedly reiterating their commitment to owning resources they believed were needed to support economic growth. Celebrating the tenth anniversary of China's entrance into the WTO in December 2011, President Hu Jintao stated, "China must strengthen its bringing in and going out.... It is extremely important to our development."[18] He offered further support to the policy at the 2011 Boao Forum for Asia: "In the next five years, China will make great efforts to pursue the strategy of 'going global.' We will encourage enterprises of different ownership structures to invest overseas in an orderly manner and carry out cooperation on projects that will improve local infrastructure and people's livelihood."[19]

China's fifth-generation leaders appear equally committed to the going-out strategy. President Xi Jinping has made a point of stressing the benefits to the host countries of Chinese investment. While in Angola, Xi noted, "It is the right time for China to implement a 'going out' policy."[20] And during a diplomatic visit to Ireland, Xi commented, "Chinese development will bring economic opportunities to all businesses of every country. We equally support both bringing in and going out and look forward to developing international trade."[21]

The combination of policies (particularly financial) put in place as much as a decade ago but sustained today, the willingness of Chinese government entities to help companies seeking investment opportunities, and the desire of Chinese corporate leaders to realize profits and be promoted can yield a result that looks very much like a coordinated strategy. As Shen Heting, president of Metallurgical Corporation of China Limited, a subsidiary of the behemoth state-owned China Metallurgical Group Corporation (MCC), told the Chinese newspaper *New Century Weekly*, "Central government enterprises that secure mines overseas are in reality securing resources for China."[22] In most cases, however, deals do not originate with the leadership but rather are driven by the individual incentives of the various players, all supported by a broader framework put in place to promote resource investment.

This is not entirely unlike the environment for many other multinationals. For example, when U.S. oil companies invest overseas, they benefit from tax provisions that treat overseas royalties like foreign taxes and can sometimes avail themselves of U.S. diplomatic help when problems arise. But Chinese support for its companies, even if it is inconsistent, is vastly more substantial and far ranging than that provided by Western governments to their firms.

Tools of the Trade

The breadth of government support and incentives for overseas resource investment is not the only thing that sets China apart. Companies also often use tools that appear novel or different as they seek to win the right to own and develop overseas resources: integration of foreign aid and resource deals, combined resource and infrastructure deals, and heavy use of "loans for resources" (most notably "loans for oil") are the most often discussed. Some of these are genuine departures from past ways of doing business, but not all of them are fundamentally new or consequential.

Foreign Aid

China provides three types of economic assistance to countries with which Chinese companies do business: grants, interest-free loans, and concessional loans. MOFCOM is in charge of allocating grants and interest-free loans; it acts together with the EXIM Bank for concessional loans.[23] As energy expert Erica Downs has noted, Beijing's financial largesse—through low-interest loans to Chinese SOEs and outright aid to resource-rich countries—has likely given its oil companies a competitive advantage.[24] Certainly provision of loans to Chinese companies engaged in extractive industries is a priority for a number of the country's financial institutions. For example, in March 2012, Jiang Jianqing, the head of the state-owned Industrial and Commercial Bank of China (ICBC), urged the government to invest more in overseas minerals in order to protect the economy from "resource bottlenecks."[25] And the president of the Bank of China, Li Lihui, said that in 2011 the bank distributed over RMB 500 billion ($70 billion) in loans to stimulate overseas mineral acquisition.[26]

Chinese officials have explicitly claimed that foreign aid is designed to "create a strategic platform for Chinese companies to go global."[27] Such government support is not unique to Chinese resource companies, but they are frequent beneficiaries. In Gabon, for example, where China has pursued investments in copper, oil, and timber, it has built clinics, schools, the National Assembly building, and the Senate building. It also supplies scholarships to Gabonese students to study in China and has sent agricultural experts through the UN Food and Agricultural Organisation South-South Cooperation Initiative.[28]

For construction and infrastructure projects, which are often packaged with resource investments to secure deals, Chinese banks sometimes provide concessional loans to countries, which then use the loans to engage the services of the Chinese companies undertaking the projects. Sometimes the firms themselves identify potential projects, while in other cases MOFCOM guides them to meet the particular needs of a host country. Such projects include a government office building in Guinea Bissau (where China invests in oil), a foreign ministry building in Yemen (where China seeks to develop oil and gas), the China-Pakistan Friendship Center in Pakistan (where Chinese companies are interested in copper, coal, and oil), and a high school in Tonga (where China invests in timber).[29]

Infrastructure Deals

The Chinese government's ability to coordinate bids that combine subsidized infrastructure projects and access to natural resource deposits creates a win-win situation for both construction companies and resource companies (though not necessarily for the savers who ultimately subsidize the loans).[30] Chinese support for infrastructure development can also have indirect value for resource acquisition; for instance, companies have made timber exports more viable by engaging in railroad and highway construction in Latin America, Africa, and Southeast Asia.[31]

Combining resource investment with infrastructure development may also help China secure supplies in a crisis. Though Chinese strategists and policy makers have not discussed the possibility in public (or, to our knowledge, in private), the existence of deeper and more enduring economic relationships that go beyond natural resources means that resource producers will be less likely to cross China down the road. This is particularly true if the arrangements involve concessional elements (as many of the infrastructure packages do) that would not be replaced by others; a foreign leader considering a Chinese request for resource supplies on special terms during a crisis would need to weigh the possibility that China might withdraw its concessional financing if the leader said no. Even if the Chinese government does not anticipate taking advantage of this dynamic, it might still eventually benefit.

Loans for Resources

Packages of resource investment and infrastructure support set China apart. Yet some of the techniques Chinese investors use are less exceptional than many assume. Attention has focused on one in particular: loans for resources.

Loans for resources are most frequently (and worriedly) discussed in the context of loans for oil. The phrase appears to imply a creeping mercantilism: instead of "cash for oil," which is how international oil markets typically function, Chinese companies appear to many to be trading loans for crude. Since these loans have long payback periods, often extending over several decades, this appears to create the sort of rigid, nonmarket arrangement that many Westerners fear China promotes, locking up oil for China over the term of the loan.

Yet the reality is far more benign and far more familiar to the global oil business. The structure of a typical loan-for-oil arrangement is straightforward.[32] The CDB provides a foreign government or state-owned oil company a loan to finance oil development. The oil producer in turn promises to sell a certain volume of oil to Chinese buyers every day until the loan is paid off, and to deposit the proceeds in an account it holds at the CDB. The CDB then withdraws its loan payment from that account.

But this is best understood as a way of providing security against default for the loan rather than as a way of increasing the security of Chinese oil supplies. The oil is typically sold at prevailing market prices and can be sold on to other countries or companies if desired, recourse the Chinese companies often take. Indeed, some loan-for-oil arrangements reduce the amount of oil that must be sold to China if oil prices rise.[33] This makes sense if the goal is to provide security for the underlying loan—higher prices mean that given loan payments can be made with lower volumes of oil sales—but it would be illogical if the arrangement was supposed to provide China with secure oil supplies.

Indeed, Western oil companies have long employed (and continue to use) a similar scheme, known as a "cash waterfall," in some of their overseas investments. The ultimately ill-fated joint Venezuela-ExxonMobil Cerro Negro oil project is a good example.[34]

In 1998, the pair financed the project in part through the sale of $600 billion worth of bonds. The strict terms of the bonds required that proceeds from oil sold by the project be deposited into an account at the Bank of New York. Those funds would be used first to pay project costs, then to pay back bondholders, and only after that to pay the project developers, including the Venezuelan national oil company PdVSA—a sequence of payments known as a cash waterfall. The Venezuelan government could still decide to nationalize the project—indeed, it eventually did—but in the interim, investors gained an extra layer of security from the cash waterfall arrangement.

The Chinese loan-for-oil arrangements share important similarities with the cash waterfall approach, but instead of using an American bank, they use a Chinese one. This is hardly a surprising choice for Chinese authorities seeking greater control over their financial dealings with foreign countries. Making it work, though, requires having Chinese companies buy the oil. (Other companies wouldn't necessarily agree to make their payments to a Chinese bank.) Ultimately, then, many requirements for mandatory oil sales to China are likely driven as much by the need to have a consumer willing to make payments to the China Development Bank (and not a Western bank) as by a Chinese desire to "secure" more oil.

Players and Prospects

Understanding Chinese overseas resource investment also requires grasping the sheer diversity of approaches applied to natural resources. In areas ranging from oil and gas to water and land, China's overseas investment strategy reveals a fractured approach. This approach also shapes the consequences of China's foreign investment on the ground.

Big Players in Oil and Gas

Chinese overseas oil production is dominated by three companies (and their subsidiaries): CNPC, China National Offshore Oil Corporation (CNOOC), and Sinopec. Smaller investments have been led by Sinochem, Zhenhua Oil (a subsidiary of the massive manufacturing, defense, and construction company NORINCO), and CITIC Energy, a subsidiary of the financial giant CITIC. These enterprises are supplemented by services companies that do not take equity stakes in overseas fields but often drill projects owned by Chinese and other companies.

CNPC is the most prominent player overseas. In 2011, it reported production of roughly 2 million barrels of oil a day, with more than 800,000 barrels of that its own equity production from projects overseas in which it had a stake.[35] (Global oil production is roughly 85 million barrels a day. "Equity" production refers to the output in which the oil company has an ownership stake, or the functional equivalent, allowing it to share in higher profits when oil prices rise; companies can also be involved in oil production as service providers, in which they charge a fee for their services but don't share in the upside potential or downside risks in the same way owners of the oil do.) Its natural gas output, meanwhile, totaled over 8 billion cubic feet (bcf) a day, out of which 1.2 bcf per day was its own overseas equity output. (World natural gas production is about 350 bcf a day.) This was still a fraction of what ExxonMobil, the largest private oil company, produced that year, when its equity share in its operations yielded 2.3 million barrels a day of oil and 13.2 bcf a day of natural gas.[36] CNOOC and Sinopec trailed CNPC in 2011: Sinopec reported 460,000 daily barrels of overseas equity oil and did not specify any overseas natural gas production.[37] CNOOC was third with roughly 85,000 daily barrels of overseas equity oil and 0.35 bcf of equity natural gas production per day.[38]

Chinese oil investment is widely distributed around the world. As of 2010, Chinese companies controlled a larger share of Kazakh oil production than they did of any other country; they accounted for 23 percent of Kazakh output.[39] (China was involved in various forms in a larger fraction of Iraqi production, but it shares its stakes with others and did not own them, instead providing extraction services to the owners.) Chinese participation exceeded 10 percent in Sudan, Venezuela, and Angola. Total overseas equity production was equivalent to 36 percent of Chinese oil imports that year, though much of the oil was not shipped back home and instead sold on world markets.

As Chinese companies expand their investments, they have tended to focus on projects with relatively little technical risk, typically buying into well-established resources where successful exploration and production is likely. This is not unusual for oil companies the size of CNOOC, CNPC, and Sinopec; their international peers, such as ExxonMobil and Shell, typically leave high-risk exploration to smaller independent companies and enter when large-scale development is all but assured.

Chinese companies are, however, willing to take large political and security risks, particularly where Western companies will not. Take the case of Sudan: though often assumed in the West to be a new frontier for oil exploration, the real risks in Sudan have long been political, not geological. Sudanese oil was already well understood decades ago as a result of extensive exploration by Western companies, which left because of unstable conditions and human rights abuses that were untenable and a source of fierce international criticism. To be certain, there are exceptions in which Chinese companies drill a handful of wells with highly uncertain prospects. Sinopec's independent exploratory drilling in Gabon, for example, was risky enough that the company stopped in 2008 without any success, while exploration in Kenya was similarly unsuccessful. In both cases, though, observers speculate that the Chinese companies drilled more as a favor to host governments than as a serious attempt to develop oil.[40]

Chinese companies also pursue international oil projects to acquire technology and managerial skills. They do this both to apply those skills in other international projects and to use them to boost their domestic production. This helps explain, in part, interest in U.S. shale oil and gas developments that have little prospect of generating exports to Chinese markets, even in a future crisis: the Chinese companies involved are interested in learning how to develop similar properties back home. (It also explains why the companies are fine with a minority stake; such stakes need not limit their ability to learn how to develop the resource.) Similar patterns can be seen in Chinese efforts to tap dense oil deposits (in Canada and Venezuela) and offshore oil deposits (particularly in Africa). Indeed, technology motives can be found in surprising places. One would not think of Angola, for example, as a target for improving oil production technology. But CNPC activities there are pursued largely in partnership with BP, which has provided important opportunities for learning skills involved in producing oil in challenging offshore environments.

China is not as influential a player in natural gas development as one might expect at first blush, particularly given its highly active efforts on oil. This appears to be due in part to technological limits. But it may also reflect weaker dependence on natural gas imports. Chinese companies have taken important roles in natural gas development in neighboring countries from which the gas can be shipped to China by pipeline. But projects further afield need to be integrated with systems for liquefying and transporting the fuel. The natural gas projects that seek to produce LNG are hugely complex and expensive and take many years to develop. They also require sophisticated efforts to market the produced gas (given the absence of a large spot market for LNG that allows buyers and sellers to connect without underlying long-term contracts). Host governments typically focus on bringing in those companies that are most capable of delivering, and Chinese companies aren't seen as being up to the task.

Moreover, in many of the world's cutting-edge natural gas prospects (such as areas off the coast of Australia or East Africa), technical risks either remain or have until recently been high. This environment appears to deter Chinese companies from participation as operators, though that may be changing. The companies can enter as equity participants later in the game; indeed, in some cases, such as in Mozambique, they have. But there are important limits to this. Project developers typically sell ownership stakes to companies that plan to take a share of the produced gas for themselves (those companies do so to hedge against uncertain natural gas prices). Since other countries (particularly South Korea and Japan) are still more prominent than China as LNG importers, they are also more likely to be sold the available equity in LNG export projects. This all may change if China shifts to become a larger LNG importer.

A More Diverse World of Mining

The two biggest Chinese companies involved in overseas mining investment are also the biggest players domestically: Chinalco (by volume) and Minmetals (by number of transactions).[41] Yet in contrast with oil and gas, where the biggest companies dominate, neither holds a majority share of the market for overseas projects; according to one Chinese government survey, only 37 percent of companies engaged in overseas mining projects are state-owned, with private companies particularly prominent in regional neighbors.[42] The line between public and private, though, is blurry, since private enterprises may enjoy significant backing from the government.[43] Furthermore, as in the oil industry, many mining industry leaders are tied to the government or the Party. For example, Guo Guangcheng, chairman of Foshun International, a large private company involved in the mining industry, also has served as a Shanghai delegate to the National People's Congress.[44]

Australia has been the top destination for Chinese minerals investment in recent years. Investment in deals valued at $100 million or more totaled nearly $30 billion between 2005 and mid-2013.[45] Eighty percent of China's direct investment in Australia is concentrated in the mining industry, of which 50 percent is invested in iron ore.[46]

Chinese minerals investment in South America, totaling nearly $17 billion between 2005 and mid-2013 (excluding small deals), is second only to its investment in Australia.[47] As of 2011, China had thirty-four major resource projects on the continent. Total FDI (foreign direct investment) in Latin America, concentrated heavily in mining, jumped sharply over the last decade.[48]

China's mining activities in Africa have also expanded significantly in the last decade in pursuit of a host of mineral resources, as sub-Saharan Africa became China's second biggest source of minerals after Australia.[49] (It remains a less prominent destination for investment.) Chinese officials are pushing for resource companies, both state-owned and private, to invest in African countries.[50]

China's neighbors to the north and the southeast are important investment destinations as well. Mongolia is playing an ever larger role in China's mineral investments. In July 2011, Shenhua Energy, China's largest coal producer, made a bid for a 40 percent share of Mongolia's massive Tavan Tolgoi reserve. Although the deal was initially scuttled after protests from Japanese and Korean bidders, it was completed in October 2013 following Mongolian elections in June.[51] China is also looking to Vietnam and Indonesia as opportunities for investment in bauxite.[52] China is the largest investor in Burma (Myanmar) with $14 billion in direct investment, a significant amount of which is directed toward the mining industry.[53]

There is no one driver behind Chinese companies' mining investments. Proximity to China is one consideration.[54] Australia, Mongolia, and Burma all offer abundant resources and geographic proximity, and large SOEs have pursued massive investments in these countries. In other cases, firms may target countries with which China has a free trade agreement (FTA). In Chile and Peru, for example, China acceded to "lopsided" FTAs in good measure to reduce trade barriers for its extractive industries firms.[55] Both countries now have substantial Chinese mineral investments. Smaller Chinese mining companies often seek out "quick profits for minimal investment," as in the Democratic Republic of the Congo.[56]

It is essential, though, to keep Chinese mining investment in perspective. As one industry journal noted in 2012, "Chinese mining investment activity outside China remains mostly marginal. China's scramble for resources in Australia, Africa and elsewhere involves minimal investment values despite rapid growth in recent years."[57] The sheer volume of global mining investment coming from China still pales next to the shares taken by players from the United States, Canada, Australia, and other established sources.

The Many Faces of Land Investment

China's agricultural investors are even more fragmented than its minerals producers. They can be divided into three types: major national enterprises associated with the central government, major regional firms supported by the provincial or national authorities, and local and private investors, usually small firms or individuals.[58]

The size of the enterprise correlates broadly with the distance it goes in securing agricultural resources. The major national companies, most notably the China State Farm Agribusiness Corporation (CSFAC) and the China National Agricultural Development Group Corporation, receive the bulk of the central government's assistance in going out and are involved in Australia, Latin America, Africa, and other distant locations. Moreover, for the larger Chinese ventures (such as those in Brazil and Australia) as much as 90 percent of the capital comes from the state-owned sector.

Provincial-level state farm agribusiness corporations (SFACs) can act independently or partner with CSFAC.[59] Perhaps the most prominent provincial SFAC is the commercial entity of the Heilongjiang State Farm Bureau, the Beidahuang Group. Founded in 1998 and based in the northeastern province of Heilongjiang, the state-owned enterprise is involved in purchases of grains, oil-bearing crops, beets, fruit, meat, milk, and marine products.[60] Beidahuang is heavily involved in overseas land investment, with notable investments in Argentina, the Philippines, and Australia, among others. In 2011 the governor of Argentina's Río Negro province signed a $1.5 billion deal (that ultimately failed) that would give Beidahuang exclusive control over the supply of soybeans, corn, and other crops from an area of up to 320,000 hectares for twenty years. In the Philippines, Beidahuang signed a deal to develop rice, corn, and other crops over an area of about 200,000 hectares in the province of Luzon. As of early 2013, Beidahuang was also reportedly looking to gain access to tens of thousands of hectares of land in Australia.

How does China compare to others in the scale and scope of its land acquisitions? According to an International Institute for Sustainable Development report, in 2007, the country's foreign direct investment in agriculture ranked third after the United States and Canada.[61] However, international agricultural investment from all countries remains less than 2 percent of total international investment in natural resources.[62]

Chinese land and agricultural investments around the world differ in form and purpose. In African countries such as Zambia and Senegal, Chinese-invested farms are often smaller-scale, as in ten hectares or fewer, and typically serve local Chinese communities, such as those that emerge around particular resource or infrastructure investments. Poor infrastructure and high transportation costs limit Chinese interest in larger-scale agricultural investment in Africa. Political challenges also affect these agricultural investment decisions. According to one Chinese official, African countries such as Tanzania, Angola, and Zimbabwe boast ample farmland, but Chinese investors are concerned about insurgents, employee kidnappings, and changing investment regulations.[63] In addition, larger Chinese agricultural enterprises, which are most interested in developing export opportunities, often face a paucity of skilled labor, as well as difficulties gaining access to pertinent information on matters such as soil quality and complex land tenure issues.[64]

Chinese companies' preference is to own land outright to ensure "product safety, lower production costs, and better profits."[65] Where owning land outright is not possible, they invest in infrastructure and processing facilities; in the case of Brazil, this allows them to purchase soybeans directly from Brazilian farmers, circumventing multinational grain companies. Here, too, challenges emerge. In Brazil, the additional costs for translation services to overcome language barriers, as well as farm labor costs—which run two to three times those of Chinese labor—can make investment prohibitively expensive for some Chinese farming enterprises.[66]

Chinese investment in agriculture generally ranks a distant second or third to that in energy or minerals in a given country. In Brazil, about 20 percent of Chinese investment is in agribusiness (as opposed to 45 percent in energy). In Australia, in 2011, $4.2 million of a hefty $9.8 billion in Chinese resource investment was directed toward agriculture. In contrast to Brazil and some other countries, however, Australia is seeking to reduce barriers to land purchases.

Water, Water, Everywhere?

Chinese companies do not go out in search of water in the same way they seek investments in land, minerals, or energy, in substantial part because water is not traded on a large scale on global markets.[67]

Instead, they influence water resources in other countries through their use of rivers that flow through China before entering other countries downstream.

Water-parched China controls the headwaters of at least ten of Asia's transboundary rivers, prominently the Yarlung Tsangpo, which becomes the Brahmaputra in India and Bangladesh; the Lancang, also known as the Mekong, in Cambodia, Burma, Vietnam, Laos, and Thailand; and the Ili and Irtysh, which flow into Kazakhstan. (The Irtysh also flows into Russia.) Downstream countries rely on these water resources for a range of agricultural, energy, and fishery needs. As local Chinese governments and companies build dams and hydropower facilities, and in some cases consider river diversions, they can drastically affect the availability of water for their downstream neighbors. With few exceptions, however, China has been reluctant to engage in discussions of water-sharing rights, asserting that it alone has the right to determine how the water is used.

It is most helpful, then, to think of the main players when it comes to water as the government agencies overseeing water policy rather than the companies implementing projects. (This contrasts with the other resource areas studied here, since the Chinese government has more control over companies operating at home than abroad.) The primary overseer of Chinese water policy is the Ministry of Water Resources (MWR), which works with eight other departments under the State Council in what has been described as the "nine dragons who administer water."[68] There are also seven River Basin Commissions (RBCs) that share in administrative authority. And decision making isn't fragmented just at the national and regional level; an array of responsibilities for water data, infrastructure, transportation, agriculture, and sustainability are devolved to local authorities in a manner that further frustrates any hope for a well-coordinated water policy.[69]

This fragmented domestic approach to water governance makes it all the more difficult to integrate concerns about impacts on other countries (and China's bilateral relations) into water policy. The extent of coordination between the Ministry of Water Resources and the Ministry of Foreign Affairs is unclear, though Chinese water experts Feng Yan and He Daming note that the lack of any "single specialized official agency in charge of China's transboundary waters" has led to "administrative overlap" and a more basic "lack of clarity in how China's water resources are managed."[70] The Ministry of Foreign Affairs lacks expertise in water issues and often defers to agencies like the MWR, the Ministry of Environmental Protection, the National Development and Reform Commission, and the State Electric Power Corporation.[71] As a result, when it comes to international water policy, the MWR—an agency with little diplomatic expertise—often plays the leading role.[72]

Water also differs from other resources in the geographical distribution of foreign impacts. (We discuss the precise patterns of impacts more thoroughly in chapter 8, which looks at how these affect international relationships and security.) Chinese companies target opportunities for oil and gas, minerals, and land in large part on the basis of where the best overseas prospects are. The locations of Chinese water-related projects, in contrast, are driven by the geography of domestic needs for water and hydroelectric power, and of domestic water resources. As a result, the impacts on other countries are incidental; China does not, for example, seek to "acquire" water resources from Kazakhstan, but the geography of domestic water resources and needs means that domestic activities affect Kazakhstan downstream.

Business Not Quite as Usual

China has followed in others' footsteps by shifting from merely buying resources through trade to investing directly overseas; in doing so, it is joining other countries, not creating a new phenomenon of its own. China's strongest presence so far is in oil, though even there, the scale of investment remains limited compared to that of other major players and will still lag even in ten years, given the strong head start that others have. China remains a minor participant in minerals and land investments, though the role of its companies is steadily growing. Moreover, averages can be deceiving: in more and more individual countries, China is either the biggest player or the largest source of new investment and growth.

Yet even where Chinese investments are relatively small, they can have new and significant consequences, in part because they differ from most others in important ways. Though many observers have exaggerated the top-down and strategic nature of Chinese investment and have overstated the novelty of some of the tools employed, it remains true that many Chinese companies (particularly the largest ones) benefit from government support that most of their competitors do not possess, thus changing the world of natural resource investments. Cheap money, which can allow Chinese companies to underbid competitors, is the most obvious aid, though that might be scaled back if the Chinese economy stumbles. The ability and willingness of many Chinese companies to call on their government for help may have more pervasive consequences, not all of which, however, ultimately help those companies get ahead.

5

China Arrives

IN MAY 2012, THE Mongolian parliament dropped a bombshell. Mongolia's vast territory, sandwiched between China and Russia and rich in resources, had long been wide open for foreign investment. Now a new Strategic Entities Foreign Investment Law would require government approval for foreign investments over $75 million in "strategic sectors" such as mining that would result in a 33 percent or greater foreign stake. Parliamentary approval would be required for any foreign majority stake.

The reaction from foreign investors was harsh and immediate. By the end of 2012, investment in Mongolia had dropped 17 percent from the year before. The government quickly revisited its decision and, in April 2013, clarified that the rule was targeted only at investment by state-owned enterprises. In fact, it was a thinly veiled attempt to protect Mongolia against Chinese investment. The powerhouse Chinese mining state-owned enterprise Chalco was attempting to buy a 60 percent share in South Gobi Resources Limited, a subsidiary of the British Australian mining behemoth Rio Tinto, for nearly $1 billion.[1] The new law was designed to stop it.

China is Mongolia's largest foreign investor; just over 50 percent of all foreign direct investment comes from Chinese companies. Moreover, approximately 90 percent of Mongolia's exports—overwhelmingly raw materials—go to China. According to Gotov Battsengel, the chief executive officer of the Mongolian Mining Corporation, "Mongolia's mining fever is driven by Chinese consumption...virtually, we have one customer."[2]

Yet such extensive trade and investment ties with China have yielded at least as much concern as enthusiasm in Mongolia, which is wary of too great a Chinese presence and influence in the country's economy. Ganhuyag Chuluun Hutagt, former vice finance minister, has said, "We will not be another Africa...we cannot afford to have one particular nation control our business."[3] Centuries of Chinese and then Soviet rule have also made Mongolians particularly sensitive to outside influence. An April 2012 poll revealed that only 1.2 percent of Mongolians believe China is the "best partner for Mongolia."[4] Human rights activist Oyungerel Tsedevdamba cites Chinese labor exports and weak environmental standards among the reasons Mongolians prefer that their country do business with other investors.[5]

As a result, Mongolia has gone to extraordinary lengths to defend itself against closer economic integration with China. It is building a railroad to bring coal from the Gobi desert to China but will use its own rail gauge rather than matching it to that of China. This means transporting coal across the border will require either changing the undercarriages of the trains or transferring the coal to trucks, adding an estimated $120 million annually to the export costs.[6] Fears of Chinese workers flooding in are pervasive, and immigration from any one country is limited to ten thousand workers. In the mining sector, companies must recruit nine Mongolian workers for every foreign worker brought in, while construction companies pay a fee of 15 percent of the foreign worker's salary to the Mongolian government. Still, according to one Chinese report, companies often prefer to pay the extra costs for their workers, viewing Mongolian workers as "lazy, alcoholic and unwilling to adhere to normal working hours."[7] Conflicts between Mongolians and Chinese are frequent.

Few countries share the history, geography, and economic complementarity of Mongolia and China. Yet the former's experience navigating the range of opportunities and challenges posed to resource-rich countries by rapidly rising Chinese investment is far from unique. In just over a decade, this investment has helped transform many resource-rich developing countries. The immediate economic benefits are easily seen in thriving mining industries, new

highways, and active ports around the globe. The ultimate impact
of this investment on the political, social, and broader economic
fortunes of these same countries, however, is less clear.

Foreign direct investment can have wide-ranging and positive impacts on economic, social, and political development.
Multinationals tend to provide higher wages than local businesses.
They also typically offer more worker training and, as a result, do
more to boost people's skills than local enterprises.[8] FDI also tends
to improve labor practices by encouraging stronger workers' rights
and the rule of law, social services, and infrastructure necessary to
support better working conditions.[9] Moreover, multinationals can
contribute to stronger environmental performance through their
adherence to higher standards (often imposed by their home governments) and use of more advanced and environmentally friendly
technologies than others might.[10]

Technology transfer is another potential positive spillover from
foreign investment, particularly when the technology gap between
the host country and the foreign investor is small.[11] One might
hypothesize that China, which deploys a vast range of technologies at home that is often appropriate to developing economies,
has the potential to be a particularly important player in raising
technology levels through its investments in resource-rich developing countries.

Foreign investment in resource production also has the potential to generate significant government revenues that can then be
spent so as to boost economic growth far more broadly. Here,
however, much depends on whether the host government is transparent and efficient—encouraging effective use of resources and
society-wide benefits—or corrupt and inefficient, which leads to
narrower distribution of benefits and often produces widespread
societal discontent.

Does Chinese investment in natural resources live up to
the transformative potential that foreign investment in general can deliver? Or does it reflect the worst of what's possible?
There is significant disagreement on this count. Media reports
tend toward extremes: the Chinese are either singlehandedly

responsible for rejuvenating the resource-rich countries of the world or plundering the world's riches and undermining global standards in labor, environment, and governance in the process. Scholars also disagree among themselves. Economist Dambisa Moyo reflects one prominent camp when she argues that Chinese investment is a boon to Africa: "China's rush for resources has spawned much-needed trade and investment...a huge benefit for a continent seeking rapid economic growth."[12] Other experts share the sentiment of the well-known development economist Paul Collier, who advised in his 2007 bestseller *The Bottom Billion*, that "natural resources are not the royal road to growth unless governance is unusually good. In the bottom billion it is already unusually bad, and the Chinese are making it worse, for they are none too sensitive when it comes to matters of governance."[13] And a third group comes down somewhere in between: political scientist Deborah Brautigam, for example, has written (focusing on Africa) that "the deciding factor in each case is likely *not* to be China, but individual African countries and their governments."[14]

The experience of a wide range of resource-rich countries with Chinese investment suggests there is an element of truth in each of the perspectives. The positive potential social and political benefits have yet to be fully realized, while at the same time the worst fears are overblown. Determining how Chinese investment in natural resources is shaping social, environmental, and political dynamics in resource-rich countries requires looking carefully both at how China behaves at home and at how resource-rich countries govern inward investment. Understanding how China's own political economy functions is essential to making sense of how its companies perform overseas. These firms and officials behave abroad in very much the same way they behave at home; changes at home are thus a central driver for changes abroad. The strength of the political and social institutions of the individual economies in which Chinese companies are investing is also critical in determining outcomes; the experience of one resource-rich country can differ radically from that of another.

Diplomat Deal Makers

In March 2013, Chinese President Xi Jinping traveled to Africa promising a new round of Chinese win-win investment, trade, and aid for the continent. This time Beijing pledged to deliver $20 billion in loans over the next three years and laid out a range of new projects in infrastructure and agriculture. At the time, China was already responsible for more than 15 percent of foreign direct investment in Africa. Such investment has earned accolades from many of the region's leaders. Former Senegalese president Abdoulaye Wade wrote in the *Financial Times*, "China's approach to our needs is simply better adapted than the slow and sometimes patronizing post-colonial approach of European investors, donor organizations and non-governmental organizations."[15]

This is Chinese business doing what it does best, with top political leaders acting as diplomat deal makers for the country's largest banks, natural resource firms, and construction companies. As in China itself, many big deals involve the central government and include state-owned enterprises, banks, and (often) local officials. A coordinated (or at least somewhat coordinated) Chinese approach can enable Chinese leaders to put together packages that appeal to a range of decision makers in resource-rich countries in ways that other potential investors often cannot. Chinese lending terms are also attractive to many countries, where they are known for "the absence of political strings, competitive interest rates, and flexible repayment schedules."[16]

China's ability to bring multiple tools to the table often leads people to conclude that it gets better deals. This isn't necessarily true. Chinese investments abroad turn a profit less often than others do; According to McKinsey, as many as 67 percent of overseas acquisitions have gone bankrupt or have failed to make a profit, surpassing the average global rate by 17 percentage points.[17] Chinese companies, as relative newcomers to overseas resource investments, may be prone to overbidding and other mistakes that undermine profitability. This can actually help the countries where they invest, at least in the short run, since the firms may be willing to invest in projects that others consistently find economically unattractive. However, it is not good for anyone over the long run, since economically unsustainable projects ultimately tend to collapse. Moreover, for Beijing, investments can sometimes be influenced by factors other than the immediate corporate bottom line; beliefs in the value of acquisitions for resource security, technology acquisition, and goodwill can all influence an investment's attractiveness.[18]

Goodwill in particular shapes relationships between China and countries in which Chinese companies invest. Doing business with China is also often a matter more of using informal relationships and personal ties than working through formal institutions or legal practices. One consequence of this is that other authoritarian states in particular find the Chinese state-centered but personalistic approach reassuring. Ties between China and leaders such as Zimbabwe's Robert Mugabe can date back decades, providing a long history of common understanding and shared interests. Alas, the willingness of Chinese firms to engage such regimes on their terms reduces incentives for those regimes to change.

China also works hard to make new friends. In Zambia, one observer commented that the Chinese are a full-service partner: they provide red-carpet trips for Zambian officials with limousines and five-star hotels, develop military ties through training of officers and weapons sales, support agricultural training and research centers, and build special projects such as stadiums and presidential palaces that attempt to serve as a constant reminder of Chinese friendship and largesse (though this sometimes backfires).[19] As a senior oil official in Mozambique noted, "The Chinese like to know that they are your friends before they invest."[20]

There are, however, real risks for China inherent in such an approach. Deals that rely mostly on personal relationships and are blessed only at the highest levels may also unravel when new leaders emerge. Gabon's President Omar Bongo, for example, strongly supported a Chinese bid to develop his country's Belinga mine, home to large deposits of iron ore. The resulting contract became known among some in Gabon as "a contract of shame" for the expansive perks it offered the Chinese partner, such as exemption from all taxes for twenty-five years. The Gabonese government (still led by Bongo) then renegotiated the deal in 2008, requiring that the Chinese revisit the project's environmental and social impact assessments. In 2009, Bongo died, ushering in new Gabonese leadership. Eventually, the Chinese lost the deal to Australia's BHP Billiton (though as of this writing BHP's involvement is again uncertain).[21]

Part of China's appeal for some resource-rich developing countries, as well, is Beijing's willingness to set aside political considerations that other countries, multilateral institutions, and even business leaders often find unacceptable. As former ambassador to the United States and deputy foreign minister Zhou Wenzhong stated in reference to investment in the Sudan, a country largely shunned by Western companies, "Business is business. We try to separate politics from business." He added: "I think the internal situation in the Sudan is an internal affair, and we are not in a position to impose upon them."[22]

What does this mean? For one, Beijing largely rejects economic sanctions against particularly repressive states that would limit Chinese investment opportunities. Thus companies are free to invest where many others are barred or fear to tread. Chinese companies are, for example, the largest investors in Sudan, North Korea, and Iran's energy sector. Beijing's stated aversion to mixing business with politics also means it doesn't pressure countries to improve their governance practices before it lends to or invests in them. (This is, of course, also true of most Western multinationals not otherwise restricted by their home governments.) And as Xi Jinping reassured African leaders, "China will continue to offer, as always, necessary assistance to Africa with no political strings attached."[23] Unlike the World Bank or other public lenders, China does not qualify its loans with requirements for budget transparency in the distribution of resource revenues. Macky Sall, president of Senegal, reflected a common view of this approach in a 2013 interview with the journal *Foreign Affairs*:

> The cooperation with China is much more direct and faster than the cooperation we have with Western countries—the United States, European countries, and other bilateral donors. There are a

lot of criteria on governance, on this and that, and a lot of pro-cedures.... That's one of the obstacles to effective cooperation: too many procedures. I'm not saying that what China is doing is better, but at least it's faster. And we need speed.[24]

This no-strings-attached approach does not win China friends everywhere, however. Some senior officials in resource-rich coun-tries are less sanguine about the willingness to ignore conditionality. Former Zambian minister of trade, commerce, and industry Dipak Patel, for example, expressed appreciation for intervention from the outside: "The World Bank can't outbid the Chinese. They always wanted conditionalities. I oversaw the privatization of 9 of 10 major industries. We actually like the conditionalities because it allowed us to be pressured into doing things."[25]

Moreover, although an integrated approach to resource invest-ment has clear benefits to Chinese companies, it also creates chal-lenges. The close ties between many Chinese natural resource companies and the Chinese state, for example, are occasionally a source of disquiet in resource-rich countries; officials and busi-nesspeople express apprehension over the large number of SOEs involved in China's overseas foreign direct investment. In some cases, there is concern that trade and investment conflict with a state-owned firm might bleed into the broader political rela-tionship, or vice versa. For example, in 2010, a political flare-up between Japan and China disrupted rare earths trade between the two countries.[26] (Rare earths are a class of elements critical to a host of energy, defense, and other advanced technologies; as of 2014, their production was dominated by Chinese mines.) As China seeks rare earth investments outside its borders in countries such as Australia, such concerns are magnified as countries worry about rising Chinese control over an important market.

In other cases, however, conflict over Chinese overseas resource investment stems from little more than a popular unease that Beijing is using Chinese companies—whether SOEs or private—to siphon off valuable resources. Mongolia, for example, worries that China is "stealing" its coal.[27]

Corruption

The relationship-based, often opaque nature of Chinese resource investments also raises the specter of corruption, and with it, significantly reduced value of resource investments to broader populations in resource-rich countries. Within China itself, corruption is viewed as both an essential element of doing business and a life-threatening disease. Xi Jinping, on taking office as Communist Party general secretary in November 2012, warned that if the Party could not rid the country of endemic corruption, it would lead to the death of not only the Party but perhaps also the Chinese state. The natural resource sector in particular offers many opportunities for corruption to flourish at home. A study by Chinese University of Hong Kong professor Zhan Jing revealed that within China itself, resource abundance—including oil, natural gas, coal, and other nonfuel minerals—breeds corruption through unclear property rights and heavy state intervention, which contributes to rent seeking. Bribery, embezzlement, and tax evasion are commonplace; even obtaining a job in the natural resource sector has a price tag attached.[28] Zhan's findings are supported by a 2010 survey of almost 7,000 Chinese officials, in which 62 percent believed the Department of Land and Resources to be the most corruption-prone of all the government bureaucracies.[29]

Corruption at home also appears to condition behavior abroad. According to economists Ivar Kolstad and Arne Wiig, Chinese foreign direct investment in resources has flowed primarily to two recipient types: OECD countries with large markets (which we explore in chapter 7) and non-OECD countries with a combination of large natural resources and weak institutions (which tends to go hand-in-hand with greater potential for corruption).[30]

The ultimate upshot of Kolstad and Wiig's analysis may be that when it comes to corruption, it takes two to tango. The 2011 investment by the state-owned China Metallurgical Group Corporation in Afghanistan's Aynak copper mine illustrates this. Following a highly competitive bidding process (in which the MCC beat out nine other firms), accusations of corruption emerged. A U.S. official claimed that the Afghan minister of mines and industry accepted $30 million in bribes for awarding MCC the contract, and James Yeager, a consultant to the Afghan Ministry of Mines and Industry, concluded that the Aynak deal had undergone a "murky and insufficient tender process" and that "bribes were paid to Afghan officials at clandestine meetings in Dubai in the Aynak tender process."[31] Yet Yeager's seventy-eight-page, in-depth review of the deal ultimately ended up highlighting wrongdoing not by MCC but rather by the Afghan minister of mines and industry.

Yeager criticized the Ministry on several grounds. The Aynak Tender Evaluation Committee was ill equipped to evaluate the bids: the members themselves questioned their fitness to participate since they lacked the skills necessary to understand the process or determine which aspects of a bid were most important. (Not one had ever been part of a tender process.) Moreover, despite substantial support for institutional development by the World Bank, "licensing [and] contracting" were conducted as if "going through the motions" in order to fulfill some expectation of market standards. The reality was that considerable deal making and personal relations were essential to securing the mine rights. And perhaps of greatest concern, the minister hired a mandated outside transaction adviser who did not have the requisite experience, and then the minister proceeded to lock documents in his office, not sharing them with the transaction adviser. Yeager raised the possibility that bids were tampered with.[32]

In contrast to the Aynak mine case, opportunities for corruption are more limited in states with better transparency and stronger governance institutions. A senior oil official in Mozambique (itself hardly known for strong institutions) claimed that when the Chinese seek extralegal options they are rebuffed, and that when China occasionally presses for new rules they get the message: "Go back and refresh."[33] In Brazil, officials have found that despite their frequent explanations to the contrary, Chinese officials and businesspeople continue to believe that, with a sweep of the pen, Brazilian officials can overcome various restrictions and regulations on foreign investment in agricultural land. The result is far less Chinese investment in Brazil's natural resources than many on either side would like.[34]

The New Colonialist?

In 2005, the Communist Party theoretician Zheng Bijian articulated a developmental path for China that differed radically from that of earlier maturing economies. Zheng claimed China had rejected the model of industrialization that relied on "high investment, high consumption of energy, and high pollution." Instead, its path forward would be marked by "economic efficiency, low consumption of natural resources relative to the size of its population, low environmental pollution, and the optimal allocation of human resources."[35] Unlike previous emerging powers, China also would not "plunder other countries' resources through invasion, colonization, expansion or even large-scale wars of aggression."[36]

Chinese officials and media promoted the theory heavily for a few years, but few analysts in or outside the country would describe Chinese natural resource investment as Zheng did. China has not managed to follow a resource-efficient, environmentally friendly developmental path; by most measures, it ranks as one of the most energy-inefficient and polluted countries in the world, and one in which unsafe working conditions and low wages are common. And Chinese companies, used to operating in such an environment at home, are prone to export their practices abroad. China has, of course, not invaded other countries to exploit their natural resources. Still, many have argued that the pattern of extracting resources abroad but shipping them home for processing is colonialism in another form. For example, Nigeria's widely respected and pro-foreign investment Central Bank governor, Lamido Sanusi, writing in the *Financial Times*, called China's practice of taking primary goods from Africa and selling manufactured ones "the essence of colonialism."[37]

Start with corporate performance on the social and environmental fronts. (We'll come back to the question of neocolonialism soon.) Chinese companies whose primary experience is within China tend to have limited experience operating at international standards for social and environmental performance. To appreciate the consequences of this, it is useful to understand something about Chinese conceptions of corporate social responsibility (CSR). In the West, CSR typically focuses on voluntary social and environmental initiatives that go beyond measures directly benefiting the bottom line or required by law. In China, CSR is typically prescribed by the government, and it encompasses a much wider range of activities, everything from ensuring strong corporate governance to following national laws when operating abroad.[38] (One way to think about this is that in China, the line between the legal and political realms is far more blurred than in the West, leading to a less clear distinction between social and legal responsibilities.) In the context of this broad conception, the results of China's national 2010 CSR survey are particularly striking. Only 5 percent of Chinese company officials surveyed said they had a high level of CSR understanding, 26.7 percent claimed a reasonably good understanding, 40 percent had heard of CSR but didn't know what it meant, and 22.9 percent said they had never heard of it. According to the survey's authors, there are several reasons for the weakness of CSR among Chinese companies: sometimes they lack an effective CSR evaluation system, sometimes there are few government incentives to encourage companies to engage in long-term CSR programs, and a third reason—perhaps offered tongue in cheek—is that "the world is not perfect."[39]

One result for Chinese companies investing abroad, as noted by Professors Chen Dun and Zhou Jialei of the Beijing Technology and Business University and China Politics and Law University, respectively, is a serious image problem: "The lack of [CSR] initiatives has tarnished the overall reputation of Chinese enterprises, brands, and the country as a whole, greatly hindering the ability for new Chinese companies to continue the going out strategy."[40] Weak Chinese practices also mean that the prospect of companies exporting social and environmental standards to the rest of the world is exceedingly small.

This is perhaps clearest when it comes to environmental performance. Extractive industries such as mining and oil and gas production are often problem-ridden regardless of who conducts them, prone to generate environmental difficulties, labor challenges, and social discontent if handled poorly. Contrary to Zheng's claim that China will somehow be different, Chinese multinationals engender at least as many problems in their drive for resources as firms from any other country do. Indeed, according to many observers in resource-rich countries, Chinese companies tend to come in below average in the corporate behavior ranks.

When it comes to the environment, this result is not surprising, given China's environmental conditions and corporate practices at home. The environment has long taken a back seat to rapid economic development in China, with low investment in environmental protection, few political and economic incentives for firms to minimize pollution, and only weakly enforced regulations and laws. As a result, China endures some of the world's worst air pollution, water pollution and scarcity, and land degradation. Pictures of Beijing's life-threatening smog or sixteen thousand dead pigs floating down Shanghai's Huangpu River in 2013 can be seen by anyone with an Internet connection. And what can't be seen is equally concerning: Beijing often refuses to release the full results of pollution studies, but without public information there is no accountability mechanism for polluters.

Without effective environmental regulations, transparency, and enforcement at home, Chinese companies are unlikely to bring strong environmental practices when they invest abroad. Instead, extractive industries bring with them the business model that has succeeded at home. One element of this is a lack of tradition in environmental impact assessments (EIAs), which are evaluations of the likely and potential environmental implications of a particular development project. Although EIAs are legally required for large development projects in China, companies frequently ignore the regulation. In many instances, they have similarly failed to comply with EIA regulations abroad.

The story of the Zhonghui Mining Group, the largest privately owned Chinese company operating in sub-Saharan Africa, reveals how difficult it is for Beijing to control the actions of Chinese companies operating abroad. In 2009, Zhonghui signed a $3.6 billion deal with the Zambian government under President Rupiah Banda to develop copper reserves in Zambia. Chinese investment in the Ichimpe copper mine, one of two projects the company planned to develop, was estimated to create three thousand jobs for Zambians.[41]

The Banda government supported Zhonghui's investments; President Banda himself reportedly called the Ichimpe mine investment a "positive development that demonstrates the relevance of private investment in the mining industry."[42] Zhonghui, although a private company, received loans from and enjoyed a close relationship with the EXIM Bank.

As soon as construction began in 2011, however, Zhonghui encountered problems. It began building the mine without conducting an environmental impact assessment, violating Zambia's 1997 EIA regulations. A change in Zambian leadership in 2011 brought increased scrutiny to a large number of previous land and mining deals. Those favorable to the new administration described the scrutiny in terms of a shift toward better government; some of those who were skeptical believed that the new administration simply wanted to nullify previous deals to reap its own payments and bribes as the various concessions were sold anew.[43] Which motivation prevailed in the Zhonghui case is unclear, but either way, the consequences were stark. The new minister of mines and natural resources, Wylbur Simuusa, told Zhonghui to "stop immediately" because the EIA and mine plan were not approved. The new government halted the Ichimpe project until Zhonghui could produce a valid EIA. By February 2012, Zhonghui had not done so, and the next month, the Ministry of Mines and Natural Resources issued default notices to Zhonghui, threatening to cancel their mineral processing and exploration licenses if they did not pay restitution. In May, the government charged Zhonghui, as well as Zambia's former minister of mines and minerals, with graft in the allocation of mining rights to Ichimpe.[44]

Whatever the ultimate reason the new Zambian government pursued Zhonghui, the company's ability to begin building a mine without an environmental impact assessment reflects weak accountability in both the Chinese and the Zambian systems. Zhonghui was able to ignore the regulations of the EXIM Bank and the warnings of the Ministry of Commerce. EXIM Bank's environmental policy, for example, calls for corporations to undertake and enforce EIAs; if a company fails to complete an EIA, EXIM Bank funding is prohibited.[45] In addition, China's Ministry of Commerce released a set of guidelines for foreign investment immediately prior to the Zambian election and identified the environment as an area for particular attention on the part of Chinese companies operating in Zambia.[46] Yet Zhonghui was able to ignore all of this.

The capacity of Zambian governance institutions was also an enabling factor. Indeed, officials and activists there remain concerned about the country's overall capacity to protect the environment, particularly when dealing with firms that do not pay careful attention to environmental regulations. According to a Zambian copper mining expert, one EIA submitted by a Chinese firm for another mine investment was approved even though the EIA was in Chinese—a language no one in the Ministry read.[47] Transparency is also a significant problem: even monies set aside for environmental protection often end up in general accounts. Environmental activists and others further observe that even if EIAs are sufficient on paper, it is a problem to ensure they are monitored for compliance. And as one activist noted, pollution in Zambia has been a long-term problem: "Penalties for pollution are far cheaper than not polluting in the first place, so companies will simply go to court."[48] Such a weak regulatory environment enables companies that are not subject to environmental rules by their home countries to pollute.

For the Chinese government, the challenge of ensuring that companies adhere to both domestic regulations and those of host countries is compounded by a second wave of investment led by small-scale enterprises. Fully two-thirds of the Chinese domestic mining industry is composed of these small firms, which operate outside the direct supervision of the central government, and whose environment, labor, and safety practices are only poorly regulated by local officials.

The reputational risk for China of these largely unregulated Chinese miners going out is significant. In March 2013, the Ghanaian sector minister for lands and natural resources, Alhaji Inusah Fuseini, warned that small, unauthorized Chinese miners were creating a "bad public image" for China in Ghana and "could damage the growing friendship between Ghana and China."[49] The Chinese ambassador reassured the Ghanaian government that Beijing was launching a campaign to discourage Chinese miners—most of whom originated from one particular county in southern China—from coming to Ghana to mine.[50] At the same time, he reflected a widely held belief within China that Ghana's problems must be addressed by the Ghanaian government. He recommended that the government tackle the problem by prohibiting local miners and chiefs from selling their land to Chinese miners, and ensuring that the Ministry of Land and Natural Resources more carefully scrutinize the licenses they grant.[51] This senior-level diplomacy notwithstanding, during the summer of 2013, the Ghanaian government, through a combined military, police, and immigration task force, led a series of often violent raids against the illegal miners, leading to the deportation of more than forty-five hundred Chinese by mid-July.[52]

The environmental consequences of weak rules in resource-rich countries can be compounded when corruption is possible. In a survey of three thousand business executives conducted by Transparency International, Chinese companies placed second only to their Russian counterparts as those most likely to bribe when doing business abroad.[53] In Mozambique, for example, one civil society activist has noted that bribery is rampant in the logging sector. He described the problem of illegal logging with regard to China as significant and the result of malfeasance on the part of both countries:

When the [Mozambican civil] war was over, the United States and other countries invested a great deal of money in de-mining [i.e. removing land mines]; the United Nations and other donors footed the bill. Then the Chinese started cutting in those areas for timber. There is no capacity to deal with it. There is a small, unprepared group linked to the Agriculture Ministry, but they have little technical expertise in forestry. There is a high propensity for bribery.[54]

As Chen and Zhou suggest, however, Chinese companies pay a steep reputational price when their environmental performance is poor. In 2005, the China Metallurgical Group Corporation paid $1.4 billion for the option to develop the Ramu nickel mine in Papua New Guinea (PNG). MCC held 61 percent of the project, while other Chinese investors as well as the Australia-based Highlands Pacific held the rest. The deal was agreed to at the highest levels between PNG's Prime Minister Michael Somare and the Chinese government. In 2010, the Chinese leadership extolled the potential of the Ramu mine to improve Sino-PNG relations. Li Keqiang, who was soon to become the premier of China, referred to the mine as representing "win-win cooperation" between China and PNG. He even went so far as to say that as a result of MCC's dedication to sustainable development and corporate social responsibility, the Ramu nickel mine was a "model for cooperation in mineral resources and other fields" between the countries.[55]

Yet the reality on the ground, like that of most mining projects in PNG, turned out to be different. The mine was beset by environmental and land tenure problems from the start. More than 95 percent of PNG land is privately owned, with much of it controlled by various tribes. According to China's Ministry of Commerce, the tribal borders are ill defined, leading to constant conflict over correct ownership; indeed, land tenure issues inflamed by past Western mining investments led to a long-running civil war.[56] In the MCC case, PNG landowners consistently asserted that their concerns were ignored and that they were falsely represented by "landowners associations who represent[ed] ... only selected clans."[57] The landholders held a large demonstration in January 2012, which ended in chaos; during the mayhem, the man whom MCC recognized as representing the landholders—despite the landholders' claims to the contrary and who had previously spent time in jail for "abusing genuine landholders"—died.[58]

Pollution also stoked discontent. MCC announced that it planned to dump 100 million tons of heavy metal and toxic mine waste into the Basamuk Bay near the mine over a twenty-year period. This method of deep-water disposal has been used at a number of mining sites throughout the world, but it is highly controversial.[59] Although the company claimed its dumping system was safe for the environment, critics immediately pointed out that 150 meters did not qualify as "deep sea" and that the EIA undertaken by MCC's partner Highlands Pacific was "sloppy," ignoring the identification of the types of toxins in the tailings, the consequences of depositing tailings on the seabed, and the impacts of the tailings on marine life.[60]

The PNG government initially attempted to protect MCC, passing an amendment to the country's environment act that prevented resource companies from being prosecuted over environmental damage. As in the case of the Ichimpe mine in Zambia, however, the advent of a new set of leaders in PNG changed the relationship between the mining company and the government. In January 2012, the newly installed government of Peter O'Neill revoked the act. The environment minister stated, "Repealing the Environment Act Amendments is a big first step for myself and the O'Neill-Namah government in restoring the proper rights of landowners to be able to protect their interests."[61] In April 2012, the minister of environment and conservation shut down the mine, citing concerns that a slurry pipeline had been built too close to a major highway and was not raised on steel supports as the law required. He admitted, under questioning by the Eastern Highlands governor in a parliamentary hearing, that there had already been problems when the pipeline was moved onto a major road.[62]

The legal battles were significant. In 2011, the National Court judge David Canning acknowledged that the dumping would seriously harm the lives and future of thousands of coastal people and that the environmental consequences of the dumping would be irreversible. But as he also noted, MCC had a permit, the dumping was permitted for ten years, and an injunction might affect investor confidence. On an appeal in December 2012, the court came down with a split decision supporting MCC's ability to dump the tailings into the sea. However, protests have continued.[63]

Land Acquisitions

The PNG experience points to the potency of any Chinese resource acquisition efforts that encounter concerns over land ownership. This is on acute display when Chinese companies' investment target is land itself.

As the Chinese seek secure sources of agricultural products, their efforts stir controversy. Grassroots and occasionally official protests related to China's overseas farmland acquisition have occurred in countries as diverse as Australia, Argentina, New Zealand, Kazakhstan, and the Philippines. In the Philippines, even though the government is eager to further agricultural trade with China, people have protested the investment. Popular opposition there led to the suspension of an agreement to lease almost three million acres of land for the production of hybrid corn, rice, and sorghum to be shipped back to China.[64] And in Kazakhstan, protests arose over an agreement to lease one million hectares of farmland to grow soy and other crops.[65] One protestor claimed that "the Chinese have only one aim—to take our land." At the same time she placed equal blame on the Kazakh government: "The Chinese are not to blame. It's our corruptible officials." Another argued, "We see the potential for a situation whereby one day, when it comes to repaying nearly $20 billion to China, we will have no money and no oil—because the oil is no longer ours. . . . We will start giving away our territory."[66]

In Brazil in 2010, the government announced a new interpretation of its land laws, which prohibited foreigners from purchasing land in Brazil except as minority stakeholders in joint ventures. This move was not explicitly targeted at China, but according to Brazilian agricultural officials the explosion of Chinese interest in land purchases contributed to the decision to revise the formal understanding of the law.[67] Importantly, some Brazilian governors and business leaders in soybean-rich states concluded that most of the Chinese companies were not serious about doing business. According to a business official, "all the local governments in China have funds for foreign direct investment that they must spend, and a trip to Brazil is not a bad way to spend the money."[68]

Chinese agricultural firms' efforts to purchase large tracts of land in Argentina have also raised both environmental and nationalist alarm bells. The failure of a $1.5 billion investment in the development of some 320,000 hectares of unused agricultural land in Argentina's Río Negro Province by Heilongjiang's Beidahuang Group reflected such concerns. The associated lease was scheduled to extend for twenty years, allowing the Chinese company to produce soy, corn, wheat, barley, and sunflowers. The deal was publicized by Río Negro Province as a "food production agreement," while local opposition called it a "land grabber's instruction manual."[69]

Challengers to the deal also raised concerns over the environment. Conservation biologist Raul Montenegro observed that Río Negro's government officials violated a number of laws, since they "didn't do any tests on the land to measure the possible impacts of these activities, nor did they consult anybody before signing the agreement." He also noted that investment by China was of particular concern to many in Argentina: "China is the country most affected by the extension, intensity, and economic impact of land degradation. So it is difficult to believe that they won't make the same mistakes with their land in Río Negro as they have in their own country."[70]

In December 2011, the Argentinian Congress passed legislation restricting ownership by a foreign individual or company at 1,000 hectares and placed a 15 percent cap on the amount of land available to foreign landowners, of which no single nationality can own more than 30 percent. Land that contains or borders major and permanent water bodies is further barred from foreign land ownership. As in the case of Brazil, the Argentinian decision was at least partly influenced by the rapid rise in Chinese demand.

Even some Chinese officials are uncomfortable with the country's overseas investments in agricultural land. Xie Guoli, a senior official at the Ministry of Agriculture, commented, "It is not realistic to grow grains overseas, particularly in Africa or South America. There are so many people starving in Africa, can you ship the grains back to China?"[71] Others fear that closer integration with the international community will breed dependency. As Minister of Agriculture Han

Changfu stated in 2012, China "will not and cannot" rely on imports to feed itself.[72]

However, these cautionary voices are drowned out by others. A few Chinese officials, for example, have spoken publicly of their desire to have their agricultural workers farm land abroad. In 2007, the head of EXIM Bank, Li Ruogu, suggested that Africa has plenty of land but not a correspondingly significant level of agricultural production. His answer: "There's no harm in allowing [Chinese] farmers to leave the country to become farm owners [in Africa]." Moreover, Li promised the bank would support this effort through investment and project development, and help with the sale of products.[73] There is a fear, not entirely unfounded (though still usually exaggerated), that China will simply export a large number of its people and, in the process, some of its problematic domestic practices. One African leader referred to an oft-cited estimate of one million Chinese farm laborers working in Africa—widely understood to be nowhere close to reality—as "catastrophic."[74]

Labor Lags

Enthusiasm for Chinese investment in resource-rich countries often centers on the potential for new jobs directly in resource production. The reality of Chinese investment as a jobs program, however, is more complicated.

Chen and Zhou's research on Chinese firms' practices overseas lays out a number of labor-related issues. They note that these companies often take advantage of low labor costs. This means they tend to gravitate toward projects that are inherently predisposed to supporting lower wages (mines of marginal quality, for example), perhaps not an economic problem for the resource-rich countries but certainly a public relations problem for the Chinese. (Many of the higher-quality resource projects have also been taken by Western firms that invested far earlier than the Chinese, often leaving the latter with more challenging mines of marginal quality.) Moreover, some of the companies tend to hire only Chinese citizens for certain tasks or operations, a practice that often results in "dissatisfaction and anger among local trade unions and workers." In addition, because the enterprises don't have experience negotiating with trade unions and are used to government support and intervention, they find themselves "largely ineffective" in managing labor disputes that arise abroad.[75]

Chinese companies often pay workers considerably less than typical rates paid by multinationals and ignore workers' rights, desires for vacation time, and need for a safe work environment. Australian scholar Graeme Smith's study of conditions in PNG mines notes that when mineworkers with previous experience at both Chinese-run mines and non-Chinese-owned mines were asked to compare the two, all reported negatively on the living and working conditions at the former in comparison to the latter.[76]

The difficulties can also be compounded by cultural factors. For example, a report prepared for the Extractive Industries Transparency Initiative (EITI) that focuses on Africa concluded that "language barriers, cultural differences and misunderstandings arising from these are impediments to communication and interaction between Chinese, African and Western stakeholders in Africa that should not be understated."[77]

The investment of China's Shougang Group in Peru's Marcona mine reads as a textbook example of many of these phenomena. The Marcona district in southern Peru is famous for its spectacular location on the Pacific Ocean. For Beijing's Shougang Group—one of the oldest SOEs (the company was founded in 1919) and the country's sixth-largest steel company—however, the lure of the remote region was not its stunning coastline but its rich deposits of iron ore.[78] The Marcona mine, with reserves of almost one billion tons of iron ore (a large-sized mine, similar to the Belinga mine in Gabon), was originally discovered and developed in the 1950s by Americans before being nationalized by Peru in the 1970s. In 1992, Shougang made history by becoming the first Chinese company to invest in Latin America with its purchase of the Marcona mine. The investment was also, for a while, the biggest foreign investment in Peru.

When Shougang arrived, Peru (and Marcona in particular) was much in need of outside assistance. Lima and its surrounding countryside, including Marcona, were embroiled in conflict between the Maoist Shining Path, a Communist insurgent organization, and the Peruvian government. Given the tumultuous environment, Shougang's decision to purchase the mine seemed particularly bold and was lauded by the domestic and international press.[79] (It also fit with the Chinese pattern of investing in resource projects with low technical but high political risks.) The Chinese government provided significant support through low-interest loans and tax breaks; Shougang paid $311 million for the mine, which by one estimate was fourteen times the mine's actual worth.[80]

The Marcona mine, run by the Shougang Group's subsidiary Shougang Hierro Peru SAA (hereafter referred to as Shougang Hierro Peru), quickly ran into trouble. As soon as the company purchased the mine, several hundred Chinese miners replaced indigenous workers who had been fired prior to Shougang assuming ownership. More importantly, the additional investment in the region's infrastructure and housing for workers that Shougang Hierro Peru had promised dropped from a pledged $150 million to a far less substantial $38 million, plus an additional $12 million fine to the government.[81] At the same time, in 1995, a combination of corruption and poor business decisions was bleeding Shougang dry back home. When workers at the Shougang Hierro Peru mine went on strike, management decided to fire the union leaders—one of whom later became minister of labor—and hired a private security force to put down the strike.[82] Shougang Hierro Peru further angered workers by clustering families into single houses that had once held only one family each, while Chinese managers lived separately in the Playa Hermosa district and ate in separate cafeterias.[83]

Shougang Hierro Peru's workers also claimed to be among the lowest paid in Peru. Over the next two decades, the Marcona mine was the site of repeated labor, environmental, and safety violations. The mine's environmental performance was not unusual, but importantly its labor record was.[84] Wage disparity among workers at the mine was a constant source of contention and strikes. In April

2007, subcontracting workers implemented a five-day work stoppage, the third strike in less than twelve months, a high rate even for the strike-prone Peruvian mining sector.[85] In 2010, sixteen hundred workers rejected a proposed bonus and went on strike; the action was the fifth within a one-year period.[86] Workers struck again in 2011 and 2012, seeking higher pay and better working conditions.[87]

Though Shougang Hierro Peru has amassed complaints and violations for its labor, safety, and environmental practices, few are complaining about its economic performance. In 2010, the company's ore production rose by 16 percent, reaching six million tons. Meanwhile, profits there rose rapidly. Shougang Hierro Peru was on track to implement a long-planned $1 billion expansion in 2013, which is estimated to increase production capacity by ten million tons.[88] *Latin Trade*'s 2011 survey of Latin America's Best Companies, which analyzed revenue growth and profit growth for companies with more than $100 million in revenue, declared Shougang Hierro Peru the best company operating in all of Latin America, because its revenues grew 124 percent to $700 million while profits rose by 456 percent to $292 million. The magazine cited Shougang Hierro Peru's ability to keep operational costs—which includes labor costs—low as a key factor in its success.[89]

Back in Beijing, however, officials were apparently concerned with Shougang's performance in Peru. In 2011, the Ministry of Commerce's Department of Outward Investment and Economic Cooperation noted that Chinese companies in Peru needed to "respect Peruvian law," "keep good relations with workers to keep disagreements from spiraling out of control," and "employ talented locals and set up fun village activities." Mining companies in particular were encouraged to "pay attention to village problems" and not "put the interests of the company above the village."[90]

How unusual is Shougang Hierro Peru's experience? A comparative study of wages there relative to those of other large Peruvian mines confirms that the company's base pay for low-skilled laborers is lower than others. But it also offers bonuses that can raise a worker's salary, and scholars have speculated that these bonuses may ultimately leave higher-skilled Shougang Hierro Peru workers paid similarly to their counterparts elsewhere. The most striking issue is the differential between old and new workers; wages for the former are $22 to $27 per day (close to the industry average of $30 per day), while the latter are paid only $15 to $17 per day (neither figure includes bonuses and benefits); this is an important source of the ongoing strikes and conflicts with the workers.[91] A detailed review of Shougang's performance also demonstrates a high rate of serious accidents and an above-average number of fines for labor violations, though less tendency to use low-paid contractors and a lower fatality rate than some multinationals have.[92]

Interviews with officials, mine workers, and civil society activists in other resource-rich countries suggest that, in fact, in many cases Chinese labor practices are substandard compared to Western multinationals, or at least they are perceived to be so. One would certainly be hard-pressed to find any case where a Chinese company was lauded for raising the bar on labor practices. A Zambian activist, for example, has this to say:

> The Australians set a high bar, trying to behave responsibly.... The Chinese operate differently. They have no definition of corporate social responsibility, they pay minimum wage, and get around long term plans and benefits for workers by hiring contractors and then rehiring them. There is no monitoring system in place to determine if people keep renewing their contracts over and over again.[93]

This perspective was supported by a former nickel mine worker, who said that the Australian companies are much safer than Chinese or Indian mining companies. He noted that when a new mine is going to open, the first thing prospective Zambian mine workers ask is, "Who is the investor?" If it is an Indian or Chinese firm, "they are less excited." According to this same miner, the Canadian and Australian mining firms are much safer.[94] Some argue that the Chinese mines are less sophisticated and use lower-skilled workers, explaining their relatively low pay. But this in itself is not the end of the story; to the extent that Chinese mining companies are not as aggressive in investing in state-of-the-art equipment, mining investment will tend to produce lower-wage jobs than others' investment does.

Chinese Migration

The strong presence of growing numbers of Chinese workers abroad can affect attitudes toward resource extraction too. Estimates of the number of workers who now seek their fortunes in the world's resource-rich countries range from the hundreds of thousands to the millions. The numbers involved in extractive industries themselves are much smaller, but the number who are active as laborers in massive construction projects can be significant. Former president of Mozambique Joaquim Chissano assessed the Chinese role in extractive industries thusly: "Everyone warns me about Chinese investment in Africa [in resource extraction]; I tell them we're asking where? We don't have any [Chinese workers in extractive industries]." Instead, he pointed out, Chinese laborers abound in construction.[95]

Large expatriate Chinese populations tend to be unpopular among the publics of countries with resource-rich economies. Requirements to use Chinese firms are often written into concessional loans; for example, one EXIM Bank loan to Angola included the requirement that 70 percent of the public tenders for construction and civil engineering contracts for Angola's reconstruction be awarded to Chinese firms, which are prone to using Chinese labor.[96] Some officials claim a motivating factor for using Chinese labor in mining and infrastructure is the fact that they will work seven days per week on longer shifts at lower pay. Spartan living conditions—temporary sheds with bunks or Chinese ships off the coast—also keep costs low. Discussions with senior Chinese foreign ministry officials yield a range of additional and illuminating justifications: "African workers have unions," "they want to go to church," "they refuse to work on weekends even for overtime pay," and "they like to sing and dance."[97] This invariably rankles local populations in the countries where Chinese laborers are sent. From the perspective of many locals, projects tied to Chinese labor remove value from the investment (though others applaud quick completion time on projects that use Chinese workers). As an expert in Mozambique noted, the Chinese practice compares unfavorably to projects funded by the World Bank or the United States Agency for International Development (USAID), which use local labor.[98]

Within extractive industries themselves, reliance on Chinese labor can exacerbate relationships with locals by adding clashing cultures to the mix. Take the case of the Ramu nickel mine in PNG. Ninety percent of the workers at the mine and 87 percent of the workers at the associated refinery reported themselves as either "dissatisfied" or "extremely dissatisfied" with their wages, claiming they earned less than both their Chinese colleagues and PNG workers in other mines.[99] The problem was exacerbated by negative cultural perceptions: PNG workers viewed their Chinese bosses as slave drivers, while the Chinese viewed the PNG workers as lazy.

Some countries have responded to concerns about Chinese workers by adopting new labor regulations that attempt to limit the potential influx. As mentioned previously, in Mongolia, immigrants from any one country are capped at fewer than ten thousand people, and foreign workers are limited as well. In 2012, Vietnam passed a new law requiring that all foreign business give priority to Vietnamese workers; local government committees will first be allowed to solicit Vietnamese workers before any foreign labor can be imported. Conflict has arisen in particular over Chinese plans to bring two thousand workers to a Chinalco-invested bauxite mine in Vietnam.[100]

The Technology and Training Bar

China's going-out strategy nominally incorporates a formal commitment to development in resource-rich countries beyond infrastructure development and resource exploitation. Chinese investment often involves putting money into manufacturing and processing industries, along with assistance in agriculture, health, and education. In three of the most challenging countries for overseas investment—Equatorial Guinea, Nigeria, and Sudan—Chinese companies have provided millions of dollars in educational assistance through scholarships and school construction.[101]

Nonetheless, more often than not, China extracts resources abroad and then ships them back home for processing, removing opportunities for technology transfer. It is this phenomenon, more than any other, that leads to accusations of neocolonialism. In some cases, the trade pattern simply reflects the facts of comparative advantage: it is economically efficient for resources to be processed in China rather than abroad. In other cases, though, the pattern is a result of tariffs on processed goods from elsewhere. This tilts the playing field and directly impedes efforts to add value to resources outside of China.

Partly in response to such concerns, the Ministry of Commerce has established a broad network of special economic zones, overseas areas in which Chinese state-owned enterprises, as well as private firms, undertake significant investment projects with support from the government. The SEZs were formally announced under the auspices of the Forum on China-Africa Cooperation in 2006, but several were already under way. They embrace a range of industries, such as mineral processing, construction materials, and logistics. Zones also incorporate industries not directly related to a host country's resources (for example, automobile manufacturing, textile processing, wood processing, and engineering).[102] They are supported by the Chinese government through tools that include financing, as well as political guidance by senior leaders, who may recommend that certain firms undertake certain projects in certain countries.

In a detailed study of China's SEZ policy, Brautigam and Tang lay out three reasons the Chinese government has promoted these development zones overseas: "Providing a platform to accelerate China's own domestic restructuring by easing the outward investment of mature Chinese firms, increasing demand for Chinese-made machinery and equipment, and reducing trade frictions by relocating Chinese production to third countries."[103]

Some zones may be explicitly tied to host governments' desires to ensure they capture some of the value-added processing associated with China's resource extraction. For example, this may have been the impetus behind the Russian and Chinese governments' decision to develop a forestry product processing industrial zone in Russia. However, these zones are not unique to resource-rich countries; nor do significant resource investments in a country go hand in hand with an SEZ.

There is debate over how well these zones are doing at reducing trade frictions and relocating Chinese manufacturing to host countries. Ana Alves, a scholar at the South African Institute of International Affairs, identifies a number of challenges to the success of these zones. In Mauritius, for example, one Chinese partner did not possess the financial capacity to implement the project, and the two subsequent firms identified by the Chinese government had no real interest in implementing the project. Even in the case of Zambia, in which seventeen companies have registered inside the Zambia-China Cooperation Zone, Alves points out that most of the companies are subsidiaries of those undertaking the onsite infrastructure development for the SEZ, rather than companies engaged in other valuable industries. Chinese developers acknowledge that they are struggling to attract investors, citing cultural and language challenges, lack of familiarity with the African business environment, and the global economic slowdown. Alves also notes there are few formal mechanisms, such as training programs, in place to actively ensure skills and technology transfer from any of the Chinese businesses to local populations.[104]

Chinese companies within the SEZs have thus not yet established themselves as important mechanisms for improving the state of native technological capacity in developing countries where China invests in resources. This confirms the fact that Chinese resource investment is much like that from other countries' multinationals: it typically has limited impact on native technological capacity, particularly beyond resource extraction itself.

The biggest exception is likely in agriculture. Since the late 1950s, China has sent as many as ten thousand agricultural technicians to

Africa. It also partnered with the UK in 2011 to launch a four-year program to help transfer agricultural technology to low-income countries in Africa and Asia.[105] China has established agricultural technology demonstration centers in several African countries, where Beijing provides training courses. It also furnishes, with low-cost loans, the agricultural machinery and equipment on which to train. In Ethiopia, for example, a Chinese-sponsored agricultural demonstration area is well on its way to fruition, with the goal of supporting experimental research, training, and demonstration of agricultural techniques. Chinese experts have taken up residence on site, and at the same time, Ethiopia is sending its own agricultural experts to China for training.

Another joint Ethiopian-Chinese technology project has transferred know-how for making charcoal from bamboo. The Chinese have benefited from selling processing machinery and charging Ethiopian workers for training; Ethiopians, in turn, have developed an entire new industry of growing bamboo to make charcoal.[106]

China Pivots

Has Chinese investment in natural resources transformed the world in the bad ways its detractors warned of—or in the good ways Chinese leaders promised and development theorists have argued are often possible? The track record is more prosaic: for the most part, the country's performance is neither special (companies do not raise the bar on environmental, labor, or financial behavior) nor disastrous (poor Chinese labor and environmental practices often simply track those of extractive industries at large).

Nonetheless, there are departures from this pattern at the margin. Chinese companies often invest in mines and projects that others won't touch, in the process delivering new income and jobs. At the same time, at best Chinese companies, which are used to lax environmental and labor rules at home, have not brought strong new practices to the countries where they invest. Even worse, in cases where host governments' institutions are weak, Chinese companies—not governed effectively by Beijing either—have too often transformed important dimensions of the countries they invest in for the worse.

Regardless of the underlying substance, though, the mixed popular review of Chinese investment in resource-rich countries—some of it rooted in reality and some of it based in misguided perception—is triggering a range of responses within China and in the countries where its companies invest. Although some Chinese officials attribute the companies' problems to a Western conspiracy, others are convinced that the country and its multinationals need to change their tactics, if not their broader approach. Consensus is growing that the firms need to operate at international standards or risk losing out over the long run. Seeing how this is unfolding requires investigating how various actors within China are taking steps to establish a new approach to investment in resource-rich developing economies.

6

Growing Good Governance

ON MARCH 17, 2013, the newly selected Chinese premier, Li Keqiang, warned that the country's continued economic growth was being endangered by corruption and an ever-worsening environmental situation. He pledged greater transparency and more public supervision, and he called on the media representatives arrayed before him in the Great Hall of the People to hold him personally accountable if the government failed to transform the situation.[1] Li's remarks reflected a changing understanding within China about the relationship between economic development and societal well-being. Officials and citizens are rapidly concluding that their own welfare is served poorly by a growth-at-all-costs strategy. Mounting environmental challenges, public health crises, and unsafe labor practices are perceived by many as too steep a price to pay for double-digit economic growth. They want Chinese business to support clean air and water, safe food, and good working conditions. In a February 2013 online poll of more than six hundred thousand Chinese by the *People's Daily*, fighting corruption, reforming health care, and protecting the environment were among the top issues citizens wanted addressed by the National People's Congress.[2] Over the past decade, ideas about how to integrate the public's demands for improvements in social welfare and public goods with economic growth have begun to evolve.

Changes at home are likely to lead to changes in how companies behave abroad. This is all the more probable as the Chinese people also become increasingly aware of their country's place in the world. The country's economic influence, expansive diplomacy, and rising military strength not only give China the ability to have more influence in international affairs but also place it under greater international scrutiny. Officials and citizens alike are increasingly sensitive to claims that, as companies become global players, their investment practices are not up to international standards, and in fact are detrimental to China's image. They are thus searching for ways to ensure that, as companies continue to invest in developing the world's resources, they are viewed as world-class competitors.

Moreover, civil society is no longer dormant. Beijing continues to define the rules of economic development at home, but the media, nongovernmental organizations, and the general public now act as watchdogs, holding local officials and business leaders accountable for their actions—and occasionally scrutinizing Chinese behavior abroad too. Civil society also engages widely with the outside world, drawing on ideas from abroad and helping weave them into the way China does business.

From the Top Down

Shifts within China are producing changes in how Beijing approaches its resource investments. Leaders are taking steps to develop a system of incentives to encourage companies to improve their performance at home and abroad. Ideals of corporate performance that go beyond short-term profits are permeating the institutional infrastructure of the economy from the top down, from the outside in, and increasingly from the bottom up.

These efforts are typically thought of in China under a very broad conception of corporate social responsibility that can encompass basic labor and environmental standards along with respect for the rule of law. Corporate social responsibility in this sense is not a new concept within China. However, the details of what it means within the country have evolved significantly over time. Before 1985, corporate social responsibility meant the responsibility of SOEs to provide health care, education, housing, and retirement benefits for their employees (in contrast with the situation in Western countries, where many of these social welfare concerns are provided for or subsidized by the state).[3] With China's accession to the World Trade Organization in 2001, however, its companies were exposed far more rigorously to the strictures of the global market and to the idea that a commitment to strong environmental protection, fair labor practices, and well-developed corporate governance was essential. The government view also evolved, shifting from interpreting Western countries' focus on standards for corporate behavior as trade protectionism to seeing opportunities for business and government to work together in addressing social needs and challenges.[4]

At the very moment of WTO accession, in fact, the United Nations Global Compact, the world's largest voluntary corporate responsibility initiative, together with the Chinese Enterprise Confederation (a government-sponsored business organization), hosted a high-level meeting in Beijing to begin the process of introducing new approaches to social responsibility to Chinese companies.[5] The Global Compact embraces ten core principles, such as "avoid human rights abuses" and "support environmental protection." Even though initially China's engagement with the Global Compact was overwhelmingly ceremonial, over the next several years, as the economy grew at home and the country's reach expanded globally, social welfare obligations gradually became more deeply embedded in a number of domestic regulations.

China also began to engage in other CSR-related international initiatives. These developments accelerated after 2006, when Beijing adopted the China Company Law. The law mandated that companies commit to corporate social responsibility.[6] Once again, this points to a sharp difference between Western and Chinese conceptions of CSR: for Western companies, CSR includes only measures that are not legally mandated.

To encourage the development of CSR, the Chinese government began to use the influence of its economic and financial institutions. The Shenzhen Stock Exchange, for example, issued a set of "Social Responsibility Instructions to Listed Companies" in September 2006, encouraging listed companies to publish CSR reports and adopt policies that protected the environment and reflected responsibility for social development.[7] The Shanghai Stock Exchange followed two years later with its own guidelines. Most of the guidelines developed by the stock exchanges were and remain voluntary. The Shanghai Stock Exchange, however, has attempted to put teeth into its efforts by requiring that companies immediately report environmental accidents and inform the exchange if they have been blacklisted by an environmental protection agency.[8] Moreover, the Shanghai Stock Exchange has pioneered its own social responsibility metric, the Social Contribution Value per Share (SCVS) rating system, which adds together tax revenues paid to the state, salaries paid to employees, loan interest paid to creditors, and donations and value added for stakeholders and then subtracts the social costs incurred from environmental pollution and other externalities.[9] The Shenzhen Stock Exchange also has detailed requirements with regard to transparency, stipulating that companies disclose information concerning the acquisition and transfer of mining rights overseas, such as evidence that their activities are in line with the laws and regulations of the host country.[10]

Yet adherence to the reporting guidelines outlined by the stock exchanges is weak. According to an evaluation of Chinese corporate social responsibility by the World Economic Forum (WEF), reporting in 2011, about 70 percent of companies listed on the Shanghai and Shenzhen stock exchanges were not following the guidelines concerning publication of CSR reports (which in principle cover activities at home and abroad), and of those that were reporting, many did not have consistent structures or provide balanced information. As the WEF report notes, the stock exchange guidelines don't provide clear guidance as to what should be in the reports, so many reports are "very loosely organized... with high level messages and little supporting data or specific examples."[11] Another study, undertaken by Chinese researchers Jiufang Tang and Pengfei Li, found that state-owned enterprises, large companies, and corporations in high-polluting sectors had the greatest level of reporting compliance. Among the reporting companies, what the companies conveyed also varied greatly, including investment in environmental protection, steps taken to have others certify their good behavior, and other matters.[12] Overall, however, they called disclosure of environmental performance information among listed companies shockingly low.

The large role of China's state-owned enterprises in the country's resource quest, particularly in the first wave of overseas investment, has also provided SASAC with the opportunity to play an important role in promoting better corporate governance. In 2007, SASAC developed its own guidelines for the SOEs that it oversaw. SASAC adopted an extraordinarily broad understanding of CSR in keeping with the Party's own priorities to develop a harmonious society, as well as to become a global leader in innovation. Thus SASAC's guidelines ranged from recommendations such as reducing layers of management and increasing investment in research and development to more traditional understandings of CSR, among them ensuring product safety and reducing energy consumption.[13]

Beijing also uses the leverage of its banking system to encourage Chinese multinationals to improve their environmental and social practices. The China Development Bank stands out for its early adoption of guidelines in these areas. In 2005, CDB required that all firms seeking loans had to undergo an environmental impact assessment and that loan contracts had to include environmental costs and standards. The CDB was also the first state-owned bank to join the United Nations Global Compact; after becoming a member, CDB expanded its loan approval evaluation process by incorporating 142 performance indicators, particularly focusing on "human rights, the environment, labor, and corruption."[14]

The EXIM Bank—the source of all Chinese government concessional loans in support of overseas resource investments—has also published several sets of environmental and social responsibility requirements for its loans. These include not only environmental but also social impact assessments for all projects under consideration. Under EXIM Bank guidelines, if an EIA falls short, the company is supposed to have to reapply for the loan. Borrowers are also required to provide ongoing reports on their projects' environmental and social impacts and ensure that they comply with host country laws.[15] Additionally, the bank notes that where local laws are not well developed, companies are required to follow Chinese or international practices.[16]

These rules appear to have some teeth: in one case, in 2008, the UK-based environmental NGO Brainforest asked EXIM Bank to look into the environmental practices of the China National Machinery and Equipment Import and Export Corporation (CMEC), which had won a tender for the Belinga mine in Gabon. Brainforest argued that the company was violating local laws and thus EXIM Bank's guidelines for financing policy. After review, EXIM Bank decided not to provide financing to CMEC for the hydropower project associated with the mine unless the EIAs could be verified.[17]

Chinese policy makers have also taken steps to encourage companies to become more familiar with the laws and regulations of countries they operate in. Ignorance of local laws and regulations is a common theme in assessments of Chinese companies' activities abroad. While calling the international performance of SOEs "commendable," SASAC Deputy Chairman Shao Ning noted that Chinese firms "generally lack international management skills" and that "they are not familiar with the foreign laws and market standards [where they invest]."[18] Culpability for the poor practices of some firms is often laid at the foot of both Chinese and host country actors: "Some [Chinese companies] ignore their responsibilities, and some countries in Africa with insufficient laws and regulations make it easy for Chinese companies to ignore their social responsibilities, pollute the environment, and fail to comply with local labor laws."[19] Beijing is attempting to rectify such challenges by educating firms and establishing additional layers of bureaucratic oversight. Responding to calls for the government to do more in assisting companies in evaluating the risks in certain countries and ferreting out information about "hidden political, economic, and social problems" in particular regions or with particular projects,[20] the Ministry of Commerce, along with the National Development and Reform Commission and the Ministry of Foreign Affairs, has since 2009 issued a detailed set of measures for overseas investment.

These guidelines include specific information about well over one hundred countries in which Chinese multinationals invest, such as the countries' development priorities, regulations governing foreign investment, and even guidance concerning how Chinese firms are perceived within the country. The Ministry of Commerce also boasts its own in-house think tank, the Beijing New Century Academy on Transnational Corporations, which conducts research and makes policy recommendations on the development of corporate social responsibility.[21] Chinese embassy staff in host countries are further nominally responsible for training staff sent by Chinese companies on local business practices and regulations, as well as community protocol and culture. They also facilitate interactions between overseas Chinese entities and local authorities to ensure compliance with local regulations.[22]

The banking supervisory body, the China Banking Regulatory Commission (CBRC), also issued an additional set of guidelines in 2012 that required banks to organize onsite investigations at least once every two years. In addition, it required that when a bank provides financing for overseas projects, it must "promise in public that appropriate international practices or international norms [with regard to environmental protection, land, health, safety, etc. of the country or jurisdiction where the project is located] will be followed so as to ensure alignment with good international practices."[23]

Yet the government has limited ability to monitor and enforce compliance with its many directives. This is partly a problem of will, but it also has deep roots in the structure of the political system: poor transparency, limited public engagement, and a weak judiciary undermine the ability of even a strong central government to regulate activities across a vast economy. This problem, already large within China, becomes far more acute for companies operating overseas. For example, China's version of the Foreign Corrupt Practices Act (a U.S. law that is designed to prevent bribery and other corruption in overseas business dealings) is the 2008 Administrative Regulation on Contracting Foreign Projects. The regulation states that a company obtaining a project as a result of "contracting any project at an illegitimate low price, or engaging in collusive tendering or commercial bribery" will be fined or have its project revoked.[24] Yet there is no institutional mechanism within the administrative or legal system to monitor or enforce the regulation.

Indeed, the banking sector also complies only weakly with its CSR regulations. In 2012, for example, the CDB signed a memorandum of understanding with the Ethiopia Sugar Corporation granting a $500 million loan to construct six sugar factories in the Lower Omo Valley. These sugar plantations are estimated to divert at least 28 percent of the Omo River's annual flow and lower the water of Lake Turkana—the world's largest desert lake—by at least thirteen meters. Analysts anticipate that once the sugar plantations and a large hydropower project planned to dam the Omo River are complete, migrations among the people of Ethiopia, Kenya, and South Sudan will breed more conflict.[25] With the exception of Chinese banks, all other international financial institutions refused to finance this development as a result of the environmental and likely social impacts.[26] In the face of such international opposition to the project, it is difficult to assert that China Development Bank is adhering to the CBRC's requirements

Chinese companies are also better—although still weak—at the more formal parts of environmental compliance—producing environmental impact assessments, following applicable regulations in the countries where they invest, and even signing up to (if not always following) international standards such as ISO 14001, which is an internationally accepted framework for establishing an environmental management system—than at those parts that are less rule-driven and anchored more in informal consultation and community engagement.[27] An informal comparison of the 2011 CSR reports of seven major Chinese mining companies bears this out.[28] For example, China National Metals Corporation (CNMC), which is listed on the Hong Kong Stock Exchange, subscribes to the Global Reporting Initiative (a framework for reporting on an organization's social, economic, and environmental performance), as well as some international standards, such as ISO 14000.[29] Yet it fails to report on a number of basic metrics, such as investment in environmental protection, investment in workplace safety, and mine fatalities. Many other mining companies or holding groups, such as Chinalco, Shenhua Group, Minmetals, China Coal Energy, and China National Gold Group, similarly publish CSR reports, but they all choose which of the relevant metrics to report.

To provide further encouragement for Chinese companies to improve their CSR efforts and publish CSR reports, the Chinese Academy of Social Sciences (CASS) has developed a rating system for CSR reports. In April 2010, CASS released the criteria on which company reports would be evaluated, among them completeness, substantiality, balance, comparability, readability, and creativity. In CASS's review of the first ten reports submitted, however, every company received either an "outstanding" or "leading" evaluation, prompting some international reviewers to raise concerns over CASS's independence and the potential for the rating system to become a "promotional tool."[30]

From the Outside In

As Beijing continues to put in place new policies and regulations in order to promote better corporate performance, it has often welcomed the opportunity to learn from and cooperate with others outside China. The Ministry of Commerce has encouraged companies to become more active in the United Nations Global Compact. In 2005, Shanghai hosted the Global Compact Leaders' Summit, and at the 2007 summit in Geneva the Chinese delegation boasted as many as one hundred members. By 2012, 299 Chinese companies had joined the Global Compact. Fu Chengyu, former head of the China National Overseas Oil Corporation, has even served on the Global Compact board.[31] Nonetheless, according to statistical analysis of a 2009 survey of the 283 Chinese firms participating in the UN Global Compact, between 2000 and 2008, only 21 percent of the firms were compliant with the Global Compact's reporting requirements, with SOEs posting a higher rate of compliance than private enterprises (though how much higher was not determined).[32]

Chinese CSR engagement in the Extractive Industries Transparency Initiative—a more ambitious effort than the others—is weaker than in other international reporting frameworks. The EITI is a coalition of governments, companies, nongovernmental organizations, and investors seeking to ensure that companies "publish what they pay" and governments "disclose what they receive."[33] The idea behind the EITI is simple: governments of resource-rich countries are encouraged to publish information about the revenues from their extractive industries (oil, gas, and mining), and these revenues are then compared to the payments (taxes, duties, royalties, bonuses, and other payments) that the multinational investors have made to the government. An independent administrator reports on and reconciles any differences that emerge. The information is made public so that people and NGOs can hold their governments accountable.[34] A country can become an EITI candidate by publishing a report reconciling the reported revenues and payments.[35]

Chinese leaders have expressed support for EITI in international forums, supported a UN General Assembly resolution that requires transparency for all member states, and agreed to a resolution at the 2009 Group of 20 (G-20) summit in Pittsburgh that supports participation in EITI.[36] However, Beijing has yet to sign on to EITI as a candidate or supporting country.[37] No Chinese company has become a member, although once states in which they operate are EITI members, some companies will comply with the EITI reporting requirements. Moreover, despite not being individual members, the companies can participate in other ways. China National Petroleum Corporation, for example, became a member of the multistakeholder board of Iraq's EITI in 2010, the first time a Chinese company had taken such a role. The Iraqi EITI group has since reported that CNPC is an "outstanding" participant and advocate for transparency in the oil industry.[38] As Erica Downs notes, the most important variable in CNPC's participation in EITI in Iraq is probably pressure from the host country, though a number of other factors might be playing into CNPC's decision. They include pressure from partners (for example, CNPC has a technical service agreement with BP in Iraq), the hope that CSR is good for business, and a serious commitment to EITI principles.[39]

Other Chinese companies have more indirect links to EITI. For example, Shenhua Coal is a member of the World Coal Association, which is an industry supporter of the International Council on Mining and Metals, which in turn is an industry supporter of EITI. A few companies, such as PetroChina, Zijin Mining, and Yanzhou Coal Mining, have also taken steps toward greater financial transparency by disclosing the taxes they pay to overseas governments, even though they are not members of EITI.[40]

There are a number of reasons behind the weak participation of China in EITI. According to a University of Stellenbosch study, Chinese officials are less aware of EITI than of the UN Global Compact, which is housed within the United Nations, an institution familiar to and respected by Chinese officials. Those officials who do know EITI often perceive it as a "Western NGO," which diminishes its impact since the government generally does not engage with NGOs. In particular, they are suspicious of the funding relationship between the Soros Foundation (which advances a range of democracy initiatives China does not support) and EITI.[41] One of the programs initially created by George Soros's Open Society Institute is the NGO Revenue Watch, which is a "leader in the development and implementation of the Extractive Industries Transparency Initiative."[42] Moreover, the Ministry of Foreign Affairs has said it is concerned that EITI principles and criteria conflict with China's stated (though inconsistently pursued) commitment to noninterference in other countries' affairs.[43]

The fact that international CSR institutions are entirely voluntary also limits their ability to shape Chinese firm behavior. For example, according to a PricewaterhouseCoopers (PwC) evaluation, EITI has had limited impact in shaping Chinese mining practices abroad, in large part because companies can often simply ignore its strictures. In Zambia (an EITI candidate), the EITI Council requires only that holders of "large scale mining licenses" participate in reporting—and many Chinese companies active in the country are small. According to PwC, only a small number of participating companies in Zambia (Chinese or other) actually submitted complete documentation. As a result, the firm found there was a "significant amount" of unresolvable discrepancies between companies' reported revenues and monies received by the government.[44]

To be certain, weak adherence to internationally recognized guidelines or even regulations is not unique to Chinese companies. Indiana University political scientist Scott Pegg, for example, argues that Chinese oil companies are not terribly different from Western oil companies. The latter, he notes, set sharp limits on their role in broader governance and transparency issues. Many firms insist that with regard to mandatory corporate disclosure of all payments made to host governments, the reporting obligation rests with the countries and not the companies; any disclosure, moreover, should be voluntary, not mandatory.[45]

In any case, international CSR networks and organizations are not the only way Chinese companies learn from the outside in. Firms learn from the experience of other multinationals, including from foreign partners in overseas resource projects and from their domestic competitors. In Peru, a Chinese mining executive noted that all the mining companies were learning from the experience of Shougang Hierro Peru, as discussed in the previous chapter. According to the Peruvian-based American scholar Cynthia Sanborn, the larger Chinese mining firms have formed an association in Peru and meet regularly at a club to exchange experiences; those with more experience lend insights to newcomers. Moreover, a cottage industry has developed in Peru to provide consulting services to mining companies, and several try to cater to Chinese needs.[46] This may help explain why the regional coordinator of Revenue Watch has found that more recent Chinese entrants to Peru's mining sector are more responsive to the needs of local people in an effort to avoid the mistakes of their predecessors.[47]

The experience of the Chinese mining company Chinalco in Peru may be one such beneficiary of Shougang Hierro Peru's missteps. In 2007, Chinalco purchased Vancouver-listed Peru Copper, acquiring the option to develop Peru's Toromocho mine, a copper mine with reserves estimated as high as two billion tons. Toromocho is located about seventy miles outside of Peru's capital city, Lima. With a $2 billion loan from EXIM Bank, Chinalco planned to bring the mine online in late 2013. Like Shougang Hierro Peru, Chinalco has faced concerns about its efforts to relocate nearby residents. In response, it has built an entirely new city, Nueva Morococha, for five thousand people, with a central plaza, school, hospital, and churches.[48] According to one estimate, the cost of resettlement to Chinalco is as high as $150–200 million. Only 8 percent of residents have thus far refused to move; the rest have supported the development of the new town and were consulted about their needs in the process.[49]

Chinalco has also brought in outside experts to help ensure that its development process runs smoothly.[50] It hired an experienced Western head and a Canadian firm to develop an environmental management system, and it invested $50 million to design and construct an advanced tunnel wastewater treatment plant.[51] It also uses local rather than Chinese labor.[52] Still, while an independent auditor found Peru's mining sector in compliance with EITI standards—the participation rate of companies signed up to EITI in Peru was over 80 percent—both Chinalco and Shougang Hierro Peru were among those missing from the list.[53]

Moreover, there were some small demonstrations in 2012 opposing Chinalco's development on the grounds that not enough homes have been built to house all the residents of the original Morococha. The local mayor is demanding that Chinalco compensate the town for as much as $300 million for the "loss of identity, culture and tradition," and he is seeking jobs for his town's residents in the new mine.[54] As of early 2013, a "No" campaign among the holdouts was under way to push Chinalco to offer more. But such conflict is endemic to the mining industry; it is hardly a unique issue for projects involving Chinese companies. Indeed, despite these challenges in the relocation process, Chinalco has earned plaudits for its approach within Peru and the broader community that evaluates multinationals' foreign investment practices.

Despite some positive signals, transforming China's business culture will take time. Beyond technical and governance challenges, there is a deeper barrier to change: many companies and policy makers are suspicious of efforts to promote better social and environmental performance for more fundamental reasons. According to a survey of twenty-two extractive companies operating abroad by the international NGO Global Witness and the Beijing-based consulting firm SynTao, many companies are concerned that transparency will reduce their competitiveness, "heighten expectations for Chinese extractive companies to address economic and social hardships in host countries," and bring "increased scrutiny from citizens, NGOs and watchdog groups."[55] As the U.S. Chamber of Commerce describes in a report on Chinese firms' CSR practices, the Chinese government retains some hesitancy about too strong a drive toward international standards, fearing they will prevent some of the companies from investing overseas.[56]

Moreover, in certain Chinese quarters, there remains a deep-seated belief that Chinese companies are unfairly targeted by the West. One op-ed published by the *People's Daily* claims: "The interest groups of some countries are quite vigilant against the investments from China and have deliberately distorted the purposes of the investments. As long as they dig out a tiny thing, they will exaggerate it immediately through the media and attack China's foreign policies."[57] The piece further calls for the Chinese media to play a public relations role, arguing that they have a "duty to provide accurate, complete and timely coverage of Chinese overseas investment projects and should be more proactive in refuting malicious reports from some Western media."[58]

From the Bottom Up

The development of better corporate social performance in most countries embraces a combination of top-down, outside-in, and bottom-up pressures for change. Governments and civil society— including NGOs, corporations, and the broader public—all contribute to developing a set of accepted norms and institutions. To date, China has been largely an exception to the rule: overwhelmingly, Chinese corporate social responsibility has been established in a top-down fashion, with only limited interaction between the key players and the people. More and more, however, citizens are raising questions about, and pushing change in, Chinese CSR practices.

The Chinese people are increasingly aware of the importance of strong corporate social responsibility. This derives almost entirely from their experience at home: corporate malfeasance within China has contributed to numerous tragedies, notoriously among them the poisoning of Sanlu milk powder in 2008, which contributed to three hundred thousand children falling ill and at least six deaths; and the 2008 Sichuan earthquake, in which thousands of people are estimated to have died as a result of shoddy construction. Daily in China, there are reports of companies responsible for serious food safety violations, environmental disasters, and corrupt practices. The public has begun to put pressure on the government to enforce higher standards of CSR through Internet activism as well as protests on the street. The environment ranks as one of the top sources of social unrest in the country. Chinese nongovernmental organizations have also become active players in enforcing corporate accountability, and whereas Chinese civil society is largely focused on improving corporate social responsibility on the home front, some media and NGOs have begun to explore the impact of Chinese investment in extractive industries abroad. A 2011 opinion piece in the *People's Daily* (which, although a Party-controlled newspaper, occasionally publishes pieces that diverge from conventional Party thinking) cautioned firms to "tread lightly when investing overseas" and pleaded for companies to "inform local residents about their efforts." It noted that "keeping a low profile tends to make things even more complicated."[59] A Chinese journalist returning from Africa echoed these sentiments: "State-owned enterprises have disregarded the accumulation of statistical data on corporate social responsibility. In responding to Western media's harsh criticisms, it is all too easy for them to remain passive."[60]

In June 2011, the Chinese environmental NGO Green Watershed traveled to Burma to evaluate investment projects. Over the course of the weeklong investigation, the NGO discovered that the reputation of Chinese companies, including in extractive industries, suffered from their close relations with Burmese officials, who were widely perceived to be corrupt. In contrast to Korean and Indian investors, Chinese businessmen paid little attention to developing contacts with the public. In visiting a natural gas development project, local residents informed Green Watershed that although Korean companies provided some social services, the Chinese companies did not; nor did they hire local workers. Even in areas where Chinese companies did invest in local services for the benefit of the local communities, they were not given credit because the projects were carried out through an unpopular government, or the projects didn't really benefit the people.[61] Green Watershed returned to China with a number of recommendations, among them the necessity of paying closer attention to the needs of local communities and communicating with them directly, as well as undertaking better conflict risk assessment given the ongoing conflicts between various ethnic groups.

The Chinese people and some business leaders are also thinking seriously about the political environment in which their companies invest, drawing into question decades of "not mixing business with politics." They are less certain that the advantages of doing business where other countries and multinationals fear to tread are worth the risks. In late January 2012, for example, the head of a major Chinese-led oil consortium was expelled from South Sudan for "non-cooperation" and twenty-nine Sinohydro workers were abducted in South Kordofan, a Sudanese border state. The abduction stirred Chinese online nationalist sentiment; one microblogger asked, "Why are militants around the world so keen on kidnapping Chinese? If they kidnap Americans, they are dead when U.S. Special Forces take action." And another netizen wrote: "We should interfere directly and rescue our citizens. Don't let Chinese people feel they are abandoned by their motherland when they go abroad."[62] The Sinohydro incident was not connected to resource development, but the episode has had broader reverberations through Chinese attitudes toward involvement abroad.

Alas, the response from the embassy in Sudan could hardly have been reassuring to those in China who expressed concern:

The Going Out strategy mainly focuses on poor third-world countries. Poor countries often have conflicts and chaos. So Chinese
workers will find it hard to avoid being affected. We must understand that a large quantity of Chinese laborers going abroad is part
of our going-out strategy. As China's economy develops, more and
more people will work overseas and thus the frequency of security
incidents involving Chinese overseas workers may grow larger and
larger.[63]

Not everyone is willing to take the risk. One of Sinohydro's top
executives, Wang Zhiping, has said the company learned an important lesson in Libya, where he estimates the conflict cost Sinohydro
at least "US$1.2 billion in suspended contracts and US$200 million
in writedowns." The company now has a "caution list," featuring
Iraq, Afghanistan, and Burma (where Sinohydro suffered a huge set-
back when its $3.6 billion Myitsone dam hydropower project was
suspended).[64] As we saw in chapter 4 as well, Chinese agricultural
firms and farmers are avoiding investment in certain countries in
Africa, where the risk of kidnapping or other violence is high.

Rethinking Chinese Corporate Culture

Chinese companies traditionally bring their experience and culture from home as they seek resources abroad, sometimes hurting
the countries in which they operate in the process—particularly in
countries where governance is already weak. But change is arising
from multiple sources. Countries in which China invests are adapt-
ing and forcing Chinese companies to shift course, a pattern that
shows no sign of abating. Pressure from home, in part in response
to the reputational damage done by Chinese firms abroad, is similarly reshaping how the companies operate. These efforts, though,
remain incomplete: weak governance in China and many of the
countries where Chinese companies invest means that efforts to
reshape corporate behavior (along, in many cases, with the behavior of other multinationals) continues to be slow and uneven.

The difficulties of investing in regions where the rule of law and institutions of governance are weak—along with the existence of big resource deposits elsewhere—are also helping propel Chinese firms beyond their traditional developing-country focus. But competing in markets such as Australia, Canada, and the United States offers its own set of challenges. Stronger state capacity means more attention to the role of the Chinese state in the firms' investments, as well as a heightened concern in many cases that Chinese firms will pose issues for national security. Stronger civil societies and legal regimes, moreover, mean sustained attention to and control over the firms' labor, environment, and safety practices. A growing segment of China's extractive industries sector is taking on these challenges, learning to adapt to new business environments, while at the same time helping reshape the investment environment in these countries.

7

Beyond the Developing World

ON JULY 23, 2012, CNOOC made a $15 billion bid for the Canadian oil producer Nexen.[1] At the time, Calgary-headquartered Nexen owned oil- and gas-producing properties in Western Canada, the UK North Sea, the U.S. Gulf of Mexico, Nigeria, and Yemen.[2] In 2011, it produced the equivalent of 207,000 barrels of oil a day out of 2.3 billion barrels of reserves.[3] The bulk of that came from oil, and more than half of Nexen's oil production came from the UK. Indeed, less than a quarter of Nexen's oil production—the product of its Long Lake bitumen project and a share in a company named Syncrude—came from Canada.[4] Yet Nexen was a Canadian-headquartered company, and roughly two-thirds of its employees were based in Canada. The takeover bid thus was subject to Canadian government review.

In the months that followed, debate raged across Canada over whether the takeover should be approved. Strong support for the deal was met with hostility similar to that encountered in many parts of the developing world where China increasingly invests. "Canada is open for business," declared one member of Parliament from the leading opposition party, "but Canada is not for sale."[5]

Debates and decisions like the one forced by CNOOC's attempt to buy Nexen are increasingly common outside the developing world. The last decade has seen a boom in Chinese investment into resource production in major developed countries. These countries typically raise a fundamentally different set of issues from investment in developing countries even as they provoke some common fears. The major developed resource producers—Australia, Canada, and the United States—have highly diversified economies. They also have relatively strong governance for environment, labor, and fiscal issues, extending not only to rules but also to enforcement. But the politics of Chinese resource investment in these countries is still often fraught and complex. Moreover, strategic concerns—these countries are typically wary of becoming subject to Chinese leverage—can play a much larger role than in most of the developing world.

Australia

China's role in Australia's energy and minerals sectors has skyrocketed over the last decade. China overtook Japan in 2005 as the top buyer of Australian iron ore. By 2011, it was importing nearly eight times as much iron ore as ten years before, a full 69 percent of all Australian iron ore exports. Purchases of bauxite have similarly jumped, rising from near zero in 2004 to make China Australia's top customer in 2007; by 2011, it was buying an extraordinary 85 percent of Australian bauxite exports. Even in coal, an area in which China is largely self-sufficient, trade has risen sharply. Coal imports, a modest four million tons a year as recently as 2007, reached nearly forty-seven million tons in 2009, just short of 20 percent of Australian coal exports, making China second only to Japan, long Australia's primary customer.[6] In the future, as Australia emerges as a leading producer of LNG, China is expected to become a major buyer. These developments have unfolded against a broader shift in Australian exports: in 2002, China overtook Japan as Australia's top partner in overall two-way trade, with flows reaching A$76.4 million between 2008 and 2009.[7]

The two countries have proven to be a strong match. Australia's large natural resource endowments but small manufacturing base pair with China's smaller resource holdings but stronger industrial capacity to take raw materials and turn them into intermediate goods like aluminum and steel. Australia's proximity to China also lowers transport costs for bulky materials. And Australia is poised to continue this role for the long haul, with the world's second-largest reserves of iron ore and fifth-largest reserves of coal. Australia's position is enhanced by the quality of its materials: Western Australia's hematite ore (a form of iron ore) requires fewer processing steps than other varieties, and Australian black coal is highly desired for its low sulfur level.[8] Australia is also well placed to supply natural gas to China; gas is considerably more expensive to transport than oil is, which makes the fact that Australia is closer to China than is the Middle East a competitive advantage. Australian natural gas shipments also have the virtue of not having to transit the narrow straits of Malacca or Hormuz, which the Chinese worry could be blocked by the United States, Iran, or others.

The Australian economy has benefited strongly both from direct exports to China and from higher prices for those commodities it sells to others. According to a 2013 report from the Reserve Bank of Australia:

> Strong growth in Asia, particularly in China, has had a profound impact on the Australian economy over the past decade. Most notable so far has been the boom in the resource sector, with commodity prices and hence Australia's terms of trade rising to historically high levels over a number of years.[9]

The benefits have, however, been uneven. In May 2012, *Bloomberg News,* noting that the Australian dollar rose 44 percent from the end of 2008 to 2012, observed that "the mining industry is thriving, but other industries—most of the nation, actually—are struggling." Much of that struggle has been driven by factors well beyond the natural resources trade; nonetheless, the resource boom undoubtedly contributes by driving up the Australian dollar, making nonresource exports less competitive in the world.[10]

Increased trade with China has gradually been supplemented by direct Chinese investment in energy and minerals, following the pattern set by Japan in the 1960s and 1970s. Australian government data covering attempts to invest at least A$100 million in distinct projects show a strong increase starting in 2006–07, leading to a peak of A$26.6 billion worth of proposed investment from China approved in 2008–09. (Australia tracks investment approvals on a July 1–June 30 year.) Chinese investment fell as the financial crisis took hold, but it still stabilized well above historic levels, in the range of A$15 billion annually. Chinese investments in Australian mineral resources also increasingly make up the vast majority of approved direct investments from China: in 2008–09, 98.8 percent of approved deals were in the minerals sector, and more than three-quarters of the investments in 2009–2010 as well as more than half in 2010–11 were also in minerals exploration and production. This contrasts with 2007–08, when barely 5 percent of Chinese investments in Australia were in energy and minerals. But despite large relative gains, China still makes up only a small fraction of new inward investment in Australia. In 2009, the peak year for Chinese investment, the total of new U.S. investment in Australia was A$93.8 billion; by contrast, only A$7.8 billion came from China.[11]

Accommodating China

China is not the first resource-hungry power to confront resource-rich Australia. It has long been a destination for investment by distant powers in mineral resources. During the 1880s, British investors poured money into the Australian minerals sector, in what has been described as the "first wave" of deals in extractives.[12] During the 1960s and 1970s, Japan acquired Australian mineral assets; Nippon Steel made numerous investments in the Pilbara region, while abundant coal reserves helped meet increasing Japanese demand for energy.

During that last wave, in 1975, amid ambivalence about Japanese investment, Australia enacted its Foreign Acquisitions and Takeovers Act (FATA). In the years since, FATA has required that a Foreign Investment Review Board (FIRB) review all Australian asset acquisitions worth more than A$100 million. Urban real estate purchases are also reviewed, and they constitute the majority of cases the FIRB handles, but we ignore them in the discussion here since their statistics obscure developments in the natural resources sector.

The FIRB evaluates investments for their consistency with the "national interest." The term was left undefined until 2010, but it now includes considerations of national security, competition, impacts on tax revenue and environmental objectives, and economic and community consequences.[13] Reviews also cover the "character of the investor"—the investor's commitment to transparent and well-supervised operations driven by commercial rather than political goals. The all-encompassing nature of this new definition of the national interest allows policy makers to retain great discretion over future assessments.

Precedent is thus more illuminating. Australia rarely rejects non–real estate investments: prior to 2011, when it blocked a buyout of the Australia Securities Exchange by the Singapore Stock Exchange, it had not rejected a takeover since Shell Australia Investments (a subsidiary of the Anglo-Dutch multinational) attempted to buy Woodside Petroleum in 2001. (The Australian government feared Shell would not develop the property promptly.)[14] Beyond actual failures, though, the threat of rejection has led companies to withdraw attempted investments and applications for their approval, leading to quasi-rejections that do not register in official statistics or reporting.

Chinese investment attempts have largely been treated like other ones: they have mostly been approved, and buyouts of small mines proceed with particular ease.[15] But five deals since 2007 were approved only with conditions related to corporate governance and control. An attempt by Sinosteel to gain approval for a takeover of Murchison Metals, an iron ore producer, was approved on condition that the Sinosteel share be kept below 50 percent, reflecting a broader Australian concern about regional market concentration.[16] A 2009 attempt by Anshan Iron and Steel Group to raise its share of iron ore producer Gindalbie Metals was approved subject to requirements that the firm support a particular infrastructure project and that there be no change to the ownership structure of a pellet plant the two firms planned to build together in China. This second condition reflected a pattern that scholars have identified in Australian policy: governments of varying political persuasions have been willing to push for some sort of reciprocity when open-ing the market to Chinese investors. Two other acquisitions—one in thermal coal and the other in iron ore—were approved with conditions on corporate governance, including the composition of boards of directors. One of those—a 2009 buyout of coal pro-ducer Felix Resources by Yanzhou Coal—also required that part of the firm be partially relisted on the Australian stock exchange by 2012, a condition that was ultimately met. A fifth acquisition was modified to exclude ore deposits in a sensitive defense-related area before being approved.

Two other deals were withdrawn after they appeared likely to be rejected or to have conditions imposed that were unaccept-able to the bidders. The Chinese company Wuhan Iron and Steel's (WISCO's) 2009 attempt to take a 50 percent stake in Western Plains Resources was sunk because of the iron ore pro-ducer's proximity to a sensitive defense area. More intriguingly, China Nonferrous Metals Corporation withdrew after it became clear the Australian government would not allow it to acquire a majority stake in the rare earth metals miner Lynas Corporation. The decision reflected strong Australian concerns about Chinese dominance in rare earth production. Rare earth metals are not particularly rare in the earth's crust, but production is currently dominated by China, and known reserves of some especially valu-able rare earths ("heavy rare earths") are highly concentrated geo-graphically.[17] Analysts have mostly concluded that scarcity of rare earth metals is not a long-run problem: substitutes can be devel-oped and deployed, and more fundamentally, new mines can be opened. If Chinese companies were to purchase a large number of prospective rare earth mines outside their territory, though, the latter source of security would be removed. This explains Australia's decision to bar CNMC from purchasing a control-ling stake in Lynas Corporation. Indeed in 2011, after CNMC's bid failed, Australia's FIRB approved a bid by Japan's Sojitz Corporation to take a stake in Lynas at a value of $325 million. Japan, unlike China, is not seen as a threat to global markets for rare earths.

Inward Investment and the Chinalco Case

China's early deals in Australia attracted attention but were still relatively low-key. But conflict within Australia over Chinese resource investment came to a head following a February 2009 attempt by Chinalco to invest $19.5 billion in the mining giant Rio Tinto, a sum that would have nearly doubled the already-record volume of Chinese investment in Australia that year. Chinalco (together with a small investment by Alcoa) had successfully invested $14 billion (gaining a 9 percent stake) in Rio Tinto the previous year.[18] The new investment would have consisted of $7.2 billion in purchases of convertible bonds and $12.3 billion in minority stakes in specific mining assets, including the world's largest bauxite mine in Queensland and a major iron ore mine in Western Australia, along with significant copper mines in Chile and the United States.[19] The deal would have raised Chinalco's stake in Rio Tinto to roughly 18 percent, and Chinalco executives would have taken two board seats.[20]

The deal came at a time when cash-flush Chinese companies were looking for big opportunities to invest in natural resources. It would have helped provide a hedge against the high iron ore and bauxite prices that were hurting steel makers and aluminum smelters, though it would not have come close to fully hedging direct Chinese exposure. Some speculated it would also have made a merger of Rio Tinto with BHP Billiton (the other Australian mining giant) far more difficult, protecting Chinese iron ore consumers from any risk that those two firms would combine and exercise massive market power.[21]

Proponents of allowing the deal to go through emphasized the broad benefits of open trade and investment. Others went further by arguing that the deal would give Australia strong access to the Chinese market. For example, Peter Drysdale, an economist at the Australian National University, argued that investments by a Chinese state-owned enterprise in Australia would further open up Chinese markets to Australian firms. Had the deal been successful, he claimed, it would have heralded "the first great Anglo-Australian-Chinese mining and metals company, probably headquartered in Australia.

This company would have been positioned to play a lead role in the Chinese market."[22]

The Australian government did not actively object to the investment, but it did not lend enthusiastic support either. Instead it emphasized that the deal was an entirely financial decision fitting the government's broader vision for free trade. During the public debate over the deal, the top economic official in the left-of-center Labor government emphasized claims that foreign direct investment had created some two hundred thousand jobs.[23]

Opponents marshaled a range of arguments. Malcolm Turnbull, the leader of Australia's Liberal (right-of-center) opposition at the time of the attempted investment, led the case against Chinalco on the basis of sovereignty. He warned that the Chinalco-Rio Tinto deal involved "direct management involvement and a high level of influence right down at the operating level of Rio's most important assets."[24] The National Party's Senator Barnaby Joyce, a prominent conservative populist, recorded at least one television advertisement with a simple one-sentence message: "Stop the Rudd [Labor] Government from selling Australia."[25]

Others focused on human rights. In a *Sydney Morning Herald* column, Peter Costello, the former federal treasurer and a Liberal parliamentarian, expressed dismay over the Chinese government's ability to control Australia's resources, and he channeled broader concerns over Chinese government policies: "In China," he wrote, "you do business with state-owned enterprises subject to political control in a country that does not tolerate political opposition, or a critical press."[26]

Those disposed against the deal had a third source of support: BHP Billiton. The Australian mining giant reportedly lobbied strongly behind the scenes to persuade Prime Minister Kevin Rudd and several top cabinet officials that the deal would cede Australian sovereignty to China.[27] At the same time, a public offer from BHP to team up with Rio Tinto in developing its iron ore assets promised to help Rio Tinto address the debt challenges that had at least partly motivated its interest in the Chinalco investment in the first place. This made the proposed Chinalco deal appear less appealing to Rio Tinto shareholders.[28]

The combination of public concern and changing commercial conditions came to a head on June 4, 2009. Faced with waning interest from shareholders and uncertainty surrounding FIRB approval, Rio Tinto announced it would not accept the Chinalco offer, incurring $200 million in breakup fees as a result.[29] In the wake of the collapse, a poll of Australians confirmed ongoing concerns. Respondents reported they were uneasy with specific Chinese investments in Australia's resources. Fifty-two percent of respondents were "uncomfortable" about the fact that China "is or will become the leading power in Asia."[30] Half of those polled believed the country was "allowing too much investment from China," compared to 42 percent who believed Australia was allowing the "right amount of investment" from the SOEs.[31] Many respondents held these views despite believing that China was economically important to Australia; a total of 63 percent of those polled described China as the economy "most important" to Australia.[32] A repeat of the same poll a year later showed declining support for Chinese investments: now 57 percent thought the government was "allowing too much investment from China" and only 34 percent thought the level of investment was appropriate.[33] Nonetheless, strong Chinese investment in Australia continued, with multiple billion-dollar-plus deals in 2011 and 2012.[34]

Canada

Over the last decade, Canadian growth has been buoyed by high global resource demand, following a pattern similar to Australia's. In 2011, oil, gas, and mining made up nearly 5 percent of the Canadian economy, while agriculture, forestry, fishing, and hunting contributed another 2 percent.[35] These figures do not include jobs up the supply chain (producing equipment and materials for resource development) or those spurred by spending of resource wealth, both of which are often larger than direct employment.

China has been a major driver of this change. In 2009, as U.S. demand declined amid recession, China passed the United States as the top buyer of Canadian ores, purchasing 24 percent (by value) to 13 percent for the United States.[36] China has retained the top position since then, on the back of strong sales of iron ore and copper, with its share in Canadian exports reaching 33 percent by 2011.[37] Chinese purchases of Canadian timber have lagged, but in 2010 China surged ahead of the United States and in 2011 became the buyer of nearly half the raw timber Canada exported.[38] This direct trade relationship has parallels to the China-Australia one, though without the massive market shares characteristic of the Chinese role in Australia's export economy.

In other areas, though, the Chinese role has been less direct. Canadian energy production has boomed on the back of high prices, and those high prices would almost certainly not have prevailed if not for Chinese demand. Yet China plays a tiny role as a buyer of Canadian oil, gas, and coal, taking a mere 1 percent of the country's product (mostly coal) as of 2011.

Chinese direct investment has largely lagged but recently came to the forefront. The first overseas investment by a Chinese oil company was actually in Canada, not Africa or Latin America.[39] Accounts vary, but in 1992 or 1993 CNPC acquired development rights in the North Twing oilfield, and in 1993, the field produced China's first barrel of overseas oil.[40] Three more small oil investments followed in as many years. But then, as Chinese companies intensified their overseas investments, Canada was left behind. There was no significant Chinese investment in Canadian energy or minerals between 1996 and 2004.[41]

This trend reversed course beginning in 2005 with the acquisition of a 17 percent stake in MEG Energy, an Alberta oil sands producer, by CNOOC for $130 million.[42] This was quickly followed the same year by Sinopec's purchase of 40 percent of Synenco, another oil sands company, for $120 million. Chinese investment in the oil sands continued to grow, and in August 2009 CNPC made the first Chinese investment in Canadian oil of more than one billion dollars, buying a controlling stake in Athabasca Oil Sands Corporation for $1.74 billion.

Investment in mines started more slowly and has trailed investment in energy. (Agriculture and forestry investment is essentially absent, and although there is debate over whether it may accelerate in the future, few are confident it will.)[43] In October 2006, Jiangxi Copper, a state-owned enterprise and the largest copper producer in China, bought a controlling stake in bcMetals for $110 million.[44] Chinese minerals investment paused until 2009, and then reemerged. That year saw nearly $2 billion of investment, including the purchase of 20 percent of Teck Resources, one of the largest mining companies in Canada, by the sovereign wealth fund China Investment Corporation (CIC). Metals investment in each of the next two years measured in the hundreds of millions. This remains a small part of the $22 billion that flowed from abroad into Canadian energy and minerals in 2011.[45]

A Precedent-Setting Case?

With the growing scale of resource production and Chinese investment has come controversy. The Canadian government has tried to stay away from debates over how it should treat Chinese investment, and whether it should be handled any differently from other foreign investment in the country. Just as the Australian debate was pushed into the spotlight by Chinalco's bid for Rio Tinto, however, CNOOC's attempt to buy Nexen in 2012 forced Canada to confront its ambivalence about Chinese investment.

The Canadian economy rode high for most of the previous decade on the back of strong world prices for the commodities it produced. This also made it the target for a large number of successful foreign investments, including from Chinese firms. Yet no Chinese investment met with significant resistance or encountered intense scrutiny from the Canadian federal government. Indeed, Canada has taken a decidedly more hands-off approach to foreign investment, including that from China, than Australia has.

Canada did, however, reject two prominent foreign investment bids in the years before CNOOC's bid for Nexen. Both were considered under the 1985 Investment Canada Act, which gave the federal government the responsibility to review all "significant" investments into Canada and allowed it to reject them if they were determined not to provide a "net benefit" to Canada.[46] Net benefit, however, is defined so broadly that practitioners have found it offers little practical guidance.

The first investment bid blocked under the Investment Canada Act was an attempt by the U.S.-based Alliant Techsystems Inc. to purchase MacDonald, Dettweiler and Associates (MDA), an aerospace firm perhaps best known in Canada as the creator of the "Canadarm," for approximately $1.3 billion.[47] When the bid was initially accepted, in January 2008, the reaction in Canada assumed the deal would sail through.[48] Four months later, though, the government stepped in and blocked the deal. Its rationale was a classic national security one: MDA produced a satellite known as Radarsat-2 that is used to monitor the Arctic, an increasing focus of Canadian national security efforts, and an area in which Canada and the United States have competing territorial claims.[49] The Canadian government also argued that since MDA had received extensive taxpayer funding (Radarsat-2 had been developed with nearly half a billion dollars in federal government money), allowing it to be sold to a foreign company would be wrong.[50] None of these decisions afforded much precedent for judging investments in natural resources (aside perhaps for any in sensitive areas).

The Canadian government made its second move to block a foreign investment, and its first to stop a foreign natural resources takeover, slightly more than two years later. In August 2010, BHP Billiton launched a hostile bid to take over Saskatchewan-based Potash Corporation, presenting an offer of $40 billion.[51] (Sinochem of China also considered a bid but withdrew.)[52] As global demand for food accelerated in the 2000s, demand and prices for potash, which is used to make fertilizer, soared; between 2001 and 2009, prices rose fourfold.[53] As of 2010 Potash Corporation was the largest potash producer and fertilizer maker in the world, with roughly 20 percent of global potash production capacity.[54]

Potash production is significantly concentrated, with two-thirds found in Russia, Canada, and Belarus.[55] (These countries are home to an even larger fraction of reserves.) Yet there was no reason to believe that BHP Billiton, which had no other stake in the pot-ash industry (or other fertilizer businesses), would act strategically to restrict production following a takeover.[56] Nonetheless, against a backdrop of political pressure from the premier of Saskatchewan (the province stood to lose royalties as a result of the purchase), the Canadian government rejected the takeover bid. Announcing the decision, the government declared it was not clear that the takeover would create a net benefit for Canada. Though legal experts gener-ally agreed that the government was required to explain its decision at greater length, it did not.[57] This, along with the political context, made it difficult to discern any precedent from the episode.

The scrutiny raised in response to the CNOOC bid for Nexen thus came as a surprise to many. In the aftermath of CNOOC's bid, the left-wing New Democratic Party, the main opposition follow-ing a 2011 federal election, argued that, as a result of its opacity and secret nature, the process for determining whether a takeover would be a net benefit for Canada was unreliable.[58] Law makers raised con-cerns about preservation of local jobs, environmental protection, and national security. Criticism from the right focused on claims that CNOOC ownership of Nexen amounted to government med-dling in the economy, something conservatives had opposed when the Canadian government was the one involved, and that some opposed when the Chinese government was doing it too.[59] As one critic put it, "Is Canadian government nationalization wrong but Chinese nationalization is fine?"[60] Others pushed back by emphasiz-ing the need for capital to support oil sands investment and the stake that Canada has in global open trade.[61]

Since 2007 Canada has also imposed special rules for invest-ments by SOEs. They are required to make commitments to matters such as transparency, decision making based on market conditions rather than political calculus (including on exports and hiring), and more general political noninterference in their opera-tions.[62] Whether such promises are adhered to after acquisitions are complete remains to be seen. (It is also unclear how one would determine compliance in some cases, such as market-based deci-sion making, where sensible people disagree about how a given company should behave.) As in Australia, though, the framework allowed broad discretion for the Canadian government in adjudicating the sale.

Public opinion also weighed in on the debate. Polling revealed the continued unease of many Canadians toward Chinese SOEs. From 2010 to 2012, opposition to foreign acquisitions of Canadian companies—already high—increased.[63] In 2010, 71 percent of those polled opposed investments from state-owned Chinese companies; in 2011 and 2012, 75.5 percent of respondents thought Chinese SOEs should not be allowed to buy controlling stakes in Canadian companies.[64] Support for China is low in a comparative sense, too. According to the 2012 poll that revealed this aversion to Chinese investment, 51 percent of Canadians were open to British companies acquiring Canadian firms, and 38 percent of Canadians polled believed American companies should be able to do the same.[65] Only the United Arab Emirates (UAE), with a meager 13 percent support, ranked lower than China.[66] These specific sentiments were backed by broader skepticism: 57 percent of respondents in 2012 did not agree that "economic benefits of Asia's investment in Canada's energy sector outweigh concerns about foreign ownership of our natural resources."[67]

There is, however, enormous variation within Canada; views of people in resource-rich provinces contrast sharply with the overall national mood. Thirty-one percent of Ontarians polled disagreed that Asian economies are vital to the well-being of Canada, but in oil- and gas-producing Alberta, 74 percent of respondents believe Asian economies are beneficial to Canadian well-being.[68] This regional variation in response to FDI dates back at least to the 1970s.[69]

It was against this backdrop that, in December 2012, the Canadian government approved CNOOC's bid to acquire Alberta-based Nexen. But it appeared to make new policy in the process. "In light of growing trends and following the decisions made today," Prime Minister Stephen Harper declared, "the government of Canada has determined that foreign state control of oil sands development has reached the point at which further such foreign state control would not be of net benefit to Canada."[70] He appeared to leave little room for exceptions, asserting that Canada "will find the acquisition of control of a Canadian oil sands business by a foreign state owned enterprise to be of net benefit, only in an exceptional circumstance." Harper also elaborated the grounds on which future proposals would be assessed. They included the degree to which any state-owned enterprise would control the target firm and the industry in which it operated, and the degree to which the firm itself was controlled by its government.

Many observers in Canada, however, assume these announcements will have limited practical effect, and the federal government will declare "exceptional circumstances" whenever necessary to allow a major deal to go through.[71] It is unclear whether any other state-owned enterprise—particularly a Chinese one—will even test it. Another large acquisition attempt will almost certainly reignite intense public debate.

United States

The U.S. experience with Chinese resource investment has been decidedly different from those of Canada and Australia. The U.S. economy is much larger than Canada's and Australia's, and resource industries play a considerably smaller role. Moreover, until recently, most U.S. resource sectors were considered relatively mature, leaving limited room for new investment; in addition, with a large pool of domestic capital available, the United States depends less on foreigners to support whatever opportunities do exist. As recently as 2008—before the financial crisis hit and resource prices plunged—foreign direct investment in U.S. mining and petroleum production stood at just under $17 billion, of which $14 billion went into oil and gas.[72] That year, roughly 0.1 percent of total inward investment in the United States came from China.[73]

Indeed, prior to 2010, Chinese firms had invested no more than $250 million total in U.S. energy firms and projects in any one year.[74] Even today, Chinese investment in basic materials, which includes minerals extraction but also encompasses manufacturing, remains tiny.[75] Agriculture has similarly stayed on the sidelines, with a mere $120 million in Chinese investment as of the end of 2012.[76]

In 2010, though, the tide began to shift on one important front: energy. U.S. oil and gas output was booming, making the United States an increasingly attractive target for energy investment. Chinese energy investments totaled $3 billion in 2010, $2.2 billion in 2011, and $3 billion again in 2012.[77] U.S. oil and gas production was being propelled upward by new technology: producers combined horizontal drilling, in which they drill down as much as a mile before turning ninety degrees and drilling sideways, with hydraulic fracturing, which uses pressurized liquids and sand to fracture dense rock and allow oil or gas to flow. As with the case of Nexen, Chinese firms were attracted by two prospects. The first was the simple ability to put more oil and gas on their books. The second, even more powerful in this case, was the chance to learn about a new technology.

Chinese firms have approached U.S. oil and gas gingerly. To date, they have taken only minority stakes in U.S. firms, or they have co-invested (with minority shares) in individual production projects. They have also worked with smaller independent operators, who are hungry for cash, rather than with major U.S. oil and gas producers. These investments in U.S. oil and gas production have gone smoothly in recent years. In October 2010, CNOOC acquired a 33 percent stake in the shale gas pioneer Chesapeake Energy in a deal ultimately worth $2.2 billion, and in January 2012 Sinopec took a similar stake in another shale gas leader, Devon Energy, for slightly more. The Chinese sovereign wealth fund CIC has also invested $500 million in Cheniere Energy Partners Limited, an aspiring exporter of liquefied natural gas. More recently, Chinese companies have begun to take minority positions in shale oil production too.

This pattern, which avoids trying to take a controlling interest in any large U.S. oil and gas producer, is likely a preemptive defense against public and political opposition. Mergers, acquisitions, and other takeovers of U.S. commodity producers by foreign entities (including the Chinese) face scrutiny from the Committee on Foreign Investment in the United States (CFIUS). Initially established through an executive order by President Gerald Ford in 1975, CFIUS now derives its power from legislation passed in 1988, which allows the president to "block foreign acquisitions of U.S. firms that threaten to impair the national security."[78] Administering this presidential authority is CFIUS, an interagency group chaired by the Treasury Department.

There is disagreement over whether acquisitions of U.S. commodities producers (or of natural resource deposits themselves) are subject to scrutiny for their strategic implications under current statute. Some analysts argue that economic issues are exempt from CFIUS oversight. Analysts Daniel Rosen and Thilo Hanneman, for example, have written that "the review process does not include national economic security, protecting U.S. economic strength as a general contribution to national power, or other considerations."[79] Others have noted that the underlying statute places no specific limits on the scope of what might be included under the rubric of national security, and they contend that economic security can play an important role.

Precedent suggests a narrow focus on espionage concerns rather than broad economic security issues. For example, CFIUS scrutiny of the acquisition of Global Crossing, a telecommunications firm, by a Hong Kong–based company with ties to the Chinese military focused on risks to secure communications for U.S. law enforcement. And a presidential order (on CFIUS's recommendation) prevented the acquisition of an Oregon wind farm by the Chinese firm Ralls Corporation, reportedly due to the wind farm's proximity to U.S. military installations rather than any energy concerns.

Only two Chinese natural resource acquisitions have attracted significant CFIUS-related concerns. Most recently, the 2012 CNOOC bid for Nexen was submitted for CFIUS review, since a small part of Nexen's holdings were in the U.S. Gulf of Mexico. After some initial noises of concern—one senator suggested that China be required to give equal access to U.S. oil and gas investors before the acquisition be allowed to proceed—the process moved forward quietly. (The lack of a rival bidder, along with the limited U.S. leverage over an acquisition of a company whose assets were mostly outside the United States, undoubtedly contributed.) The main concerns raised during the process related to intellectual property, cybersecurity, and proximity of some drilling platforms to sensitive military installations; however, CFIUS approved the deal in February 2013.

For Chinese companies and political leaders, though, the 2005 attempt by CNOOC to acquire California-based Unocal looms largest, and it still colors their thinking. On June 23, 2005, CNOOC made an unsolicited $18.5 billion bid to acquire Unocal, which was equal to $67 per share—all in cash—and resoundingly trumped Chevron and UNOCAL's provisional April 2005 deal worth $16.5 billion in cash and stock options. CNOOC and Chevron began aggressive lobbying campaigns in Washington during June and early July 2005. On June 30, the House of Representatives passed a resolution calling for a "thorough" CFIUS review of the deal, and CNOOC filed a voluntary notice with CFIUS on July 2.[80] On July 19, Chevron upped its offer by $1.2 billion, to $63.01 per share, from about $60.50.[81] CNOOC countered with an offer of $69 per share, but according to the *Associated Press*, the company would increase the offer only if "Unocal agreed to pay the $500 million cost of terminating the Chevron deal and lobby for the deal in Congress."[82] CNOOC ultimately withdrew its bid on August 2, a little more than a week before UNOCAL's board agreed to accept Chevron's revised bid on August 10. Ultimately, CNOOC's bid was not blocked by CFIUS but was instead rejected by Unocal in favor of a competing offer that did not raise similar regulatory risks. This has not stopped many people in both China and the United States from misremembering the episode as one in which CFIUS actually rejected the acquisition.

The CNOOC-Unocal experience cooled Chinese interest in major U.S. oil and gas acquisitions. Days after the U.S. House of Representatives voted to approve a resolution calling for President George W. Bush to block the CNOOC-UNOCAL deal on national security grounds, China's Foreign Ministry issued a strongly worded written statement:

> We demand that the U.S. Congress correct its mistaken ways of politicizing economic and trade issues and stop interfering in the normal commercial exchanges between enterprises of the two countries....CNOOC's bid to take over the U.S. Unocal company is a normal commercial activity between enterprises and should not fall victim to political interference.[83]

In August 2005, a CNOOC spokesman in Hong Kong was quoted, saying about the UNOCAL deal, "Are we pissed off? Yes."[84] More than a year and a half after the UNOCAL bid failed, *Reuters* reported that a senior Chinese official and vice chairman of the National Development and Reform Commission, Zhang Guobao, had an angry exchange with the American ambassador, saying "If the United States would not allow CNOOC to purchase Unocal, will not itself guarantee China a steady energy supply, and opposes Chinese purchases of Iranian oil and gas, how can China survive?"[85]

Learned lessons can still be observed in changed tactics on the part of Chinese oil companies. In particular, companies shifted to taking minority stakes in American firms rather than making outright bids. Fu Chengyu, the chairman of CNOOC who led the ill-fated 2005 bid for UNOCAL, later successfully led CNOOC's entrance into the U.S. shale industry through two joint ventures with the American firm Chesapeake Energy in 2010.[86] These agreements gave CNOOC minority stakes in shale fields in Wyoming, Texas, and Colorado.[87] Fu, who has since been moved to head up Sinopec, pursued a diversification strategy focused on multiple smaller investments and pursuit of minority stakes, with a particular focus on taking advantage of "[tapping] foreign management expertise," that was shaped by the lessons of the UNOCAL bid—a lower-key strategy that has seen success.[88]

The one area other than oil and gas in which Chinese investment might raise strategic concern is rare earth metals. As in Australia, it is reasonable to worry that Chinese companies may not focus only on resources where China is relatively poor but also target minerals where it already has a strong position—most notably rare earths. The risk is that through commercial acquisitions China could eliminate competition in areas where it has already attempted to exploit a near-monopoly position. Projects underway with high concentrations of heavy rare earths—essential to many defense and clean energy technologies—are found in China, Canada, the United States, South Africa, and Sweden.[89] With only five or six proposed heavy rare earth projects "sufficiently advanced in their development to have a shot at making it into production," and only one in the United States, acquisition of even one U.S. venture could have upended the structure of the international market.[90] Any attempt by China to do that would likely provoke strong opposition within the United States.

With limited exceptions, then, U.S. precedent is one of a relatively hands-off approach to acquisitions, but also one in which particularly sensitive acquisition attempts are discouraged (and thus usually avoided) in the first place. The United States has not shown an interest in imposing extensive conditions on investment in the same way Australia has. Nor have U.S. policy makers expressed concern about excessive SOE activity in strategic energy industries in the way Canada has. But U.S. policy has not been aggressively tested since the unfolding oil and gas boom made the country a far more attractive target for investment. If a Chinese company breaks precedent and attempts to take over a major U.S. producer, it will be a novel test of whether the United States sticks to past practice or develops new rules of the road.

China Learns and Adapts

The experiences of Australia, Canada, and the United States with Chinese resource investment have differed decidedly from those in the developing world. Rather than focusing on environmental, labor, or fiscal challenges, these countries have emphasized national sovereignty and "strategic" concerns in their governance of Chinese investment. So far all three countries have taken a largely ad hoc approach, developing policy on a case-by-case basis shaped by a mix of national interest calculations and political and popular pressures. Canada and Australia have had tougher decisions to confront, with big Chinese acquisition attempts in recent years, while the United States (as of late 2013) has been spared any major acquisition attempts since 2005. Each country has adapted at the margin to Chinese companies' efforts to invest, but none has shifted radically. Instead it has been China and its companies that have had to change most. The United States, however, has not recently been forced to reckon with high-profile Chinese investments in the same way Canada and Australia have. It is thus arguably the most likely to go through significant change in response to Chinese investment in the coming years.

The strategic questions related to China's resource quest facing established powers such as the United States, and regional powers such as Japan, are, however, much broader than those the United States shares with Canada and Australia. As the world's sole superpower, the United States is invariably drawn into international relationships and security challenges around the world. China's neighbors are also inevitably facing strategic challenges. As we will see in the next two chapters, China's resource quest is already altering that landscape, both close to China and further from its shores.

8

Security and Politics in China's Backyard

IN THE MIDDLE OF THE 2000s, a new security threat appeared to emerge. With resource prices rising rapidly, and shortages seemingly imminent, scholars and pundits began to warn of "resource wars." China featured prominently in those warnings: Beijing, people suggested, was far less committed to markets than the United States and would be much more willing to use force as it battled others for the remaining scraps of an ever smaller resource pie.[1]

Indeed, one camp of analysts now argues that, with global resources insufficient to meet growing world demand, countries may be destined to go to war over control of available supplies.[2] An opposing camp, however, insists that the prospect of resource wars is largely if not entirely nonsense.[3] They argue that modern history shows few instances of war over resources. Moreover, they note, since most resources are now traded on world markets, ownership is far less important than one might assume. Countries can secure resources simply by paying the market price, leaving no need for them to go to war in order to acquire them.

The market-based critique of the resource wars warning is powerful. So long as resource prices do not rise astronomically (and few analysts foresee such a development), it will be far cheaper to acquire resources by paying market rates than by engaging in armed conflict. And even strong price rises compared to what prevailed a decade ago leave resource costs relatively modest relative to the overall size of big economies, including those of the United States and China.[4] To the extent that China is afraid prices will rise intolerably, it can hedge

SECURITY AND POLITICS IN CHINA'S BACKYARD   139

its exposure by buying access to deposits on commercial terms, precisely the approach many Chinese companies have taken in recent years. Unless the world changes radically, it will not pay to invade foreign lands in order to win their natural resources.

At least as important is the fact that there are only a few resource-rich territories China could control militarily assuming it wanted to. We will see in the next chapter that Chinese capabilities to project power well away from its borders are primitive. For the foreseeable future, the country will not even have the option of trying to take resources in the Middle East, Africa, or Latin America militarily. This makes wars involving China over much of the world's resources implausible at the current time.

But this does not mean growing Chinese demand for natural resources will not have wide-ranging consequences for international relations and security; we shall see in this and the following chapter that it certainly will. Resource wars, though, are far down the worry list. And the most likely flashpoints for militarized conflict will not arise far abroad in the Middle East or Africa; they will be found much closer to home. Indeed, the biggest consequences of Chinese resource demand, for the traditional worlds of international relations and international security, are being felt in China's backyard.

The South and East China Seas

The South and East China Seas play a special role in Chinese thinking about oil and gas. This is in part because some in China believe they hold large petroleum deposits. To understand what is happening in the South and East China Seas, it is essential to disentangle the multiple motives drawing China and its neighbors to focus on the area: beyond natural resources, sea lane security, national defense, and basic nationalism all drive Chinese actions.

Most of the petroleum deposits in these areas lie in places claimed by both China and neighboring states. Thus, they present diplomatic and security challenges that resources within recognized Chinese territory do not. But their locations near China—and, in particular, in areas that do not require transport through the Straits of Hormuz or Malacca to reach Chinese consumers—make them particularly appealing for domestic strategists who are worried about physical security of supplies. Issues in the South and East China Seas are also complicated by the fact that China (or others) could plausibly use military or other coercive means to gain control over the resources there.

A Resource Guessing Game

There is considerable debate over the actual potential of the petroleum resources in the South and East China Seas. Any estimate inevitably carries a high degree of uncertainty, given the paucity of seismic study and exploratory drilling in the regions. An oft-cited U.S. Geological Survey (USGS) estimate from the early 1990s claimed that there were 28 billion barrels of oil in discovered reserves and undiscovered resources in the South China Sea.[5] (Discovered reserves include oil and gas that companies have identified and that can be extracted at prevailing prices; undiscovered resources are oil and gas that are generally known to be extractable with current technology but that have not been firmly established by producers.) More recently, a 2010 USGS assessment of undiscovered resources in areas in the South China Sea arrived at an estimate of 11 billion barrels of oil and 145 trillion cubic feet of natural gas.[6] These are sizable but not massive figures; by comparison, probable but undiscovered North American conventional resources have been estimated at 63 billion barrels of oil and more than 400 trillion cubic feet of natural gas—figures that do not include recent developments in shale gas and tight oil.[7]

Chinese estimates are typically much higher than Western ones, so much so that CNOOC has called the region the "Maritime Daqing," after the massive onshore oilfield that once powered the Chinese economy and still produces much of its domestic oil.[8] The U.S. Energy Information Administration (U.S. EIA) reported in 2008 that "one Chinese estimate suggests potential oil resources as high as 213 billion barrels of oil" along with natural gas resources of 2,000 billion (two quadrillion) cubic feet; another, it said, claims

225 billion barrels of oil equivalent solely in the area of the Spratly Islands.[9] Wang Yilin, then the head of CNOOC, reportedly stated in late 2012 that the South China Sea "could hold 17 [billion] tonnes [125 billion barrels] of oil and 498 [trillion] cubic feet of natural gas."[10] The most bullish numbers appear to come from the Chinese Ministry of Land and Resources, whose high-end estimates reportedly exceed 400 billion barrels of oil and 700 trillion cubic feet of gas.[11] This would make the South China Sea the biggest pool of undiscovered oil in the world, well ahead of the former Soviet Union, the Arctic, or the Middle East. If Chinese and other regional leaders genuinely believe such estimates, it is easy to understand why they are so interested in claiming the resources.

East China Sea resources are similarly speculative; indeed they are perhaps even more poorly understood than South China Sea oil and gas. CNOOC's 2011 annual report claimed proven reserves of 68.4 million barrels of oil equivalents in the area.[12] Similarly, in 2012 the U.S. EIA estimated there were even odds that the East China Sea contained at least 60 to 100 million barrels of well-understood and economically recoverable oil, along with 1–2 trillion cubic feet of natural gas.[13] Chinese estimates of "undiscovered" resources are much higher, clocking in at between 70 and 160 billion barrels of oil for the East China Sea, rivaling Chinese estimates of oil and gas in the South China Sea.[14] Once again, though highly speculative, it is not surprising that these sorts of estimates draw policy makers' interest.

Whose Oil and Gas Is It?

China has made claims to the vast majority of the South China Sea tracts that contain most of the area's oil and gas fields.[15] These claims overlap with ones by Taiwan, the Philippines, Malaysia, Brunei, and Vietnam. Some areas are contested only by China and one other nation; others are claimed by as many as four nations. The broadest disputes are between China and Vietnam, both of which claim the entire sea (excluding others' coastal areas) for themselves.[16] The East China Sea is superficially simpler—it lies between China and Japan and is primarily contested by those two countries and Taiwan (with marginal involvement from South Korea)—but because it brings two major powers into conflict, it may be more consequential.[17]

The focus of conflict between China and Japan in the East China Sea has been a set of islands referred to as Senkaku in Japan and Diaoyu in China. The islands are uninhabited and administratively under the control of Japan, which has regarded them as part of its territory since 1895. (Between World War II and 1972, however, they were under the control of the United States.) China, for its part, argues that records from envoys dating back at least to the Qing dynasty demonstrate the islands are within the "border that separates Chinese and foreign lands."[18] In 2008, in a move that appeared to defuse territorial tensions, China and Japan agreed to the joint development of the Chunxiao/Shirabaka gas field in a disputed area of the East China Sea.[19] The decision, however, never led to development, and tensions have escalated since then.

They reached a new high in September 2010 when a Chinese fishing boat, piloted by a drunken captain, collided with two Japanese patrol crafts. Japan arrested the fishing boat captain and held him for two and a half weeks before releasing him.[20] The Chinese response in the intervening time was sharp, and widely seen as excessive given the nature of the underlying infraction. The Foreign Ministry postponed the gas field development negotiations with Japan, calling the arrests and detentions "absurd, illegal, and invalid."[21] Chinese tourists canceled trips to Japan en masse, and there were protests outside Japanese schools and diplomatic missions in China.[22] The central government in Beijing suspended all exchanges or interactions between Chinese officials and their Japanese counterparts, and the foreign minister said in a statement that Japan had "seriously damaged Sino-Japan bilateral relations."[23] Premier Wen Jiabao, in New York for the United Nations General Assembly, called on Japan to release the fishing captain "immediately and unconditionally."[24] Shortly thereafter China blocked rare earth exports to Japan.[25] Finally, on September 24, 2010, the Japanese government announced it would release the fishing captain, who was brought home to China on a government-chartered plane.[26] However, tensions remained high, as China continued to block Japan's rare earth shipments. The shipment restrictions continued for seven weeks before being lifted in mid-November 2010.[27]

Escalation has continued on both sides. In September 2012, the Japanese government announced it had purchased three of the Diaoyu/Senkaku islands from their private (Japanese) owner, which was completed in order "to maintain the Senkakus peacefully and stably," according to a statement by the chief cabinet secretary.[28] The *PLA Daily* characterized Japan's purchase as "the most blatant challenge to China's sovereignty since the end of the second world war."[29] Shortly thereafter, the Ministry of Foreign Affairs issued a White Paper that strongly asserted China's unequivocal sovereignty over the islands:

> [The purchase] severely infringed upon China's sovereignty and ran counter to the understanding and consensus reached between the older generation of leaders of the two countries. It has not only seriously damaged China-Japan relations, but also rejected and challenged the outcomes of the victory of the World Anti-Fascist War [World War II].[30]

Tensions in the East China Sea intensified in the following months. In February 2013, Japan accused China of having locked radar "capable of aiding weapon strikes" on a Japanese ship and helicopter near the islands, charges China denied.[31]

The U.S. position on the dispute reflects both U.S. commitments to Japan, under the 1960 Treaty of Mutual Cooperation and Security, and concern about the balance of power in East Asia. Washington's official position is that the islands are covered by the defense treaty but is ambiguous beyond that.[32] As a U.S. State Department spokesperson stated, "We don't take a position on the islands, but we do assert that they are covered under the treaty."[33]

A spray of islets and atolls claimed by multiple coastal parties is also the focus of tensions in the South China Sea. The sites are contentious because sovereignty over land features and islands provides the claimant country with the basis to claim surrounding expanses of water and seabed.[34] Two areas have drawn the most concern: the Paracel Islands, which are occupied by China and claimed by Vietnam; and the Spratly Islands, which are claimed in their entirety by China, Taiwan, and Vietnam, in part by Brunei, Malaysia, and the Philippines, and occupied in part by all claimants except Brunei.[35] China's claim to the Spratly and Paracel islands rests on "historical usage," "first discovery," and "effective exercise of sovereignty."[36] Other countries present a variety of arguments.

The South China Sea has already seen conflict over the various rocks and land features; indeed it was more intense in the 1980s and 1990s, when China clashed with both Vietnam and the Philippines. The first confrontation resulted in approximately eighty Vietnamese deaths; the second, in which China seized a feature known as Mischief Reef, led to a series of tit-for-tat responses that threatened to spiral out of control.[37]

As in the case of the East China Sea, tension in the South China Sea has been intensified by the combination of resource claims and accompanying disputes over control of critical waterways. In 2002, Association of Southeast Asian Nations (ASEAN) members and China declared that, by signing a Declaration on the Conduct of Parties in the South China Sea, they would pledge to "reaffirm their respect for and commitment to the freedom of navigation in and overflight above the South China Sea...[and] undertake to resolve their territorial and jurisdictional disputes by peaceful means, without resorting to the threat or use of force."[38] But tensions in the South China Sea have risen in recent years, characterized by incidents involving "fishing vessels, oil exploration vessels, paramilitary maritime law enforcement vessels, naval ships, and military aircraft" among others.[39]

China has also taken steps to increase administrative control over various islands. It has installed an administrative center on Woody Island (which the Chinese call Yongxing Island) in the Paracel Islands and revitalized an aircraft landing strip. In July 2012, *Time* reported that China planned to station troops on Woody Island, a move described as an attempt to "extend Chinese administrative control over the resource-rich Paracel, Spratly and Macclesfield Bank island groups... [which are] claimed by China and five neighboring countries and have been the source of increasing confrontations in the region."[40] Moreover, in early 2010, according to some press reports, Chinese officials began describing their territorial claims in the South China Sea as a "core interest." The term was formally defined by State Councilor Dai Bingguo in 2009 at the U.S.-China Strategic and Economic Dialogue: "For China, our concern is we must uphold our basic systems, our national security; and secondly, the sovereignty and territorial integrity; and thirdly, economic and social sustained development."[41]

Over time, the number of core interests explicitly claimed by China has expanded. Originally, during the early 2000s, officials used the term to refer to Taiwan, when the territory's people appeared to be moving toward *de jure* independence. By 2006, it evolved to incorporate Tibet and Xinjiang, two regions in China with sizable and restive minority populations. In 2010, Dai reportedly told U.S. Secretary of State Hillary Clinton that the South China Sea was one of China's core interests. And in 2013, a spokesperson for the Ministry of Foreign Affairs claimed that the Diaoyu/Senkaku Islands in the East China Sea were a core interest: "The Diaoyu Islands are about sovereignty and territorial integrity. Of course, it's China's core interest."[42]

Before that statement, in December 2012, the provincial government in Hainan (which is in charge of administering the South China Sea) raised the stakes when it announced that China had the right to intercept ships going through the South China Sea, but "only if they were engaged in illegal activities (though these were not defined) and only if the ships were within the 12-nautical-mile zone surrounding islands that China claims."[43] The rule was based on China's territorial claims to certain islands in the region. Since it claims the Paracel and the Spratly islands (of which various islands are also currently occupied by a number of countries) as well as the Scarborough Reef, the twelve-nautical-mile zone "surrounding islands that China claims" would include maritime areas that important sea lanes traverse. Some naval experts have expressed worry that China might "enforce these new rules fully beyond the

12-nautical-mile zones."[44] This would run directly into longstanding U.S. commitments to keep such waters open to international commerce—including resources trade. Indeed, the problems could run deeper. The United States and China disagree over whether countries can regulate foreign military activities in their exclusive economic zones (EEZs), the swathes of ocean adjoining their borders where they have an exclusive right to economic activity. The United States says no, but China (along with a small minority of countries, among them nearby Malaysia and Vietnam) says yes.[45]

Chinese claims, if successful, could embolden Beijing to take steps with security ramifications that go well beyond disputes about undersea oil. Nearly 50 percent of global trade passes through the South China Sea on its way to markets.[46] The majority of Chinese, Japanese, and Korean oil imports pass through the waters too, making free passage of commerce through the region essential to those countries' security.[47] The East China Sea is similarly vital to Japan; as one analyst has written, "no sea lanes are more important [to Japan] than those that traverse the East China Sea."[48] Meanwhile, for China, the stretch of the East China Sea from Taiwan to the southern islands of Japan has become a leading focus of naval modernization efforts aimed at denying adversaries access in the event of an intense conflict.[49]

Law to the Rescue?

Many hope that international law will impose a resolution to the conflicts over resource ownership. This would, however, be a strong departure from historical precedent. (Moreover, even if international law were applied, it would not remove the potential for intense territorial conflict.) Despite the existence of extensive rules regarding the demarcation of EEZs in international waters, there is actually little experience with using international law to settle disputes over offshore oil and gas ownership.

For example, Qatar and Iran, though both parties to the UN Convention on the Law of the Sea (UNCLOS), settled their dispute over the boundaries between their respective claims within the massive Pars gas field through a bilateral agreement signed in 1969.[50] Perhaps the greatest progress in dividing up resources has come among the states bordering the Caspian Sea. But even this has seen only mixed success, and pairs of countries have generally negotiated directly rather than working through international law.[51]

If the countries of the South and East China Seas regions somehow agreed to use UNCLOS to adjudicate boundaries, then a second challenge would arise: it is ambiguous. Japan and China, which have both ratified the UNCLOS, define their territorial claims in the East China Sea using UNCLOS measures but rely on different measures from the convention: in December 2012, China submitted a claim to the UN Commission on the Limits of Continental Shelf (a body established by UNCLOS) detailing how the Diaoyu/Senkaku islands are situated in the zone encompassed by China's continental shelf, which it asserts is a "natural prolongation of China's land territory."[52] In principle, a successful claim over the islands would allow China to establish zones of 200 nautical mile radius extending from every islet. Japan has similarly focused on the fact that the islands are within the "exclusive economic zone extending westward from its southern Kyushu and Ryukyu islands"—and could apply similar principles.[53] If the commission agreed that the continental shelf expanse is part of an extension of China's land territory, this would give China a useful tool in arguing its claim over the islands. But even though the UN commission assesses "the scientific validity of claims," it does not have any authority to resolve disputes. Ultimate responsibility for territorial resolution falls back on China and Japan.[54]

Given the sometimes-contradictory claims to various South China Sea islands and maritime zones, it should not be surprising that, as in the East China Sea, delineating maritime boundaries in the South China Sea is complex—and also that UNCLOS does not offer much help. Some maritime divisions have been reasonably settled. For example, Thailand and Vietnam came to agreement in 1977 about the division between their EEZ and continental shelf boundary in the South China Sea/Gulf of Thailand area.[55] Similarly, Indonesia and Vietnam agreed to a continental shelf boundary in

2003.[56] But the South China Sea islands remain hotly contested, and even though the Philippines brought its territorial dispute with China before an arbitral tribunal under UNCLOS in January 2013, China has reportedly refused to accept international arbitration.[57] UNCLOS, thus, does not figure as a significant tool to resolve the territorial claims.

Despite all the factors contributing to the potential for conflict—speculation regarding resource wealth and the strategic value of the regions in particular—most analysts still deem large-scale armed conflict unlikely. At a minimum, though, the coming years are unlikely to see any side stand down; and with various military forces operating in close quarters, the possibility of error, confusion, and crisis escalation will be ever-present. Moreover, attempts to resolve tensions that focus purely on commerce and law and ignore broader strategic realities may not result in stable outcomes (even if in theory some consider them ideal). The South and East China Seas are likely to remain a potential area of conflict, with energy prominent, for years to come.

Oil and Gas in Central Asia

In part because of the vulnerability of the sea lanes through which much of its natural resources flow, China has increasingly focused on boosting resource production in neighboring countries, and bolstering land-based links for resources trade. Central Asia is at the center of this effort. As with the South and East China Seas, though, there is far more than resource development in play.

Central Asia is rich in oil and gas. Kazakhstan alone holds about 2 percent of the world's proven oil reserves, equivalent to roughly six years of Chinese imports; unproven resources are likely much larger. Turkmenistan holds 11.7 percent of the world's proven gas reserves (or almost one-third of all of Europe and Eurasia's gas), equivalent to nearly twenty years of Chinese demand.[58] In 2011, Kazakhstan produced 1.8 million barrels of oil a day, and Turkmenistan contributed another 200,000. Turkmenistan and

Uzbekistan each produced 6 billion cubic feet of natural gas a day, while Kazakhstan added another 2 billion, collectively about a third of Chinese demand.[59]

But Central Asian energy has long been fraught with challenges. Central Asian countries lack independent access to international markets. The post-Soviet Central Asian states—Kazakhstan, Uzbekistan, Turkmenistan, Kyrgyzstan, and Tajikistan—stand out in this regard. When the Soviet Union collapsed, more than half a century of rule from Moscow left Central Asian oil and gas producers reliant on a pipeline network directed toward supplying the Russian industrial machine. This gave Moscow extraordinary power over the economic fate of resource-rich Central Asian nations, and hence immense political influence.

There are only two ways out of Central Asia that don't run through Russia. The first is to the west. Oil and gas can be piped under the Caspian Sea, then through some combination of Azerbaijan, Armenia, Georgia, and Iran, and on through Turkey to the rest of the world; alternatively, it can be moved through Turkmenistan and Iran to world markets. The other option is to sell to China in the east.

Trapped on All Sides

In the 1990s, the United States became deeply involved in promoting the western option. Its central goal was to bolster the independence of Kazakhstan, Kyrgyzstan, Tajikistan, Turkmenistan, and Uzbekistan as they emerged from Russia's shadow. Historian Daniel Yergin writes, "For the United States and Britain, the consolidation of the newly independent nations was part of the unfinished business of the post-Cold War and what was required for a new, more peaceful world order."[60] He also argues against claims that the U.S. motive was economic, a popular belief in Moscow at the time. ("Some Russians also believe, or at least half believed, that the United States had deliberately orchestrated the collapse of the Soviet Union," he writes, "for the specific purpose of getting its hands on Caspian oil.")[61] U.S. military experts have come to similar conclusions: "The

driving force behind U.S. policy," argued Stephen Blank, a professor
at the U.S. Army War College, in 2007,

> is anti-monopoly, while the driving force behind Moscow and
> Beijing's policies is quintessentially monopolistic in nature. This
> American policy of defending the independence, integrity, and
> security of these states extends the long-established vital geostrategic
> interest of the United States in forestalling the rise of any Eurasian
> empire in either continent that could challenge it.[62]

Few would debate that Russia has sought to keep Central Asian oil
and gas under its own control. But the view from Beijing is considerably more complicated. Central Asia plays a special role in Chinese
security and economic thinking. Chinese involvement in the region
is best understood by looking at a full range of commercial, strategic, and domestic security concerns, rather than just at oil and
gas. Doing so reveals that energy-related commerce is usually inter-
twined with security goals that go well beyond a desire for reliable
oil and gas supplies.

Chinese relationships with Central Asian countries were focused
on traditional security concerns long before China became dependent on resource imports. Long-standing concerns about its (and
its neighbors') ethnic minority Uyghur population, along with
unresolved territorial concerns, drove Beijing's regional policy
during the 1990s.[63] Beijing saw unrest by the Uyghur population
in Xinjiang Uyghur Autonomous Region as a threat. Uyghurs had
been seeking greater autonomy in China for decades. During the
1990s, though, neighboring countries with large Uyghur populations suddenly achieved independence. According to one source,
Central Asia holds three hundred thousand Uyghurs, with more
than two-thirds located in Kazakhstan.[64] Beijing feared the potential for an "orange revolution" in China, and in particular that the
new political openness in Central Asia could provide an outlet
for Uyghur independence efforts that might spill across the border into Xinjiang.[65] China took the prospect of violence seriously
and has since 1998 deployed hundreds of thousands of troops in

the Xinjiang region.[66] It has also cooperated with regional governments in efforts to "counteract terrorism, separatism and extremism," both bilaterally and multilaterally, first through the "Shanghai Five" and later through the Shanghai Cooperation Organization (SCO), which includes China, Russia, Kazakhstan, Kyrgyzstan, Tajikistan, and Uzbekistan.[67]

Chinese engagement with Central Asia has also diverged sharply from its conflict with its South and East China Seas neighbors over regional oil and gas resources. Chinese security policy toward Central Asia has lacked a fierce desire to claim land on behalf of China. As China security expert M. Taylor Fravel observes, with the fall of communism in Central Asia, China eagerly developed enhanced security ties rather than acquiring disputed land.[68] In contrast to its current policy toward the Diaoyu/Senkaku Islands, Beijing did not take a hard-line approach on border disputes in Central Asia. Those issues were viewed as second-tier matters; creating stability along the border between Central Asia and the Xinjiang region, Beijing believed, trumped other concerns.[69]

A New Way Out

Chinese involvement in Central Asian oil and gas has thus occurred in an already established context dominated by traditional security concerns. International oil companies bought up resources immediately after the fall of the Soviet Union. But CNPC, the first Chinese company to enter Central Asia, did not make its first oil or gas field acquisition, Kazakhstan's Aktobe field, until 1997. Since then, CNPC has been the most active Chinese oil company in the region. In 2005, it bought a 67 percent stake in PetroKazakhstan, a Canadian-based company focused on Kazakh oil, for $4.2 billion.[70] That was followed in 2009 by the joint purchase (with KazMunaiGas) of MungistauMunaiGas for $2.6 billion.[71] Sinopec, CNOOC, Sinochem, and CITIC have all acquired smaller stakes in the Kazakh oil and gas production industry. (CIC has also acquired portfolio interest in Kazakh oil and gas.) By 2010, Chinese companies owned a larger share of oil production in Kazakhstan than in any other country.[72] Still, with the share at 23 percent, the Chinese position was far from dominant. Moreover, even with Kazakhstan so physically close to China, not all of its equity production was shipped there; CNPC makes oil shipment decisions on the basis of profit opportunities rather than blindly sending its oil to China.[73]

The remainder of Chinese oil and gas investment in Central Asia has focused on Turkmenistan. In 2009, the China Development Bank agreed to loan Turkmengaz $4 billion for the development of the South Yolotan, or Galkynysh, gas field, secured by payments for exports of natural gas to China.[74] CNPC and Turkmengaz are jointly developing the field, which began supplying gas in September 2013.[75] This is reportedly the only instance of a Chinese loan "directly linked to an upstream role for a Chinese NOC [national oil company]."[76] But CNPC has still not been able to secure an equity stake in the project; it operates as a service provider.[77]

Chinese efforts to build pipelines that connect its markets to Central Asia are probably of greater strategic importance to Beijing than oil and gas investment itself. These pipelines can also do considerably more to change the international economic and security landscape. Two pipeline projects have occupied center stage. The China-Kazakhstan pipeline runs from the Atyrau port in northwestern Kazakhstan to China's Xinjiang province in the northwest. It covers a total of 1,384 miles and has a capacity of 240,000 barrels a day of crude oil, equal to about 5 percent of Chinese oil imports.[78] Developed by the Sino-Kazakh Pipeline Company, a joint venture between CNPC and KazMunaiGaz, this was China's first transnational pipeline.[79] The underlying agreement was signed in 1997, and the line became operational in 2006. In 2007, China and Kazakhstan agreed to an extension by about 400 miles westward.[80] This began operating in 2009 and extended the pipeline to oilfields in western Kazakhstan near the Caspian Sea.[81] The capacity is currently being expanded and is expected to reach 400,000 barrels a day by 2014.[82]

The second major pipeline project is the Central Asian Gas Pipeline (CAGP), which brings natural gas from Turkmenistan, Uzbekistan, and Kazakhstan (this last primarily a transit country) to China. It runs for 1,130 miles and has a capacity of 3.8 billion cubic feet a day of gas.[83] The CAGP became operational in 2009 and connects to another pipeline at the border of China that runs eastward. In 2011, China imported 1.4 bcf a day from the CAGP, far below its full capacity.[84]

Experience with the CAGP shows how Chinese state entities can spur construction of infrastructure that is seen as critical to resource security. The CAGP is financed by a loan from CDB.[85] It is further backed by a commitment from China to buy a minimum quantity of gas delivered by the pipeline; proceeds from those sales will likely be directed first toward paying off the loan.[86]

Whatever the underlying motivation for building these pipelines—commercial or strategic—the pipelines can serve a similar function to those the United States has tried to support from Central Asia to the West, increasing the independence of Central Asian countries by giving them an alternative to Russia. In this sense China, which is able to combine political support for pipeline construction with financial muscle and a ready market, may have more ability to achieve what were once U.S. ends. But there are large differences between the two countries' courses: establishing fixed pipelines to China increases Central Asian dependence on Beijing, making Central Asian states more vulnerable to Chinese influence and politics, including decisions to halt purchases down the road. Moreover, whatever the motive, increased pipeline-based supplies from Central Asia could raise the stakes and difficulty for any U.S. (or Indian or Russian) effort to cut Chinese oil and gas supply lines during a future war.

China has developed a strong and expanding set of resource arrangements with its Central Asian neighbors that not only helps ensure access to energy supplies but also enhances Beijing's broader security interests. Although conflict is unlikely to emerge surrounding Chinese engagement in Central Asia's energy resources, its management of shared water resources has provoked consternation in at least one of its Central Asian neighbors—and several other countries in the region as well.

Water Fights

Shared water resources pose their own distinct challenges. In some ways these challenges are even more acute than those related to oil and gas in Central Asia and the South and East China Seas. Both China and its neighbors can choose to procure oil and gas from beyond the South and East China Seas if they choose to do so. Meanwhile Chinese investment in Central Asian oil and gas can be done in a way that creates benefits for all the parties involved. Water, in contrast, comes far closer to creating inescapable and zero-sum competition. Damming of rivers to generate hydroelectric power alters how water flows, which can harm fisheries and agricultural activity downstream. When river waters are permanently diverted for irrigation, energy production, or similar operations that permanently consume the water (unlike hydroelectric dams) can harm those who share the water resources more than damming for hydroelectric power. This potential for real damage is often compounded by poor or nonexistent information sharing between China and others with which it shares rivers. Real problems are exacerbated when a lack of information makes them less manageable, and phantom problems can become a source of conflict when there is insufficient information available to sort out myth from reality. Three cases shed light on these issues and help distinguish inevitable conflict from situations where more potential for cooperation exists.

The Ili and Irtysh

China and Kazakhstan share around twenty rivers. The most notable are the Ili, which begins in China's Tianshan Mountains and passes through Kazakhstan into that country's Lake Balkhash, and the Irtysh, which starts in the Altay Mountains in China and runs through Kazakhstan before joining up with the Russian Ob River. Both rivers factor prominently in China's plans for development in the sensitive Xinjiang region. In 2000, China launched an ambitious campaign of "Western Development" to promote economic growth across six provinces and five autonomous regions in the west of the country. Vital to this strategy has been a set of massive programs seeking to raise economic productivity in the Xinjiang region as part of the government's effort to blunt separatist and anti-Beijing sentiments. A core focus of this effort has been on agriculture and oil production, both of which require large amounts of water. China has been building canal systems that divert increasing amounts of water from the Ili and Irtysh toward these purposes.

Information about Chinese activities is fragmentary and inconsistent, but analysts largely agree that the plans threaten to be of significant detriment to Kazakhstan, and to a lesser extent Russia. The Ili and Irtysh both provide water for crucial agricultural and industrial sections of central and eastern Kazakhstan. According to Stephen Blank, diverting large amounts of water from the Ili and Irtysh will "slash freshwater inflow to eastern and Central Kazakhstan," putting the sixth-, seventh-, and eighth-largest cities in Kazakhstan "on the brink of full water deficiency" while "[drying] up the Irtysh-Karaganda canal," which figures prominently in Kazakhstan's own hydroelectric power production.[87] Chinese diversion of water for its own economic purposes thus poses risks to economic development downstream.

Fears extend to environmental consequences as well. Lake Balkhash, one of the world's largest, receives well over half of its inflow from the Ili River.[88] The United Nations Development Programme (UNDP) has warned that a fall in the lake's water supply could turn it into an "environmental tragedy comparable to the Aral Sea disaster," and Eric Hagt at the Center for Strategic and International Studies has written that "the shallowing of the rivers and shrinkage of the Balkhash and Zaysan Lakes [in eastern Kazakhstan] could have environmental repercussions such as salinization and micro-climate change—similar to the problems of the Aral Sea region."[89] The Aral Sea, straddling Kazakhstan and Uzbekistan and once one of the four largest lakes in the world, essentially disappeared as a result of Soviet irrigation projects.

Efforts at bilateral cooperation between China and Kazakhstan have yielded some meaningful outcomes for water quality monitoring, but a resolution to the issue of allocation remains elusive. Shortly after Kazakhstan's independence in 1991, the Kazakh ambassador to China, Murat Auezov, attempted but failed to negotiate an agreed approach. His government later tried to bring in Russia, whose Omsk region relies on the Ob River flowing from the Irtysh, into a set of three-party negotiations. But Russia demurred. Public sentiment in Kazakhstan escalated against Chinese activities in the late 1990s as news of the canal plans began to sound alarm bells, and finally a framework agreement was signed in 2001 to facilitate transboundary cooperation.[90] The agreement did not, however, cover measures relating to the allocation of water between the two countries—the most crucial of several transboundary issues to be resolved. Instead, a Sino-Kazakh consultative commission was created. The Chinese side rebuffed Kazakh efforts to trade free and subsidized food for allowing the natural, unimpeded flow of river water. In 2006, the commission produced a draft on water quality dissemination responsibilities between the two countries, a precursor to a 2011 Agreement on Water Quality in Transboundary Waters between China and Kazakhstan, obligating both sides to monitor water quality.[91]

Still, the Kazakh government continues to push the Chinese side to negotiate. Kazakh vice minister of agriculture Marat Tolibayev underscored the urgency of the situation in December 2012: "Water diverting is growing exponentially and we understand that procrastination [with regards to a possible agreement] is getting more dangerous for Kazakhstan and we are trying to secure an agreement in 2015." Yet the two sides have been unable to come to an agreement on proper sharing of the resource.[92]

In January 2013, an agreement was reached to construct waterworks facilities that would aid in "equitable distribution" of water resources on several of the transborder rivers.[93] China and Kazakhstan are also conducting scientific research on transborder river issues. The research is expected to be completed in 2014, with an eye toward informing later agreement.

Disputes over the Ili and Irtysh are likely to constitute an early test of whether technical cooperation can facilitate agreement between China and its neighbors on more fundamental resource issues. Current engagement between China and Kazakhstan should help yield a better understanding of which Chinese activities would leave Kazakhstan relatively unharmed and which can come only at the expense of Kazakh prosperity. At that point, any resolution will depend on decisions in Beijing and Astana. China could, in principle, simply take whatever water it wishes, since Kazakhstan lacks the capability to stop it. But Kazakhstan may be able to leverage Chinese interests in investing in and developing Kazakh oil and copper resources, as well as exert political pressure through the Shanghai Cooperation Organization Forum.[94]

The Mekong River

The Mekong River presents a different sort of challenge. Starting in the Tibetan-Qinghai Plateau, the Mekong flows 3,050 miles south through China's Yunnan Province, where it is called the Lancang River, into Southeast Asia; the river crosses Burma, Vietnam, Laos, Thailand, and Cambodia before emptying into the South China Sea. About a quarter of the water originates in China and Burma; so does roughly half of the total sediment, the material responsible for creating fertile agricultural conditions downstream.[95] More than seventy million people reside in the Mekong basin, variously depending on it for drinking water, fish, irrigation, transportation, energy, and agriculture.[96]

Four of the downstream countries—Vietnam, Laos, Thailand, and Cambodia—have long attempted to manage their competing interests through the Mekong River Commission (MRC), a multilateral organization established in 1995 to help cooperatively manage the river's resources. (Burma, which like China currently holds observer status in the MRC, has indicated its interest in joining the organization.) The MRC is characterized as relatively toothless—it has no enforcement powers—but has nonetheless helped on occasion to avoid unnecessary conflict between its parties' interests.[97] (If, for example, benignly adjusting the way one party removes water for agriculture can preserve another's fisheries, a body such as the MRC can help identify opportunities to avoid conflict.) The emergence of China, though, has complicated the situation.

In recent years, China has embarked on an ambitious set of dam projects along the Lancang River. It has built five operational dams; as of early 2013, three more were under construction, and as many as twenty-three others are being contemplated.[98] The project that has garnered the most attention is the Xiaowan Dam, which was completed in 2010.[99] It is the world's tallest arch dam, and the electricity it generates travels as far away as Shanghai.[100] The Nuozhadu Dam, which will have an even larger reservoir than Xiaowan, began early operations as of early 2013 and was slated to be fully operational by 2014.[101] These dams threaten to interfere with the seasonal floods on which millions of farmers in Cambodia, Laos, and the Mekong Delta region of Vietnam rely.[102] Some analysts also worry that the dams will remove essential sediment from the river.[103] Indeed, many experts have expressed alarm at the potential economic and environmental consequences of damming the upper Mekong, focusing in particular on seasonal disturbances. A 2009 report from the United Nations Environment Programme warned that the Chinese dams, by storing large amounts of water for release later, "will largely eliminate the Mekong's annual food pulse [a concentrated period of food production]."[104] Most affected would likely be Cambodian fisheries, which account for approximately 16 percent of the country's GDP.[105]

Local communities have gone further in protesting the Chinese dam projects. Uncharacteristic droughts and floods are now frequently blamed on Chinese dam building.[106] "Many local people and groups that monitor the dams in China point the finger at the dams as one of the main causes of drying up of the river," says Srisuwan Kuankachorn, a co-head of Towards Ecological Recovery and Regional Alliance, a Thai environmental group. He blames Chinese hydropower projects for drying up river transportation lanes, destroying fisheries, and damaging cropland.[107] Yet the weight of evidence on this front runs against blaming the dams for the damage. Yunnan province (upstream in China) has experienced droughts at the same time the downstream countries have.[108] Jeremy Bird, chief executive officer of the Mekong River Commission, has said that "China's dams have not caused this problem"; other sources come to a similar conclusion.[109]

Greater transparency and technical cooperation might help reduce unnecessary conflict; at a minimum, questions like those over whether Chinese dams are causing drought could be more definitively resolved. Attempts have been made to draw China closer to the MRC for precisely this reason. For many years of the MRC's existence, China refused to share much data. In 2010, during a severe drought, development expert Alan Potkin reflected widespread views when he urged the Chinese to "come clean on how much water they are diverting at Xiaowan and, in the future, at Nuozhadu."[110] "Even Chinese academics in favour of hydro-power," an *Economist* article noted, "complain that nearly all information to do with these rivers, even the amount of rain that reaches them, is treated as a state secret."[111] At the end of 2010, MRC pressure and a bout of negative publicity led the Chinese government to release more dam-related information, but controversy still remains.[112]

Some conflicts are unlikely to be amenable to technical resolution. Dams naturally smooth out seasonal variations in water flow, but that is precisely the problem for downstream fisheries and in some cases agriculture. More information on Chinese plans could help countries downstream mitigate some of the resulting damages, but it will not come close to eliminating them. Resolving these more difficult conflicts will likely come down to basic power politics, an area where China has far more leverage than its neighbors. Divergent interests among downstream parties—Thai hydropower generation, for example, may actually benefit from the Chinese dams—make even a united front from MRC members unlikely. And, unlike the case of Kazakhstan, the other parties to the conflict do not have mineral riches to offer China as bargaining chips (though they may be able to offer some concessions on contested territorial boundaries). These dynamics will not lead to so-called water wars involving China, since

Beijing can get what it wants without any such thing (and the down-stream countries are far too weak to challenge China), but they will inevitably generate new conflicts within the region.

The Brahmaputra

If one does want to find potential water wars involving China, the natural place to look is its face-off with India over the Brahmaputra. Yet this is perhaps the best example of a situation where the substantive conflict is almost entirely an invention of the participants, and transparency could go a long way to making the prospect of resource conflict go away.

China and India are both rising powers; they also share an old and complex security relationship. The crux of their dispute over water has centered on the Brahmaputra, a 2,000-mile river shared by China, Bangladesh, and India. The river, whose upper reaches are known in China as the Yarlung Tsangpo, starts in Tibet, runs eastward for hundreds of miles before turning sharply westward, then drops through the Himalayas to flow through the Indian province of Assam, and eventually merges with the Padma, Ganges, and Meghna into the Bay of Bengal.[113] Chinese planners have been eyeing the Brahmaputra's hydro potential for years, while Indian analysts, aware of the extent to which their country depends on the river's flow, are growing vocal about the threat they believe Chinese ambitions pose.

For years, Chinese engineers have developed proposals that might exploit the river to help address the country's heavy energy needs. (In 1995, the Chinese Academy of Engineering Physics even proposed using a series of nuclear explosives to create a canal through mountain ranges north of the river to irrigate the Gobi Desert.)[114] The country has already built a handful of smaller dams along the river and its tributaries.[115] Most attention, however, is directed toward the proposed Motuo Dam, a thirty-eight-gigawatt hydropower plant that would be installed at the Great Bend of the Brahmaputra, where the river makes a U-turn from east to west. (A typical nuclear power plant generates one gigawatt of power.) The Great Bend's natural hydropower potential comes from the fact that the water drops nearly two miles as it turns south, creating a natural source of potential energy.[116]

Chinese planners argue that the project would benefit the world; Zhang Boting, deputy general secretary of the China Society of Hydropower Engineering, notes that it could save 200 million tons of carbon dioxide emissions annually, roughly equivalent to 2 percent of the country's emissions in 2011.[117] Hawkish Indian analysts, however, have speculated that the dam is linked to an even more ambitious plan supported by some in China to divert significant quantities of water from the Brahmaputra to the Yellow River in order to help alleviate water shortages in Northern China. Their fears center around the western portion of the notional South-North Water Diversion Project.[118] The idea was discussed internationally as early as 1986 and was championed in Li Ling's 2005 *Tibet's Waters Will Save China*.[119] But given the area's rugged terrain and the long, hard route from the Yangtze to the Yellow River, many officials and analysts have questioned the project's cost and feasibility. In 2011, Wang Shucheng, a former minister of water resources, stated that the plan would not happen, given its difficulty and lack of necessity.[120] In October of that year, Vice Minister for Water Resources Jiao Yong stated that "considering the technical difficulties, the [lack of] actual need of diversion and the possible impact on the environment and state-to-state relations, the Chinese government has no plan to conduct any diversification project in this river."[121] Tashi Tsering, a Tibetan environmental law expert, has also held that the diversion scheme is infeasible; "The laws of physics will not allow water diversion from the Great Bend," he argues.[122] And environmental expert Isabel Hilton has argued that even the worst-case outcome is far less dire than many have claimed:

> Even were this project to be pursued... it would not turn off the tap: only 14 percent of the Brahmaputra's flow is in the river at the point at which it enters the gorge.... Were the Chinese, by some engineering miracle, to divert the entire flow of the river from within their territory, it would still only account for a small percentage of the river's resources.[123]

China has apparently not yet begun construction on the Motuo Dam or the diversion scheme. The specter of the project has, however, still alarmed many in India. Brahma Chellaney, a security expert at the Centre for Policy Research in New Delhi, has emerged as the most vocal critic. "Diversion of the Brahmaputra's water," he wrote in 2009, "is an idea that China does not discuss in public, because the project implies environmental devastation of India's northeastern plains and eastern Bangladesh, and would thus be akin to a declaration of water war on India and Bangladesh."[124] Many Chinese security analysts have not helped calm fears but instead have fanned the flames: "If Americans use Taiwan to pressure China," wrote one commentator, "why can't China use the Yarlung Tsangpo to balance India?! To pull this out in critical moments, how could we not?"[125]

Both sides have attempted to forge cooperative agreements to help defuse tensions. After a 2000 mudslide in Tibet, the two countries signed a memorandum of understanding. Under this agreement, China agreed to share information concerning water level, rainfall, and discharge from three river stations twice a day with Indian agencies, and to warn the Indian Water Ministry before the execution of any diversion plans.[126] Another agreement was made in 2006 to share transborder flood season data.[127] Meanwhile, China and India have participated in an annual series of Abu Dhabi dialogues from 2006 to 2009 focusing on promoting water cooperation among seven countries in South Asia.[128]

China has continued to press forward with its hydropower development plans. On January 23, 2013, the government approved an energy development plan for 2015 that included the construction of three new hydropower facilities on the middle reaches of the Brahmaputra River in Tibet.[129] After details were shared with Indian policy makers, particularly regarding the "run-of-the-river" nature of the plants (they will not affect the flow of the river), Indian prime minister Manmohan Singh publicly declared that India had no problem with the development.[130]

Ultimately, the technical challenges associated with the most threatening schemes for the Brahmaputra mean that acute conflict over the river is unlikely. But this does not mean worries about water will not severely strain the China-India relationship.

China's quest for water and energy will likely lead to heightened tension in an emerging great power relationship unless further steps are taken to reassure India that Chinese intentions (and impacts) are benign. To the extent that China is reluctant to participate in joint discussions of water management and impacts, it will also fan broader fears of unilateralism—well beyond water issues—in the region.

Striking a Balance Between Cooperation and Conflict

China's quest for natural resources has transformed political and security relationships close to home—even as the prospects for military conflict stemming from attempts to secure natural resources have been exaggerated. Interests in oil and gas are compounding broader and more influential security conflicts (along with simple but often intense nationalism) to raise the odds of conflict in the South and East China Seas. And China and its neighbors, like others before them, are unlikely to find international law providing an easy way of resolving their differences. Nonetheless, as China engages in minor standoffs and crises with neighbors, it may learn to manage them, reducing the risk of future escalation. Weighing against this positive trend, though, is rising Chinese nationalism and military capacity, making confrontation appear increasingly attractive to many in Beijing. This risk could intensify if the Chinese economy or political leadership substantially weakened, since that could tempt the Chinese leadership to distract citizens from problems at home by provoking international confrontation.

But not all of the security consequences of China's quest for resources in its near abroad are negative. China's quest for oil, gas, and ores in Central Asia is transforming regional politics in a more cooperative direction, as trade and investment align leaders' interests (if not always those of their people). Meanwhile, China's thirst for water is affecting relationships with a range of downstream neighbors. Here power relationships are unlikely to be transformed— China is both militarily dominant and upstream of its rivals—but new modes of cooperation could still emerge to shape behavior and forestall conflict.

Whatever happens in China's near abroad, though, will not be the end of the story. The political and security consequences of China's resource quest are increasingly being felt further from home as well.

9

Security and Politics Abroad

IN FEBRUARY 2011, AS a wave of revolution swept North Africa and the Middle East, Libya began to descend into civil war. The previous month, oil prices had risen on broad fears about regional turmoil and intense worries that the Suez Canal, controlled by an unstable Egypt, might be closed. Now Libya was becoming engulfed: oil production plummeted, foreigners fled, and the UN Security Council weighed whether to intervene.

In Beijing, policy makers were increasingly under stress. Several oil production sites in Libya controlled by CNPC had come under attack, but China could do little to protect them.[1] The Chinese government had to cobble together a hasty rescue mission that included chartered aircraft, ocean liners, and ships owned by Chinese enterprises to evacuate thirty thousand Chinese nationals in Libya.[2] Most oil exported from the Middle East was destined for Asia, but China, with no blue-water navy, remained entirely dependent on the United States to keep the Suez Canal and other critical sea lanes open. China's relative impotence only underscored the impression that without the U.S. military exertions to keep the global resource trade going, Beijing could well see the Chinese economy collapse.

Indeed, although resource competition and cooperation between China and its neighbors provide the most immediate opportunity for China's resource quest to alter international relationships, the consequences of efforts to secure resources are being felt much further away. They are being driven primarily by steps taken to ensure safe transport for the resources China needs, and by entanglements stemming from resource investment and trade relationships abroad. These will only intensify as China becomes a stronger commercial and military power in the coming years.

Securing the Seas

Popular discussion of how China's natural resource challenges collide with international security typically focuses on the countries in which its companies do business. But the more fundamental challenge facing China's resource security may have less to do with whether those companies control overseas resources and more to do with whether they can get those resources back to China. Today we take it for granted that resources produced in one part of the world can easily be shipped to any other that wants them. But this is far from a given, and it is certainly not something Chinese strategists take for granted over the long haul.

International trade has always been underpinned by power. Absent some source of physical security for overland routes and high seas corridors, anarchy reigns and threats of theft and piracy can make trade prohibitively costly or even impossible. Similarly, without someone to provide security in critical commodities-producing regions, instability can disrupt producers' ability to extract supplies. Moreover, when a single power (or a group of powers) controls a particular trade route, it can choose to prevent others from using the channel if it so desires. This has often been the case: empires have protected privileged trade routes and excluded others from using them; countries have discriminated in choosing whom and at what price to allow use of their territory as a transit point for trade; and, in wartime, combatants have used their ability to block access to trade as a tool for achieving their war goals. Similarly, when great powers have provided stability in critical commodities-producing regions, they have often insisted that the commodities produced there be sold only to them or their allies (or perhaps to others through their exclusive trading companies).

Since World War II, the United States has underwritten a different sort of global order. It has chosen to make trade routes and commodities sources accessible to all. The decision to do so facilitates the growth of globalized markets. But doing so is a choice, not an inevitability, and it is something many Chinese strategists fear might change in the future.

The emergence of China as a leading consumer of imported commodities has itself brought the durability of this arrangement into question. The U.S. government has declared its continuing commitment to stability in critical regions, but many Americans wonder why the United States should bear the costs of maintaining freedom of the seas when Chinese consumers appear to benefit from easy trade at least as much as Americans do. This inclination can be particularly strong when the trade routes in question carry goods destined for China but not for the United States. The Strait of Malacca, for example, carries little, if any, oil bound for the United States but was the conduit for 77 percent of Chinese oil imports as of 2009.[3] Why, many Americans will inevitably begin to ask, should the United States pay to keep these sea lanes open? Similarly, the United States conducts military, diplomatic, and aid operations in critical commodities-exporting regions, particularly the Middle East and Africa, with benefits (when U.S. strategy succeeds) not only to its consumers but also to China. Skepticism of such activity is likely to become particularly acute in cases where little of the commodity production in the relevant regions is actually shipped to the United States. The predicament is increasingly likely for U.S. oil and gas imports from the Middle East and Africa and as U.S. oil and gas production rises.

Many Chinese are just as skeptical of the current arrangements. The United States has, so far, kept critical sea lanes open, regardless of the destination of the commodities that flow through them, but this might not remain the case indefinitely. Over time, if the United States were to withdraw from providing universal sea-lane security, China might be left without reliable trade routes for critical commodities imports, particularly if it has not developed the naval capabilities required to take over the task itself. Similarly, although the United States has so far remained committed to promoting stability in exporting regions (albeit with mixed success in practice), there is no guarantee it will continue to do so. Were the United States largely to withdraw from the Middle East, for example, China might find its energy supplies considerably more volatile.

Chinese concerns about possible U.S. retrenchment have increased in recent years as Western analysts have begun projecting that North America might become energy self-sufficient, creating at least a possibility of the United States reducing its overseas commitments, even though U.S. officials insist it will not. And at least as worrisome to Chinese leaders is the prospect that during an armed conflict the United States would use its naval dominance to cut China off from commodities imports critical to both its economy (and hence social stability) and its war-making capacity. Some in China may also fear that the United States could interfere with critical resource-producing regions in Central Asia in times of acute U.S.-China conflict.

The Geography of Resource Trade

Chinese vulnerability to interdiction of vital resource supplies depends critically on where those supplies come from. Resources that come from the Middle East and parts of Africa—primarily oil and gas—are the most fraught. Some must pass through the Bab el-Mandeb, a narrow passage with Yemen on one side and Djibouti and Eritrea on the other. Resources from Egypt and Sudan must pass through here; flows from North Africa (Libya and Algeria) also pass through this waterway after having transited the Suez Canal.[4] Other Middle East oil and gas must pass through the Strait of Hormuz, a twenty-one-mile-wide waterway pinched between Iran and Oman, and often a focus of global worries about the free flow of oil.[5] Everything that passes through either of these two waterways must also transit the Strait of Malacca, bordered by Singapore, Malaysia, and Indonesia, on its way to Chinese ports. Alternative routes are possible (and occasionally but not intensively used); in principle some ships can pass through the Sunda and Lombok straits, both within Indonesian waters, or, in the extreme, travel around the east coast of Australia (between Australia and New Zealand) in order to reach China.

Resources shipped from the Americas travel different routes. Shipments from the west coast of North and South America transit the Pacific Ocean and thus avoid the most notorious chokepoints in Southeast Asia and the Middle East. (They must still, however, pass through the South or East China Sea on their way to Chinese ports.) Many resource shipments from the east coast of the Americas can use the Panama Canal to transit to the Pacific Ocean and onward to China. But oil shipments typically must take another route, because oil tankers are usually too large to pass through the Panama Canal. Instead tankers travel across the Atlantic and around the Cape of Good Hope at the southern tip of Africa. They then must pass through the narrow sea lanes of Southeast Asia—usually the Strait of Malacca—before reaching Chinese shores.[6]

Resources extracted from Africa follow similar routes, ultimately entering the Indian Ocean before crossing Southeast Asia. Many of the resources shipped from Australia, by contrast, pass to the east of Australia and Papua New Guinea before entering Chinese waters through the East China Sea. But resources that ship from the country's west coast—notably iron ore—pass through Southeast Asian sea lanes instead.

Sea-Lane Control

This diverse set of sea lanes through which Chinese resources pass poses a steep challenge to Chinese military planners, who would rather not rely on the United States for secure transit. Yet China's ability to project power—to replace the United States as a provider of sea-lane security or stability in faraway resource-producing regions—remains severely limited. The Chinese military continues to focus first on contingencies involving Taiwan, in particular the ability to prevail in a cross-straits conflict, along with the capacity to influence Taiwanese decisions more generally.[7] Ground forces are focused on internal security and perimeter defense.[8]

Chinese leaders have, however, long desired broader capabilities. A 2011 study from the U.S. National Defense University described the evolution of China's naval strategy as "from the 'near-coast defense' strategy prior to the mid-1980s to the 'near-seas active defense' after the mid-1980s, and then to the advancement of a 'far-seas operations' strategy by the mid-2000s."[9] These evolving goals are reflected in statements by China's leaders since the early 2000s. President Jiang Zemin said in 2001 that although China should continue to improve its near-seas active defense, the People's Liberation Army Navy should also "in the long run pay attention to enhancing the far-seas defense and operations capabilities."[10] In 2002, when Hu Jintao succeeded Jiang as president, he continued to press in a similar direction.[11] In 2004, President Hu addressed the senior leadership of the People's Liberation Army (PLA) and put forth a new vision for a defense policy that encompassed the idea of "far-seas" capabilities in an expanded conception of "China's national interests beyond its geographic borders," which was later codified in a series of White Papers and in the Communist Party constitution.[12] A 2006 editorial from the *PLA Daily* reported that "China's national interests are spreading everywhere in the world, into the open seas."[13] More recently, President Xi Jinping has drawn significant attention with his increasing emphasis on developing a world-class military, declaring that China "must ensure there is unison between a strong military and a prosperous country."[14]

But goals have not been consistently matched by capabilities. The U.S. Department of Defense reports annually on Chinese military capabilities; its 2012 report reflects mainstream thinking well. China has just begun to build a substantial capability to operate in open but nearby waters. "Over the past five years," the Pentagon reported, "China has begun demonstrating a more routine naval and civilian enforcement presence in the South China Sea." This comes after decades of interest in the area unmatched by the ability to project power into it. It is being followed slowly by broader capabilities. "By the latter half of the current decade," the Pentagon study projected, "China will likely be able to project and sustain a modest-sized force, perhaps several battalions of ground forces or a naval flotilla of up to a dozen ships, in low-intensity operations far from China."[15] A flotilla that size would be able to conduct counter-piracy operations but not "project and sustain large forces in high-intensity combat operations far from China."[16] In particular, it would not be able to clear the Strait of Hormuz or any other chokepoint in the face of a deliberate state-led effort to close it. Investment in technologies such as aircraft carriers (which would have little or no value in a confrontation over Taiwan) and nuclear-powered submarines (which can stay away from port for an extended period of time) point in the direction of wanting more influence far from Chinese shores.[17] Having already launched one aircraft carrier in 2012, in April 2013 China announced its intention to develop a second, more powerful carrier. Yet the U.S. Department of Defense still foresees a far weaker capacity to project power well away from China than the United States and others enjoy.

Indeed, there remains significant debate within China over how much to invest in the ability to undertake naval operations in distant waters, and substantial uncertainty abroad over just how much sea-lane security figures into defense plans.[18] Xi Jinping's first visit to a military installation as president was to the naval base on Hainan Island. He called on the soldiers to be prepared for military struggle and to "nurture [a] fighting spirit." At the same time, the State Oceanic Administration laid out its plans for expanding maritime power through the purchase of new vessels and planes.[19] Chinese naval leaders and journals may speak frequently of the need to boost investments in sea-lane security, but part of this is inevitably bureaucratic jockeying for funds. Others want to steer money toward different defense priorities, and some undoubtedly fear that investment by China in a blue-water navy would merely invite countermeasures from others.[20] The net result could well be greater expenses but a similar military balance.[21] All of this suggests it is unwise to expect a fundamental change, in which the dominant role of the United States would be altered by a much stronger Chinese presence in securing high-seas resource trade anytime soon.

The Gulf of Aden Test

China is, however, slowly becoming more involved in distant missions, which over time could give it greater ability to secure its own resource trade. For example, despite China's lack of military assets in the Mediterranean area, the PLAN and PLA Air Force (PLAAF) were still able to contribute to the rescue effort of Chinese nationals in Libya in February 2011. Beijing was able to divert one missile frigate from the PLAN's anti-piracy task force off the coast of Somalia and provide four PLAAF transport aircraft from Xinjiang.[22]

There has been just one extended deployment of naval forces far from China's coastal seas; it gives important insight into China's limits and how it might work with others abroad. In 2008, Chinese ships suffered seven pirate attacks in the Gulf of Aden, a passage between Yemen and Somalia that ships must cross after exiting the Bab el-Mandeb en route to the Indian Ocean. In November 2008, a Chinese fishing ship was attacked and seized by Somali pirates, and a month later pirates attacked a largely empty cargo ship in December 2008.[23] On the same day, Chinese sources told state-controlled media that China was preparing to deploy PLAN vessels in response.[24] A spokesman for the Foreign Ministry, Liu Jianchao, stated a day later, "Piracy has become an international enemy that poses severe threat [sic] to international navigation, maritime trade and security."[25] He expanded on the new challenge: "During the first 11 months of this year...twenty percent of [Chinese ships] were attacked. This year, there are seven hijack cases involving China...to date, there remains one Chinese fishing boat and 18 crew members held captive."[26]

In response, China dispatched its first Chinese Naval Escort Taskforce (CNET) to the Gulf of Aden at the end of 2008, and the country's first counter-piracy effort in the Gulf of Aden became operational in January 2009. It was the first long-distance deployment by the PLAN.[27] As of August 2013, fifteen such task forces (each lasting about four months) had been deployed to the Gulf of Aden to provide escort convoys and protection to commercial Chinese vessels.[28] Beijing claims that its task forces have completed more than 500 escort missions for over 5,000 Chinese and foreign vessels, and salvaged or rescued over sixty ships."[29]

These deployments appear to be directly connected to concerns about pirate attacks on Chinese vessels rather than to broader concerns about piracy in general. This sets Chinese involvement apart from others', which has been aimed at safeguarding ships in general, including participant countries' own vessels only incidentally. Recent Chinese media reports reinforce the idea that China's counter-piracy activities are directly related to the number and frequency of pirate attacks on Chinese ships. For example, in 2010, *China Daily* reported that China was increasing its counter-piracy activities after "a series of pirate attacks on Chinese ships in the past two weeks."[30]

The focus on Chinese ships does not mean, however, that China has acted entirely independently. In particular, some have argued that the deployment was helped considerably by the existence of a UN framework. They point out that passage of several UN resolutions in 2008 assuaged Chinese worries that deployment to the Gulf of Aden might carry international repercussions.[31] Interest in having its activities legitimated by an international framework, however, has not extended to a desire to participate in internationally directed operations. Several of those—such as EU and NATO efforts— are exclusive to members of the organizations. But others, such as CTF-151, which at various times has been led by the Thai, Danish, South Korean, Pakistani, Turkish, and U.S. navies, are not.[32] China has also declined requests to join collective command efforts to patrol the International Recommended Transit Corridor (IRTC), the preferred passageway for ships traveling through the Gulf of Aden. Defense Ministry officials have, however, said that China is "willing to strengthen intelligence and information exchanges and, when necessary, take part in humanitarian relief operations with all countries, including the United States." To this end, China has been a member of the multilateral Contact Group on Piracy off the Coast of Somalia (CGPCS) and also participated in Shared Awareness and Deconfliction (SHADE) meetings, forums convened by other countries to improve information sharing, increase coordination, and avoid redundancy.[33]

As China participates in more overseas missions, then, it appears to be partly drawn into the sorts of collaborative efforts other countries typically pursue, but it has not been fully integrated. Other countries have not had to change how they pursue high-seas security. Yet Chinese involvement in high-seas security efforts is starting to change some of the details of how high-seas security functions, with at least a very small amount of the burden increasingly shared.

A "String of Pearls"

The Gulf of Aden deployment also brought Chinese capabilities and limitations into stark relief. The PLAN has been able to protect Chinese ships transiting through the Gulf of Aden. Yet that endeavor—opposed only by weakly armed pirates—has stretched the limits of PLAN capabilities. The PLAN has also been forced to improvise arrangements for supplying and maintaining naval capabilities thousands of miles away from their home bases. The deployment has thus "highlighted the need for shore-based logistics support for PLAN forces operating in the Indian Ocean," in the words of one U.S. analyst.[34] Others have gone further and divined a Chinese plan for overseas naval bases.

Much of this has revolved around the so-called String of Pearls. This strategy did not originate in China; it is an idea first expressed in a 2004 report, *Energy Futures in Asia*, produced by a contractor for the U.S. Department of Defense. The term has since become common to U.S. and others' thinking about Chinese strategy in the Indian Ocean. One scholar describes it as indicating "China's growing geopolitical influence through efforts to gain access to ports and airfields, develop special diplomatic relationships, and modernize military forces" extending through the full sweep of the Indian Ocean, from the Strait of Malacca to East Africa.[35]

Speculation has focused on Chinese commercial engagement with a string of countries—Burma, Bangladesh, Sri Lanka, Pakistan,

Mauritius, and the Seychelles, among others—that dot the boundary and interior of the Indian Ocean. In some cases, notably with Sri Lanka and Pakistan, contractors have been involved in the construction of port facilities that have raised suspicions that Beijing is intending to develop distant naval bases. Without exception, though, the speculation rests on thin ground.

Take the much-talked-about Chinese involvement in Pakistan's Gwadar port. In early 2013, reports that a Chinese company would take over the management of the port from the Singapore Port Authority raised widespread alarm.[36] Yet there is little evidence China will actually be building and maintaining a naval base on the rim of the Indian Ocean in Pakistan. Indeed, the *Financial Times* reported in 2011 that Pakistan had requested that China build a naval base at Gwadar, and China did not accept the offer.[37] (This pattern reflects a pervasive dynamic whereby Pakistan pushes China to develop Gwadar, playing on energy security concerns, but repeatedly fails; Gwadar is currently a "port to nowhere," with no infrastructure connecting it to the rest of Pakistan.)[38] A 2012 RAND report prepared for the U.S. Air Force noted that the various ports under development by China "are not military bases." Instead, it argued, "they could serve as supply depots for China's naval forces, enabling it to conduct operations further from its shores."[39]

It is far from clear that China has an interest in overseas bases; at a minimum, any desire to build up bases would need to be weighed against the backlash it is likely to spur. Citing the Chinese government's longstanding policy against overseas bases in keeping with its emphasis on nonintervention, senior U.S. naval analyst Daniel Kostecka noted in 2011 that "there is no substantive evidence in Chinese sources or elsewhere to support the contentions of commentators, academics, and officials who use [the String of Pearls concept] as a baseline for explaining Beijing's intentions in the Indian Ocean." Instead, he argues, Chinese strategists are debating whether to create "places," not full-fledged bases.[40] This is a common view among specialists, though it is far from universal. The Chinese scholar Shen Dingli, for example, has written, "Setting up overseas military bases is not an idea we have to shun; on the contrary, it is our right."[41]

To be certain, there is more to the speculation about Indian Ocean activities than the belief that China desires to secure its flows of energy from the Middle East. India in particular worries that Chinese activities are aimed at bolstering its position in future combat between the pair. This concern has been particularly acute for Chinese-funded efforts to develop a port in Sri Lanka, efforts that one analyst describes as looking "like a dagger pointed directly at India."[42] Yet if that port were developed into a robust base, its proximity to India could be more liability than asset during conflict, given weak capabilities to defend it against air attack.[43]

In any case, for the time being, Chinese aspirations to provide security for the resource trade are far from being translated into real capabilities. A serious effort to be the lead supplier of security for the sea lanes that it depends on would require not only a logistical network to support them far away from China but also far more investment and technological progress in ships and accompanying aircraft.

How might this change beyond the next decade, as Chinese blue-water naval capabilities develop further? Analysts have occasionally suggested that the United States and China should ultimately share the burden of sea-lane security. The idea may seem appealing in principle, since both countries benefit from secure sea lanes. But it is far less likely to be attractive in practice. For the United States, sharing sea-lane security ultimately means entrusting the security of some important trade routes to China. U.S. strategists, though, are likely to be at least as skeptical of any Chinese commitment to keeping trade routes open to all as Chinese strategists are currently of U.S. promises to do the same (despite the long U.S. track record of providing open access to sea lanes for trade). Any U.S. decision to cede control of critical Middle Eastern and Southeast Asian sea lanes would also come with grave consequences for U.S. allies in the region. Japan and South Korea depend critically on Middle Eastern and Southeast Asian sea lanes for imports of oil, gas, and other commodities. It is difficult to imagine their comfortably relying on China for the free flow of goods that are vital to their economies.

Moreover, absent major changes in the rules of international trade, U.S. withdrawal from providing Middle Eastern stability and Southeast Asian sea-lane security could well have dangerous economic consequences for the United States. Shortfalls in commodities imports to China caused by problems in producing regions or critical transit routes would leave China looking to replace its supplies with materials from elsewhere. That scramble would make the commodities in question scarcer for all consumers—the United States included—with resulting economic damage to all. The only way out of this would be if the world essentially divided itself into trading blocs that privilege U.S. consumers over Chinese ones during such a crisis. This makes the prospect of U.S.-Chinese sharing of sea-lane security even more remote.

Pipeline Politics Beyond Central Asia

China has, in principle, an alternative option to relying on U.S. provision of sea-lane security to ensure reliable access to resource supplies: when it comes to oil and gas, it can use pipelines. Pipelines are all but a necessity when moving oil and gas from Central Asia. China has, however, endeavored to build pipeline routes for oil transport even where seaborne commerce is common. This is almost certainly driven by fears that it could lose access to the Strait of Malacca during a conflict with the United States or another foreign power. But the Chinese track record in these more purely strategic (rather than also commercial) efforts has been mixed.

Chinese strategists have talked in particular about four areas: pipelines from Russia, a pipeline through Burma, one traversing Thailand, and a pipeline through Pakistan. Only the first two have been successful so far. The East Siberia-Pacific Ocean (ESPO) pipeline carries oil from Siberia to Chinese refineries in Daqing and Fushun.[44] The shipments are priced according to market-based rates. The ESPO pipeline differs from other Chinese efforts in that it makes at least some economic sense independent of worries about sea-lane disruptions during wartime, and it does not cross areas marked by political instability.

China has also successfully built a pipeline from the Indian Ocean port of Sittwe in Burma to Yunnan province. In 2007, after many years of discussions, China and Burma agreed to the construction of a $1 billion natural gas pipeline (to be supplied by Burmese gas; Burma is a relatively large but underdeveloped resource holder) and an accompanying $1.5 billion oil pipeline. CNPC owns a narrow majority of the project.[45] The project has encountered challenges in Burma related to land acquisition, a common problem for pipelines around the world but one made worse there by the lack of clear benefits for the local population.[46] The economics of the oil pipeline have also been repeatedly questioned.[47] And even the security advantages remain unclear to many Chinese; as one researcher at the China University of Petroleum noted, "The Sino-Myanmar [Burma] pipeline does little to relieve China's dependence on Malacca, as the 22 million tons of oil imports are just a drop in the ocean compared with China's large energy consumption."[48] Yet in 2013 the pipeline was successfully brought into service, perhaps demonstrating that Chinese companies can be called on to pursue strategically important projects that are designed to improve resource security even when those projects' economics and actual security benefits are not transparently compelling.[49]

Two other prospects have not been so fortunate. The only other pipeline that doesn't encounter politically fraught lands is a notional one crossing the Isthmus of Kra in southern Thailand; this potential pipeline, though, does more to illustrate that many talked-about projects never materialize. A 1.5 million barrel a day pipeline across the isthmus was approved by the Thai government in 2004; in principle construction was to begin in 2008.[50] (Chinese planners have also talked about the possibility of building a canal that would traverse it, a prospect that has been discussed in Thailand for fifty years.)[51] The project has some plausible underlying logic, since it could cut down on tanker costs for moving oil from the Middle East to East Asia. But no domestic Chinese players have ever seriously pushed for the project, and no work has ever been done on implementing the pipeline.

A final pipeline from the port of Gwadar in Pakistan (west of India) through to China has also been discussed for many years.[52]

Yet instability in Pakistan—not only security challenges but more fundamentally the lack of a predictable government with which to deal—has prevented progress. It is not clear whether much would happen even if this roadblock were cleared away, given the weak economics of any prospective pipeline, and the proliferation of new supply routes into China's west. Moreover, even if the pipeline reduced Chinese exposure to interdiction of seaborne oil, it might introduce a new vulnerability: Pakistani maps of the notional route suggest it would be highly vulnerable to Indian land forces during a future Sino-Indian conflict.[53]

Chinese-backed pipelines might eventually lessen the country's dependence on seaborne imports, but there is little chance they will eliminate them. China will continue to depend on seaborne oil and gas for the indefinite future. It will also continue to rely on metallic ores and agricultural products (which cannot be moved through pipelines) to be shipped through international waters.

Entangled Interests

China's resource quest can also lead it to become entangled in events far from home through its companies' investments overseas—and this can, in principle, have broad consequences for international security and international politics that go beyond bilateral relationships. This dynamic has been most pronounced for Chinese investments in oil and gas. China is far from alone in having its oil interests create consequences for international security and politics—the United States has often been drawn into the same nexus—but with China still in the early stages of deepening its investments abroad, the consequences of Chinese involvement, though already apparently different, are not yet well understood.

Civil War in Sudan

Sudan has been engulfed in intermittent civil wars since its independence more than fifty years ago. In early 2003, a conflict centered on the Darfur region in the west of Sudan broke out. It led to hundreds of thousands of civilian deaths over the course of the next seven years and to international calls for action to halt it.[54] The Sudanese government in Khartoum supported Janjaweed militias with arms, even incorporating some irregulars into its Popular Defense Forces.[55] Although Khartoum agreed to disarm the militias on multiple occasions, Janjaweed fighters continued to be a brutally effective government proxy in Darfur.[56]

During that time, CNPC maintained a large ownership stake in Sudanese oil production. CNPC involvement in the Sudanese oil sector dates back to an agreement on oil development with the government of Sudan in 1995.[57] In 1996, CNPC won another trio of development blocks in a competitive international auction, and in 1999 the project began producing oil for shipment to Singapore, turning Sudan from an oil importer into an oil exporter. After that, the role of CNPC in the Sudanese economy grew steadily. By 2009, CNPC held a stake of at least 35 percent in each of five developments, in addition to majority shares in a petroleum refinery and a petrochemical production facility. In 2009, China imported roughly 50 percent of Sudanese oil production.[58] This was about 16 percent of CNPC's 2009 equity production.[59]

The result was strong mutual dependence between CNPC and the government of Sudan. The relationship between Chinese oil interests and Khartoum came under stress during the Darfur conflict but never reached a breaking point. (China has also faced a new set of geopolitical difficulties following South Sudanese independence that may be a harbinger of broader challenges to come.) Rebels attacked Chinese oil fields at least three times between 2004 and 2008, raising concerns about security and drawing Beijing deeper into Sudan's politics.[60] One rebel commander warned, "We carried out operations in the oil regions before and warned the firms and individuals that whoever is there is considered a legitimate military target."[61] Yet Sudanese oil production climbed during every year of the conflict.[62] Indeed, there is no indication that the attacks and abductions had a major impact on daily production, or even that they were surprising given the high degree of political risk the Chinese NOCs naturally encountered while operating in Sudan. Similar abductions occur with some frequency in the Niger Delta, another conflict-prone area with major oil interests.

The Chinese government, consistent with its past support for Sudanese sovereignty, shunned initial international mediation efforts in Darfur favored by the United States, the UN, and others.[63] However, by the mid-2000s, China's standard noninterference policy gave way to more direct diplomatic pressure on Khartoum. One Chinese scholar described this strategy as "influence without interference."[64] Starting in 2004, a series of senior Chinese envoys visited Sudan and urged Khartoum to end its support of Janjaweed militias. The government of Sudan balked at the requests.[65] In response, Chinese diplomats took a new approach: they began to withhold their veto power and abstain from UN Security Council votes on Darfur. China did not veto UNSC Resolution 1556 in July 2004, which implicated Khartoum directly in the Darfur conflict; UNSC Resolution 1564, which even threatened Sudan with oil sanctions; or UNSC Resolution 1593, which urged that the International Criminal Court begin an investigation in Darfur.[66] In total, China abstained from eight of the twenty-two UNSC resolution votes from 2001 to 2007.[67] It voted in favor of all the others.[68]

Yet this willingness to let resolutions pass does not tell the full story: China appears to have successfully softened some of the most important resolutions that did pass as a condition for its abstention. UNSC Resolution 1706, for example, was designed to expand the UN peacekeeping mission to Darfur and deploy an international force to the region. China abstained from the vote but steered the resolution so that Khartoum was given the opportunity to approve the UN peacekeeping force.[69] The result was at least a seven-month delay in the start of the peacekeeping mission, since the government of Sudan stonewalled. Many analysts argue the delay was an important strategic buffer period for Khartoum to increase its strength in the region and perhaps may have been part of a tacit agreement with China.[70]

Some observers have speculated that China's effort to weaken resolutions was influenced by pressure from Chinese NOCs (or a proactive desire from the government to help the NOCs) to smooth over the Sino-Sudanese diplomatic relationship.[71] Resolving this is essentially impossible, since China has not faced similar situations with countries in which it has no oil interests. At a minimum, though, oil interests did not lead China to take decisive action to block UN efforts in Sudan.

The Chinese government also continued to supply small-arms ammunition throughout the conflict despite a bar from the Security Council against assistance to any of the parties involved.[72] Heavier weapons, including helicopter gunships and attack aircraft, came from Russia and Belarus. (China has also been accused of training Sudanese fighter pilots in the use of Chinese Fantan fighter jets delivered in 2002, prior to the UN restrictions.)[73] The roles of Russia and Belarus suggest that, moral issues aside, Chinese leverage through the option of denying arms sales to Sudan may have been limited; Khartoum appears to have had other major suppliers willing to provide it with an ample volume of arms. Regardless, any connection between arms sales and Chinese resource development would have been tenuous at best; China did not need to sell arms to Khartoum to secure access to resources, since Chinese companies were the only ones willing to develop Sudan's oil.

Ultimately, the experience of Darfur does not support claims that the combination of Chinese resource interests and Beijing's UNSC veto will always prevent international intervention in civil wars and other human rights challenges. But the possibility that China will make such interventions slower and more difficult cannot be ruled out.

Preventing a Nuclear Iran

Chinese oil and gas interests have also been blamed for Beijing's reluctance to pressure Iran to curtail or forgo its nuclear-weapons-related activities. Chinese uranium and technology suppliers have a long history of assisting the Iranian nuclear program, extending to well before China was dependent on imported oil.[74] Though such assistance has stopped in recent years, China continues to be the strongest voice among the permanent Security Council members against aggressive economic sanctions targeted at Tehran.

China has been highly active in the Iranian oil and gas sector. CNPC is responsible for developing the northern half of the large Azadegan oil field, the biggest one found in Iran in decades.[75] A CNPC subsidiary (CNPC International) was also important in helping Iran blunt the consequences of sanctions by taking over majority ownership and responsibility for development of the southern half of the field from INPEX, a Japanese company that had previously held a 75 percent interest but withdrew under international pressure between 2006 and 2010. It does not, however, appear to have moved forward much with development. Meanwhile Sinopec is the major foreign equity participant in Yadavaran, the other major Iranian oil prospect, an arrangement it entered into in 2007.

As tensions with Iran intensified, with oil- and gas-related sanctions particularly prominent, Chinese energy-related interactions with Iran have sent inconsistent messages. With the withdrawal of Western firms following nuclear-related sanctions, CNPC was left as the largest foreign oil company active in Iran and moved ahead with its North Azadegan investment.[76] In July 2012, Iran announced that Chinese companies planned to invest $20 billion to develop Azadegan and Yadavaran, with an ultimate production goal of 700,000 barrels of oil a day.[77] Chinese companies also continued work on several less promising fields.

But Chinese companies have proven more willing to exercise restraint elsewhere. In September 2011, press reports indicated that Chinese companies had deliberately refused to invest in new projects, including opportunities abandoned by Western firms thanks to sanctions.[78] (Azadegan and Yadavaran were existing projects.) Perhaps the greatest controversy has focused on the South Pars gas field. Iran, home of the second-largest natural gas reserves in the world, has concentrated on expanding production from its South Pars field, which is estimated to contain 47 percent of Iranian reserves.[79] In March 2013, the U.S. EIA noted that "Phase 11" of the development, a joint effort between CNPC and the Iranian national oil company, aimed for completion in 2016 and, with capacity of two billion cubic feet of natural gas a day, for supplying Iran's first liquefied natural gas exports.[80] In June 2009, CNPC had signed a $5 billion contract to develop the project, replacing the French company Total, which was ejected after what Iran considered unacceptable delays.[81] Beginning in 2011, however, Iran began to warn CNPC over what it saw as inadequate progress with the project.[82] CNPC responded by citing stability concerns and difficult operating conditions, and in July 2012 it pulled out of the project, at least temporarily.[83]

Were there underlying motives related to international efforts to isolate Iran? The evidence is mixed. In September 2012, Wu Bangguo, chairman of the Standing Committee of the National People's Congress, led a delegation to Iran that included CNPC's president, Zhou Jiping. It was reported that Iran agreed to CNPC's withdrawal from the South Pars project and promised to provide another block of oil or gas in exchange at a later date.[84] The *International Oil Daily* reported in September 2012 that CNPC withdrew because of war concerns and an inability to find gas buyers, quoting a CNPC source as saying "CNPC can't find buyers for gas production from South Pars, so that's why we can't start production on there."[85] In September 2012, *Caixin Online* also reported that critical equipment for the South Pars project, such as natural gas compressors, would need to be purchased from European countries or the United States, but sanctions would have prevented delivery to Iran.[86]

Meanwhile, pending Chinese efforts to buy into U.S. oil and gas production also may have played a role. With U.S. oil and gas production on the rise, Chinese companies were interested in investing in U.S. prospects; some worried, though, that they could be denied permission to invest if the U.S. government disapproved of their activities in other countries of concern, most notably Iran. In October 2010, press reports suggested that the Chinese government "informally instructed" firms to slow down after the United States imposed unilateral sanctions on Iran. A source linked the instruction to the 2010 $2.2 billion shale gas deal between the U.S. firm Chesapeake Energy and CNOOC (which was involved in North Pars but has almost entirely extricated itself), saying "The political pressure came directly from the government...and I believe it's logical to draw a link with these U.S. deals."[87]

Whether Chinese reluctance to support stronger Security Council sanctions against Iran has been tied to its interest in Iranian oil and gas is more difficult to determine than whether the presence of Chinese companies has helped Iran avoid the impact of investment-focused sanctions. China has a long-established pattern of avoiding support for Security Council sanctions against countries for what it judges to be their internal activities, a pattern that extends well beyond countries in which Chinese companies maintain oil interests.[88] Moreover, some (controversial) scholarship on nuclear proliferation also suggests that Beijing may not be particularly eager to prevent Iranian nuclear progress either, as a simple matter of geopolitical calculation.[89] That said, to the extent that the Chinese government is interested in slowing the Iranian nuclear program, the prospect that oil and gas interests of powerful Chinese companies might be endangered by aggressive moves surely weighs in the leaders' calculus.

It is also important to distinguish here between an interest in investing in Iran and a desire to continue buying oil and gas from the country. Losing investment positions, particularly after Chinese companies have sunk considerable time and money, is a major blow. Losing the ability to buy Iranian oil is, at least in principle, far less problematic; Chinese refiners can simply source oil from the broader market. Nonetheless, to the extent that leaders worry about the ability to source new supplies this way (a fear that, however unreasonable, extends well beyond China), fears of losing the ability to buy oil from Iran may genuinely scare decision makers in Beijing. Moreover, it is far from clear that other countries would have been enthusiastic about oil-related sanctions had China not been in a position to continue buying oil; many in Western governments considered continued Chinese purchases to be critical to squaring efforts to squeeze Iran with the need to keep oil markets well supplied and prices from rising sharply. The alternative to Western sanctions that China does not fully comply with may have been no sanctions at all—and with even less impact on Iran.

The standoff with Iran suggests that the existence of major Chinese energy firms weakens Western abilities to affect the behavior of countries such as Iran by imposing sanctions directly on energy. But it also demonstrates continuing Western leverage, both through the critical role of U.S. and European firms in providing high-technology equipment and through the ability of the United States to use access to its own oil and gas reserves as leverage. Whether Chinese involvement in resource markets has also led Beijing to water down otherwise tough sanctions is more difficult to determine from experience thus far.

Mixing Politics and Trade

Increasing Chinese demand for resources is also likely to change relations between China and major producing countries even where it has no investments on the ground. These go well beyond the market impacts we explored earlier. Instead, they will have much broader consequences for international politics too.

Economists have long argued that the geography of oil trade does not matter much. If a consumer faces a producer that refuses to sell it oil, the consumer can easily buy from others. Similarly, if a producer faces a consumer that refuses to buy its oil, it can easily sell to others. Analysts have casually extrapolated this logic to other resources. But there are two problems with this: not all resource markets are like the oil market, and economics is not the only source of friction for oil. The upshot is that as China becomes a much bigger buyer of natural resources, more and more countries will want to curry favor well beyond the commercial sphere. This may have broad consequences for international relationships, particularly between China and the Middle East.

China occupies a far more dominant position as a consumer in minerals markets than it (or any other country) does in oil markets. Chinese refusal to buy iron ore, bauxite, copper, or other minerals from any reasonably sized producer could leave the producer with great difficulty in finding alternative customers; it is not illogical, then, for minerals producers to want and seek good relationships with China.[90] To be certain, this risk has been reduced by the move toward spot markets in minerals in recent years. And China itself could be hurt by too broad a refusal to buy minerals that are critical to its industry. Nonetheless, the risk here is greater than for oil.

What about natural gas? The consumer side of the liquefied natural gas market is far more diversified than it is for minerals. This makes China less central. But LNG terminals are typically built with long-term supply contracts attached. This means new additions to supply must find interested consumers to take the other side of long-term contracts. In Asian LNG markets, Japan and South Korea are vastly preferred to India or China as customers; they are seen as having a long track record of amicable dealings with suppliers and a clear pattern of not defaulting on contracts.[91] As a result, LNG project developers can more easily take Japanese and South Korean commitments to buy gas to potential financiers when looking for financing. But attracting Chinese buyers still remains an important goal for many producers, and because those buyers (and many sellers) are government owned, this deal making can take on a political cast. This is most consequential for new or growing producers (such as Australia or Mozambique) that need to secure new buyers for their additional supplies. Suppliers with low-cost gas and contracts in place—Qatar chief among them—will not need Chinese buyers to achieve their goals.[92]

The politics of oil markets are subtler. Under almost all circumstances, flexible markets mean countries should not care whether they sell oil to China or to other consumers. They also should not worry about building strong relationships with China in case they want to have the option of selling China oil in emergencies. But the recent experience with oil-related sanctions against Iran suggests that some producers are reasonable to want good relations with China. In recent years, many of the biggest oil consumers in the world collectively declined to buy Iranian oil. More consequentially, perhaps, broader sanctions interfered with oil tanker traffic and with settlement of payments for Iranian crude. The consequence was a steep drop in Iranian oil sales and revenues. Had Iran been on bad terms with China and India, leading them to consider joining the effort, there is a reasonable prospect that the damage to Tehran would have been even worse. Indeed, other countries, particularly in the Middle East, that (in contrast with Iran) are not engaged in defiant behavior also worry about this "security of demand."[93] When oil sales are the lifeblood of an economy, even a tiny chance that markets won't suffice is enough to encourage political efforts to backstop relationships with major oil buyers. The result is likely to be closer ties between China and major oil producers in the coming years.

A Slow Evolution

China's quest for natural resources is beginning to have consequences for international politics and security far from its shores. But those developments are largely unfolding more slowly than ones closer to home. China is subtly changing the world: it is making it tougher for Western countries to influence others through sanctions on resource investments; adopting new approaches to international cooperation in the few instances where it participates in security missions far from home; and redrawing the patterns of resource trade, changing political attitudes in the countries it does business with in the process. But China itself is also shifting, becoming more trusting of international markets and reliant on the U.S. power that underpins them, and learning that seeking friendly relations in resource-producing countries can sometimes run counter to the goal of promoting stability.

In the coming decades, though, China is likely to shape the international environment more. The Chinese military will become more capable—particularly if a strong Chinese leadership provides the resources needed for rapid expansion—and with that will come increasing interest, at least in some powerful Chinese quarters, in becoming less reliant on the United States for security in resource-producing regions or on the high seas. Chinese companies will become less dependent on U.S. and European ones for the technologies they need to produce resources abroad—and hence will have greater ability to undermine Western sanctions. And as resource trade between China and other regions, particularly the Middle East, continues to rise, foreign leaders and strategists will concern themselves more than ever with ensuring that their relationships with China are strong.

IO

Resource Strategy in a Changing World

AT THE OUTSET OF this book we asked a simple pair of questions: is China's natural resource quest changing the world? Or is China itself being changed as it seeks secure supplies of natural resources abroad? The reality is that both types of transformations are under way—and often in surprising forms.

Changing the World

China has already changed the world through its rapidly rising consumption of a host of natural resources. Contrary to the prevailing belief in some quarters, it does not secure them mainly by buying up resource deposits abroad, but rather it procures resources through trade. Indeed, the consequences of this, primarily in the form of rising prices for commodities ranging from oil to iron ore, are the largest that China's resource quest has had—and are more far-reaching than the impacts of investment abroad. China has also changed the very structure of critical markets, but not as Chinese policy makers sought or international observers feared. A decade ago, many people worried that China would steer the global oil trade away from its market-based foundations, yet this hasn't happened. Meanwhile, the emergence of thousands of small Chinese steel mills ultimately led to a much more transparent and competitive system for trading iron ore—an outcome that Beijing actively resisted.

Chinese investment abroad has also transformed resource-rich economies, but more subtly than what Chinese leaders promise or skeptics of Chinese investment often warn about. Resource investment in most sectors and countries remains a small part of their overall FDI pie. Moreover many of the tools China uses—for example, loans tied to resource production—are variations on ones that Western firms use too. And Chinese firms' labor, environmental, and financial practices are often no worse (but certainly no better) than what some of their competitors bring to bear.

Yet Chinese firms regularly export the ways of doing business that they have learned at home. Indeed, this is a theme pervading China's natural resource quest: understanding Chinese behavior abroad requires understanding Chinese behavior at home. The same political and economic practices that shape its development model at home are reflected in Chinese behavior when investing in natural resources abroad. The central government and state-owned enterprises, which set the strategic direction for the domestic economy, are similarly powerful actors in establishing the overall strategy for China's international actions. As a matter of broad policy, these players approach the country's resource needs through a loosely coordinated trade, aid, and investment strategy that mixes a powerful role for market forces with a much stronger role for the state (including state-owned companies) than is familiar in the West.

Just as in China, though, significant economic activity takes place outside the central government's purview. Large SOEs typically (though not universally) explore resource investments as purely commercial endeavors, though still helped by Beijing through cheap capital and other assistance. And smaller nonstate firms—either private ones or those supported at the provincial or township level—are increasingly going out not as part of a coordinated effort to ensure Chinese resource security but with a mind to heed Deng Xiaoping's 1992 admonition to get rich quick. Even individual Chinese, like the gold miners who caused trouble in Ghana, now independently seek their fortunes abroad, relying on personal funds and connections to support their ventures. When things go awry, Beijing only reluctantly becomes involved.

Institutional weaknesses within China, including in the areas of environment, labor, transparency, and the rule of law, are often exploited by Chinese firms when they operate at home. Similarly, firms often take advantage of weak state capacity abroad. Chinese players often assume it is the responsibility of the host government to enforce its own environment, labor, and governance rules. In this respect they are not so different from many other multinationals. Yet unlike Western multinationals, which sometimes export relatively good social and environmental practices when they invest abroad, Chinese companies have little to contribute on this front.

The impact of China's resource quest on international politics and security has been more modest thus far. Warnings of resource wars and political tie-ups with resource-rich despots have largely come to naught; claims that Chinese pursuit of natural resources has been a core contributor to civil conflicts like the one that raged in the 2000s in the Sudan fail to withstand scrutiny. Yet there is little question that China's resource quest is changing the international political landscape in important ways. Willingness on the part of Chinese companies to invest in some Iranian oil and gas production has helped blunt the impact of Western sanctions. Chinese efforts to build pipelines that circumvent the Strait of Malacca are lessening— though far from eliminating—Chinese vulnerability to potential resource cutoffs in wartime. Conflict with neighbors in the South and East China Seas—driven in part by pursuit of resources and a desire to secure the sea lanes through which they are transported—is becoming more heated every year. Chinese efforts to use large volumes of water from rivers that cross international boundaries have stoked tensions with some neighbors, even as pipelines that connect China with nearby oil and gas deposits draw Beijing closer to others.

Changing China

As China has ventured abroad, though, it is not only the world that is being changed. China is changing as well.

This is already apparent in efforts to respond to the high commodity prices spurred in large part by China itself. Since the mid-2000s, Beijing has sought with some success to improve energy efficiency and rebalance the Chinese economy away from heavy industry, in part as a way to blunt the impact of sky-high costs. It has also pressed to increase its domestic resource production, most notably in grain, helping blunt the global impact of its rising resource demand.

The impact of the resource quest on China itself can be seen far more broadly in Chinese efforts to invest globally. Chinese firms' behavior is being altered by the laws and regulations of the countries where they invest, as well as by those countries' capacity to enforce their rules. Firms' interactions with other multinationals are also shaping Chinese behavior. In the oil and gas industry, for example, companies are partnering with foreign firms to acquire access to advanced technology and skills. In the mining industry, some of them have hired Western experts to help them address weaknesses in their corporate social responsibility practices.

Yet a consistent pattern remains: where state capacity to enforce laws and regulations on the books is stronger, the Chinese government and enterprises have been forced to adapt and comply. Where governance is weaker, Chinese behavior generally fails to move the bar. In some cases, China has been forced to confront this dichotomy in the face of rapid changes abroad, leading to bigger shifts in strategic thinking. China's experience in countries where there has been a significant government transition—particularly from a friendly authoritarian to a more democratic ruling party, as in Burma—is contributing to a debate within China over the traditional wisdom of not mixing business with politics. Some Chinese business leaders, as well as NGO activists, are reassessing the trade-off between the short-term economic gain from working with unpopular authoritarian governments and the longer-term damage to China's reputation and ability to do business when those regimes fall.

These trends are amplified by the diffusion of new ways of thinking that are taking hold within China itself. Corporate social responsibility has begun to rise on the domestic agenda, and some firms have extended that by beginning to place greater emphasis on adopting better practices abroad. Nongovernmental organizations in China are also in the first stages of investigating, reporting on, and in some cases advising firms investing abroad on issues of corporate social responsibility. Once again, China at home is influencing China abroad.

Experience in the world is also changing how China approaches the political and security entanglements that come with being a big consumer of imported resources. Chinese leaders today are more comfortable than their predecessors in relying on international markets to secure resources, even when those markets are underpinned by U.S. power. (They are, to be certain, still often jittery, particularly when thinking about the prospect of resource security during war.) Some argue that they are gaining instructive experience in handling crises, such as those that have flared up in recent years in the South and East China Seas, though the willingness to provoke appears still to be increasing, and the risk of heated conflict remains dangerously high. Chinese policy makers are also gradually becoming more open to data sharing and other technical cooperation that might defuse conflicts over water.

New Horizons

If would be foolish, of course, to assume that the next twenty years of China's resource quest will mirror the previous twenty. Indeed the changes already afoot point to further transformations down the road.

Rapidly rising Chinese resource demand no longer comes as a shock to the global system—and, as a result, radical price rises mirroring those seen over the last decade are unlikely. Indeed, if China successfully rebalances its economy and further boosts the efficiency of its resource use (or indeed, if there is a sustained slowdown in the economy), those moves could contribute to weaker resource prices over the coming decade, a mixed blessing for resource consumers and producers around the world. China may also continue to transform the structure of markets—many eyes are on the prospect for a transparent market in natural gas—but there the odds are lower.

The biggest changes in the offing for Chinese resource investment stem from its growing scale. Over time, investment positions will grow, as companies develop new resource deposits and buy existing ones from others. (This expansion could, however, slow if the Chinese economy weakens, not as a result of lower demand for natural resources, but because of tighter credit.) Indeed, it is easy to forget that a mere five years ago China was a tiny player on the resource investment scene. Moreover, as Chinese oil and gas firms raise their technological capabilities, their ability to access resources requiring more sophisticated drilling techniques will also grow. Even firms' improvements in corporate social responsibility practices may open more investment doors, in developing and advanced industrialized countries alike.

Change is also in the offing on the political and security fronts. It was not long ago that China lacked the military capacity to rattle sabers over resources and other concerns in the South and East China Seas. This is no longer the case, and Chinese assertiveness is now increasingly threatening to spark instability, a trend that might be exacerbated by economic or political weakness at home, which could create new incentives for international confrontation (though perhaps sap funds from the military at the same time). Further abroad, as China accumulates a wider portfolio of investments, and as its companies become more technically capable of replacing Western ones, China's interest in stability abroad—and its ability to undercut Western sanctions—will grow.

Over the long haul, however, the biggest prospective changes may come on the high seas. To date, China has not had the option of supplanting the United States in its role as protector of global resource flows. Over the next decade, however, China plans a significant expansion of its naval capacity, including the deployment of several aircraft carriers. This naval expansion will, in principle, enable China to play a far more active role as a maritime power with global reach, a role currently played only by the United States. (This is highly unlikely to be matched by a similar capability to intervene on land, something that the United States has used, with a mixed record, to try to promote stability in resource-producing regions, most notably the Middle East.) Moreover, the outcome of an active Chinese debate over establishing a more permanent military presence overseas will be a significant factor in China's longer-term security posture globally. All that said, however, China will still have limited military resources for the foreseeable future, and it is likely to focus them first on its top-tier concerns: preventing Taiwan from becoming independent, forestalling any blockade of its near seas, and advancing its related interests in the South and East China Seas. This—along with the backlash that a more active global role would undoubtedly provoke—augurs against China trying to supplant or match the United States as guarantor of safety on the seas anytime soon.

Responding to China

China's resource quest has consequences for nearly every country in the world. Each country will need to form its own response: to decide what challenges and opportunities China's resource quest creates for it and how best to respond. Countries will potentially be affected as resource consumers, resource owners, resource investors, and geopolitical players—and they would be well served to develop responses in all of these dimensions. The United States will be implicated in all four ways.

Resource Consumers

Many countries, including the United States, are most directly affected by China's natural resource quest through higher prices for many of the resources that their residents and businesses consume. High resource prices are not always problematic for all countries; high iron ore prices, for example, don't impose a special burden on the United States, because it is a net iron ore exporter.[1] Other countries in similar positions for individual resources might be similarly indifferent to China. But high prices for other resources pose challenges.

High oil prices, for example, hurt the United States and the rest of the oil-importing world.[2] They raise their oil import bills and sap strength from economies in the process. High oil prices mean bigger oil price spikes too—and large oil price spikes can do severe damage to national economies. For the United States, this will remain true even if the country were to become self-sufficient in oil, a distant but not entirely implausible possibility that experts have recently begun debating. The United States is part of a global oil market, and disruptions overseas can lead to price spikes at home. Moreover, even if the United States became oil self-sufficient, rapidly rising prices would still strip U.S. consumers of cash, leading to damage to the broader economy; windfalls to oil producers wouldn't fully offset that.

The biggest thing the United States and others can do to reduce their vulnerability to high oil prices is to follow the lead of the European Union and Japan by reducing the amount of oil they consume. This can be done in a variety of ways, including creating or sustaining stricter fuel economy standards for cars and trucks, raising taxes on gasoline and diesel, increasing government support for innovation in efficient vehicles, or a combination of the three.[3]

Countries can also help reduce (or at least restrain) oil prices by working together—which means also with China—to reduce their demand for oil. Some efforts will be policy-driven. For example, the United States spurred a G-20 effort that encouraged all participants (including China) to reduce wasteful fossil fuel subsidies, including those that encourage excessive consumption of oil. Others will be technical: the United States and China, for example, have a joint forum in which they pursue harmonized standards for electric vehicle charging, with the goal of allowing innovations in the two countries to build on each other and accelerate progress.

High prices for rare earth metals—or, the equivalent, scarcity of rare earths—can hurt a host of high-technology and defense-related industries that rely on them. The United States, Japan, South Korea, and European countries such as Germany with strong technology sectors are particularly vulnerable. Here the biggest thing these countries can do is make sure the market is allowed to respond by boosting supplies. The United States and Canada, for example, have deposits of rare earth elements that can help alleviate shortages, and companies are already starting to invest. Policy makers should ensure that environmental and other rules don't unnecessarily restrict or slow development of those deposits. At the same time, Washington and others should follow Tokyo's lead to invest substantially in research on recycling rare earths. Recycling technologies are nascent and offer substantial potential payoff.

The last big area in which countries should pay attention as consumers is the continued openness of world resource markets. Thus far, China has not made world markets more rigid; indeed, for several mineral ores, it has actually (if inadvertently) made them more flexible. Still, as Chinese companies come to control larger amounts of resource production overseas, the possibility exists that Beijing will try to shift to more rigid trading arrangements, undermining the ability of the rest of the world to respond flexibly to major supply disruptions. Other market-minded countries should make sure they continue to support open markets for natural resources, even in areas (such as natural gas) where some (notably in the United States) have recently been tempted to erect barriers to trade. Interference with resource markets would weaken the United States and others legally and politically when trying to oppose problematic Chinese actions. Strategists should also keep watch on anti-market developments in China.

Resource Owners

For many resource-rich countries, developing and developed alike, Chinese resource demand has been a critical source of revenue, even as the global economy as a whole has suffered through a serious financial crisis. Yet China's natural resource quest also challenges these same countries as owners of vast volumes of natural resources. Commodities markets are driving the most immediate impact; high prices for a range of resources are prompting expanded production of everything from oil to soybeans to rare earths. Policy makers must decide whether to abet the trend by opening up more public land to resource extraction or development. This can make sense—the economic benefits of opening up lands to resource development rise when resource prices go up—but countries will still need to take care with environmental protection as it brings new areas into resource production.

A group of resource-rich countries as diverse as the United States, Mongolia, and Vietnam moreover perceive security concerns when considering significant levels of Chinese investment in natural resources. In the United States, for example, U.S. companies are not the only ones seeking to boost oil and gas production. A host of multinational resource producers have already entered the U.S. market. So far, Chinese companies have been careful to take minority stakes in joint development projects. As a result, there have not been any major confrontations since the CNOOC-Unocal debacle in 2005. If, however, a Chinese company seeks majority control of a major U.S.-based oil- or gas-producing company, policy makers will have tougher decisions to make.

There are good arguments for and against allowing ever-greater Chinese access in the United States. Chinese investors help boost U.S. resource production by bringing in capital. Moreover, as Chinese companies become more deeply involved in U.S. oil and gas production, the United States gains some leverage over them, because it can then link continued access to those companies' performance in areas of concern (such as Iran) abroad. At a more basic level, by allowing Chinese investment in domestic oil and gas, the United States strengthens its hand in encouraging others to be open too.

On the opposing side, there are concerns that during a major confrontation between the two countries, Chinese companies that control U.S. oil and gas production could exert leverage by shutting down production or by threatening to cause accidents. Similar fears over how China might exploit its resource investments during a political or military conflict exist in Vietnam, Mongolia, and elsewhere as well. And even though greater economic engagement can reduce the odds of such a confrontation, it cannot eliminate the possibility. The best approach may be the one apparently taken during the CNOOC takeover of Nexen, with the Chinese company required to function as if it were a minority owner when it comes to corporate operations, despite having a controlling financial stake.

The United States, Canada, and other rare earth producers should also be careful in the case of any attempted Chinese takeover of a major rare earth production operation. Given China's dominant position in the industry, and its past willingness to abuse the position for commercial and geopolitical leverage, rare earth producers should not allow China to acquire scarce deposits.

As Chinese commodities firms seek to enter and compete in the U.S. market, as well as those of other countries with strong governance such as Australia and Canada, there will also be an opportunity to enhance their environmental, labor, and corporate governance performance standards. For the United States, over the medium term to the long run, a bilateral investment treaty—currently under negotiation with China—would provide a strong legal framework for ensuring best practices by Chinese firms. Participation in the Trans-Pacific Partnership, which Beijing is currently exploring, could be another important means of raising the performance standards of those firms. In the nearer term, the United States is in the process of becoming EITI-compliant—joining other EITI-compliant countries such as Mongolia and Peru—which will help ensure that any Chinese firms investing in extractive industries in the United States will operate transparently.[4] Canada, which has explored the possibility but not yet actively pursued it, should follow.

Resource-rich countries are also confronting public debates over the benefits and costs of exporting nonrenewable resources to China. In Africa and Latin America, this has manifested itself in popular concerns about land purchases tied to food exports. In Kazakhstan, the public has voiced worries over land purchases and oil exports. In the United States, there is little concern about exports in areas such as minerals or agricultural commodities—indeed, these will usually be celebrated—but natural gas exports have already become controversial, and this controversy may eventually spread to the prospect of oil exports.[5] Proponents of allowing exports cite the opportunity to capture economic gains from trade and to shake up politicized world gas markets; they also warn that constraining U.S. natural gas exports would undermine leverage over China and others in trade negotiations and arbitration, since U.S. export constraints would likely violate U.S. WTO obligations. Skeptics of allowing exports argue that barring natural gas exports could help U.S. consumers and manufacturers; they contend that blocking exports would help the United States wean itself off oil and reduce its carbon pollution.

The weight of evidence and particularly the risks to the world trading system suggest that the United States would be better off if it allowed exports of natural gas without restricting potential customers. In particular, if the United States were to give strong preference to friends and allies (such as Japan and India) over China, it would undermine growing Chinese confidence in markets as a provider of resource security, potentially undermining U.S. interests in the longer run.

Overseas Investors

China is now the largest driver of resource demand, but it is certainly not the only player. How should the United States and other countries, whose firms often compete with the Chinese for the right to develop natural resources overseas, respond to this resource quest? It is easiest to identify dangerous ideas that countries should avoid. In particular, they should not get into a race to the bottom with China by providing low-cost financing to resource firms as a way of competing with Chinese banks. Doing so would take money from average citizens and hand it to firms whose profits are far more narrowly shared. More useful are efforts such as those by U.S. government agencies (among them the U.S. Export-Import Bank) and similar agencies from other OECD countries to bring China in line with OECD financing standards.

More difficult is the question of whether countries should lower any transparency and environmental standards they impose on their resource companies that operate overseas, in order to allow them to compete with Chinese firms on a level playing field. Such a step could make some sense; forcing companies to adhere to overly high standards might lead them to lose bids, with the net result being development by Chinese companies and low environmental and social performance to boot. But this view is shortsighted. The presence of multinationals with high standards can prompt host governments to improve their own laws, and strong host country governance can in turn improve Chinese performance. Moreover, China pays a reputational cost when its firms don't adhere to host country laws. Its companies are increasingly learning from the "outside in"; over time, the presence of other multinational firms alongside Chinese ones is likely to lift performance by all.

One area in which the United States, in particular, might do better is in ensuring that U.S. diplomats are more active in helping U.S. companies win opportunities to develop resources. Government support for overseas resource developers has ebbed and flowed, reaching a high point in the second term of the Clinton administration, before declining through the Bush and early Obama administrations. Basic steps such as supporting U.S. commercial delegations on state visits should be adopted. And although the United States should not emulate China's practice of providing below-market financing for large-scale infrastructure and resource development projects, the administration could help U.S. companies compete by arranging resource-based trade and investment missions that include not only extractive industries but also U.S. construction and other infrastructure-related firms.

We saw earlier that many Chinese firms and the government itself have already begun to recognize the importance of adopting international standards for corporate social responsibility. Some are producing CSR reports, opting for third-party certification, and joining multiple international CSR framework organizations such as the Global Compact and the Global Reporting Initiative. The United States and other resource-rich countries with strong state capacity, such as Canada, Australia, and Norway, can help by assisting those countries with weaker capacity to develop their own enforcement capacity through training and encouraging compliance with international reporting standards such as EITI. The United States could also consider requiring that Chinese state-owned firms, as well as other countries' state-owned enterprises, adhere to the same financial and other disclosure standards as are followed by publicly traded U.S. firms when they invest in the United States. Similar requirements could also be enforced in other countries with strong and transparent financial regulatory systems.

The Great Power

The United States must also respond to China's resource quest as a great power. (Japan, India, and perhaps Russia will need to respond to China as regional powers, and other countries will feel compelled to respond to China as geopolitical players too. As with the case of the United States, determining the right contours for each will require looking carefully at the particular predicaments, needs, responsibilities, and abilities.) The United States feels the repercussions of events in almost every part of the world, thanks to its global security, economic, and diplomatic presence. It also remains responsible, by its own choice, for providing stability and security for friends, allies, and others in many resource-producing areas and sea lanes around the world. It is thus inevitably affected by many of the broader consequences of Chinese efforts to secure natural resources.

The South and East China Seas are the most likely places where serious armed conflict involving China might occur in a resource-rich region. But competition for resources is unlikely to be the sole (or even central) driving force in any such confrontation. To be certain, to the extent that resource competition can be tamped down—including through deference to international law—the potential for conflict will be reduced. The United States can increase its credibility in calling for such efforts by ratifying the UN Convention on the Law of the Sea. That said, as we argued earlier, UNCLOS is unlikely to resolve resource conflicts in the South and East China Seas. The U.S. approach to the region will need to be informed by this, and by considerations that extend well beyond natural resources (and hence beyond the scope of this book).

Additionally, the United States can play an important role in providing technical assistance to help ameliorate resource-based conflict in the region. Its efforts through the Lower Mekong Initiative, which includes all the downstream countries that share the Mekong River—Burma, Cambodia, Laos, Thailand, and Vietnam—are a good example. By furnishing technical assistance to these countries—modeling the potential impacts of climate change, forecasting other potential impacts, and promoting a sister-river agreement between the Mekong River Commission and the Mississippi River Commission—the United States is enhancing the leverage of these countries in their efforts to push Beijing to be more transparent. It is an important mechanism as well for strengthening the substance of the U.S. rebalance to Asia.

The United States will be drawn in far more decisively when it comes to the question of sea-lane control. As we argued earlier, as China comes to depend far more than the United States on certain sea lanes (particularly the Straits of Hormuz and Malacca), it may be tempting for the United States to invest less in protecting them and attempt to shift responsibility to China. This would be unwise. In the short run, China does not even have the ability to replace the United States as the protector of commerce on the high seas—and for oil in particular, the United States would still be hurt by disruptions in the Middle East and Asia.

In the longer run, as Chinese naval capabilities grow, the United States should still seek to maintain a dominant role in sea-lane security. Entrusting critical sea lanes to China would essentially mean abandoning U.S. allies and, so long as many resource markets remain global, also expose the United States. That said, the United States should use every opportunity to develop its relationship with the People's Liberation Army. The 2012 joint anti-piracy exercise between the U.S. Navy and the PLAN is one such example, and an invitation to the PLAN to attend Rim of the Pacific 2014, a multilateral exercise off the coast of Hawaii, is another. These joint exercises are the foundation for ensuring sea-lane security in the future. Meanwhile, the United States should seek Chinese cooperation—diplomatic and economic rather than military—in efforts to promote economic stability in important resource-producing regions, notably the Middle East, even as the two countries differ over the appropriateness of political change.

Further, the United States needs to adapt to the way Chinese investment is affecting global efforts to confront challenges such as the Iranian nuclear program. U.S. technological superiority in extractive industries gives it some leverage, both because countries value U.S. companies as critical investors (despite having China as a theoretical alternative) and because even Chinese companies often rely on U.S. equipment (which can be withheld through sanctions). Sustaining this strength is important. We also saw that opportunities for Chinese companies to invest here give U.S. diplomats leverage by providing something the United States could threaten to take away if Chinese companies don't cooperate with international pressure against other states. Opportunities for these companies to invest in the United States may also reduce pressure for them to seek out problematic investments abroad.

Looking Ahead

China's demand for resources will not abate anytime soon. Beijing plans to bring hundreds of millions of people still in poverty into the middle class, further develop its infrastructure and industry, and build its diplomatic and military presence abroad. No matter how efficiently the country uses its own resources as well as those of the rest of the world, its economic development will continue to exert a profound impact on the availability and price of commodities, and have broader consequences for governance, international relations, and global security.

Not every consequence of China's resource quest will be relevant to every country, and wise leaders will take care not to be drawn into conflicts in which they have little or no stake. Yet many countries—and particularly the United States—will find themselves challenged by China's resource quest along multiple dimensions as a result of the many ways in which they themselves interact with the world. Leaders need to understand all of these dimensions and take steps to respond as the world is transformed by China's growing presence and pursuit of natural resources.

The rest of the world cannot determine the outcome of China's resource quest. It can, however, help ensure that China's impact is as broadly benign—or even beneficial—as possible. Understanding the reality of China's resource quest, good and bad, in all its facets, is essential to achieving that goal.

NOTES

Chapter 1

1. All dollar figures are in U.S. dollars unless otherwise noted. Edward Wyatt, "Ex-ConAgra Unit Settles with U.S. Over Artificial Oil Trade," *New York Times*, August 16, 2010.

2. One might point out that it was U.S. corporations, not the U.S. government, that produced and traded overseas resources. But this does not change the fact that U.S. power helped companies gain access to resource-production opportunities and, more important, helped ensure that resources produced overseas by anyone could be reliably shipped to consumers in the United States.

3. Andrew Gordon, *A Modern History of Japan: From Tokugawa Times to the Present* (New York: Oxford University Press, 2003), 245–246.

4. United States International Trade Commission, *Steel Industry Annual Report on Competitive Conditions in the Steel Industry and Industry Efforts to Adjust and Modernize: Report to the President on Investigation No. 332-289 Under Section 332 of the Tariff Act of 1930* (U.S. International Trade Commission, 1991); and International Iron and Steel Institute, *Steel Statistical Yearbook 1983* (Brussels, Belgium: International Iron and Steel Institute, 1984).

5. Daojiong Zha, "China's Energy Security: Domestic and International Issues," *Survival* 48, no. 2 (Spring 2006): 182. From the article: "International reaction to China's pursuit of supply security through offshore energy sources, particularly oil and gas, has put Beijing on the defensive. In some ways this is a repetition of the Japanese experience in the 1970s and 1980s, when there were serious debates about the impact on the world's economic and political structures of Tokyo's pursuit of high economic growth."

6. The discussion of Japanese investment strategies here is drawn largely from Raymond Vernon, *Two Hungry Giants: The United States*

and Japan in the Quest for Oil and Ores (Cambridge, MA: Harvard University Press, 1983).

7. Ibid., 84.
8. Ibid., 96–97.
9. Ibid., 100.
10. Ibid., 101.
11. For example, Decca Aitkenhead, "Dambisa Moyo: 'The World Will Be Drawn into a War for Resources,'" *Guardian*, June 24, 2012; Clifford Krauss, "Chinese and U.S. Demand Drives Commodities Surge," *New York Times*, January 15, 2008; and "A Ravenous Dragon," Special Report: China's Quest for Resources, *Economist*, March 13, 2008.
12. For example, George W. Bush, *National Security Strategy of the United States of America*, March 16, 2006, http://georgewbush-whitehouse. archives.gov/nsc/nss/2006/index.html; U.S. House of Representatives, "Congressional Record-House: June 30, 2005" (Washington, DC: Government Printing Office, 2005), H5515; and Heriberto Araujo and Juan Pablo Cardenal, "China's Economic Empire," *New York Times*, June 1, 2013.
13. For example, U.S. Senate, "Energy Trends in China and India: Implications for the United States," Hearing before the Committee on Foreign Relations, S. HRG. 109-326, July 26, 2005 (Washington, DC: Government Printing Office, 2006), 24; and John Lee, "China's Geostrategic Search for Oil," *Washington Quarterly* 35, no. 3 (Summer 2012): 75–92.
14. For example, Dan Blumenthal, "Is China at Present (or Will China Become) a Responsible Stakeholder in the International Community?" paper prepared for "China Becoming a Responsible Stakeholder," Carnegie Endowment for International Peace, Washington, DC, June 11, 2007, http://carnegieendowment.org/files/Bates_paper.pdf, 6; Jonathan Watts, "China's Exploitation of Latin American Natural Resources Raises Concern," *Guardian*, March 25, 2013; George Obulutsa and Fumbuka Ng'wanakilala, "Africa's Trade Ties with China in Spotlight as President Xi Visits," *Reuters*, March 24, 2013; and Joshua Partlow, "Afghan Minister Accused of Taking Bribe," *Washington Post*, November 18, 2009.
15. For example, Leszek Buszynski, "The South China Sea: Oil, Maritime Claims, and U.S.-China Strategic Rivalry," *Washington Quarterly* 35, no. 2 (Spring 2012): 139–156; Brahma Chellaney, *Water: Asia's New Battleground* (Washington, DC: Georgetown University Press, 2011); and Edward Wong, "China Quietly Extends Footprints into Central Asia," *New York Times*, January 2, 2011.

16. For example, David E. Sanger, "China's Oil Needs Are High on U.S. Agenda," *New York Times,* April 19, 2006; Tania Branigan, "China's Role on World Stage Is No Cause for Alarm, Says Barack Obama," *Guardian,* November 14, 2009; and "China Faces Charges of Colonialism in Africa-Asia Pacific," *International Herald Tribune,* January 28, 2007.

17. For example, Kenneth S. Deffeyes, *Hubbert's Peak: The Impending World Oil Shortage* (Princeton, NJ: Princeton University Press, 2008); Kevin G. Hall, "Mideast's Own Oil Consumption Helping to Drive Prices Up," *McClatchy Newspapers,* April 17, 2008, http://www.mcclatchydc.com/2008/04/17/34056/mideasts-own-oil-consumption-helping.html#.Uikc6FeGVyI; and Ed Wallace, "Blame High Oil Prices on Speculators and Bernanke," *Bloomberg Businessweek,* April 19, 2011, http://www.businessweek.com/investor/content/apr2011/pi20110419_786652.html.

18. For example, Daniel A. Summer, "Recent Commodity Price Movements in Historical Perspective," *American Journal of Agricultural Economics* 91, no. 5 (2009): 1250–1256.

19. For example, John Seaman, "Energy Security, Transnational Pipelines, and China's Role in Asia," Asie Visions no. 27, Institut français des relations internationals, April 2010; and Trevor Houser, "The Roots of Chinese Oil Investment Abroad," *Asia Policy* no. 5 (January 2008): 141–166.

20. For Japanese resource investment strategies, see Raymond Vernon, *Two Hungry Giants: The United States and Japan in the Quest for Oil and Ores* (Cambridge, MA: Harvard University Press, 1983).

21. For example, Barry Sautman and Yan Hairong, "Barking up the Wrong Tree: Human Rights Watch and Chinese Copper Mining in Zambia," *Pambazuka News* no. 563, December 12, 2011, http://www.pambazuka.org/en/category/features/78660; and Ton Han Shih and Jennifer Cheng, "China in Africa, No Worse Than Others," *South China Morning Post,* August 15, 2012, http://www.scmp.com/article/999184/china-africa-no-worse-others.

22. For example, Sara Schaefer Munoz, "Colombia Investigates Corporate Land Deals," *Barron's,* June 30, 2013, http://online.barrons.com/article/SB40001424127887323689204578571832721057220.html; and Damien McElroy, "Protest at the Great African Land Grab," *Telegraph,* October 4, 2012.

23. For example, Ana Cristina Alves, "China and Gabon: A Growing Resource Partnership," China in Africa Project Report no. 4, South African Institute for International Affairs, 2008.

24. For example, Brendan Taylor, "Storm in Teacup over South China Sea," *The Australian,* May 11, 2012, http://www.theaustralian.com.

au/opinion/world-commentary/storm-in-teacup-over-south-china-sea/
story-e6frg6ux-1226352425072.

25. For example, Isabel Hilton, "Diverting the Brahmaputra—Much
Ado About Nothing?" China Water Risk, February 9, 2012,
http://chinawaterrisk.org/opinions/diverting-the-brahmaputra-m
uch-ado-about-nothing/.

26. For example, Bates Gill, "China Becoming a Responsible Stakeholder,"
paper prepared for "China Becoming a Responsible Stakeholder,"
Carnegie Endowment for International Peace, Washington, DC, June
11, 2007, http://carnegieendowment.org/files/Bates_paper.pdf.

27. For example, Daniel J. Kostecka, "Places and Bases: The Chinese
Navy's Emerging Support Network in the Indian Ocean," *Naval War
College Review* 64, no. 1 (Winter 2011).

28. For an example of the former, see Evan A. Feigenbaum, "China's
Military Posture and the New Economic Geopolitics," *Survival* 41, no.
2 (Summer 1999): 71–88.

Chapter 2

1. Hok-lam Chan, "The Chien-wen, Yung-lo, Hung-his, and Hsuan-te
Reigns, 1399–1435," in *The Ming Dynasty, 1368–1644*, vol. 12, ed.
Frederick W. Mote and Denis Twitchett (Cambridge Histories
Online, 1988), 232–236.

2. Christopher A. Ford, *The Mind of Empire: China's History and Modern
Foreign Relations* (Lexington, KY: University Press of Kentucky, 2010),
106–107.

3. Mark Elvin, *The Pattern of the Chinese Past* (Stanford, CA: Stanford
University Press, 1973), 217.

4. John K. Fairbank, "Introduction: Maritime and Continental in
China's History," in *Republican China, 1912–1949*, vol. 12, ed. John
K. Fairbank and Denis Twitchett (Cambridge Histories Online,
1983), 17.

5. Emma Jinhua Teng, *Taiwan's Imagined Geography: Chinese Colonial
Travel Writing and Pictures, 1683–1895* (Cambridge, MA: Harvard
University Asia Center, 2006).

6. Ramon H. Myers and Yeh-chien Wang, "Economic Developments,
1644–1800," in *The Ch'ing Dynasty to 1800, Part One*, vol. 9, ed.
Willard J. Peterson (Cambridge Histories Online, 2002), 589.

7. Peter H. Calkins, "Twenty-Three Centuries of Chinese Trade,"
Canadian Journal of Agricultural Economics 48 (December 2000),
465.

8. Elvin, *Pattern of the Chinese Past*, 215–219, 289–293.

9. Ibid., 217.

10. Jonathan D. Spence, *The Search for Modern China* (New York: Norton, 1990), 57.
11. Ibid., 601.
12. Robert B. Marks, *Tigers, Rice, Silk, and Silt: Environment and Economy in Late Imperial South China* (Port Chester, NY: Cambridge University Press, 1998), 86; and Elvin, *Pattern of the Chinese Past*, 221.
13. Edward Barbier, *Scarcity and Frontiers: How Economies Have Developed Through Natural Resource Exploitation* (Cambridge, UK: Cambridge University Press, 2011), 271–272.
14. Myers and Wang, "Economic Developments," 607.
15. Marks, *Tigers, Rice, Silk, and Silt*, 183, 254–255.
16. Ibid., 91–96.
17. Myers and Wang, "Economic Developments," 639.
18. Elvin, *Pattern of the Chinese Past*, 218.
19. Phillip V. Allingham, "England and China: The Opium Wars, 1839–60," http://www.victorianweb.org/history/empire/opiumwars/opiumwars1.html.
20. David C. Wright, *The History of China: Second Edition* (Westport, CT: Greenwood Press, 2011), 100–101.
21. Paul S. Ropp, *China in World History* (Oxford: Oxford University Press, 2010), 107; and Phillip A. Kuhn, "The Taiping Rebellion," in *Late Ch'ing 1800–1911, Part 1*, vol. 10, ed. John K. Fairbank (Cambridge Histories online, 1978), 301–307.
22. Ibid., 117.
23. Teng, *Taiwan's Imagined Geography*, 207.
24. Ropp, *China in World History*, 116–117.
25. Ibid., 120–122.
26. Morris L. Bian, *The Making of the State Enterprise System in Modern China: The Dynamics of Institutional Change* (Cambridge, MA: Harvard University Press, 2005), 52.
27. William C. Kirby, "Continuity and Change in Modern China: Economic Planning on the Mainland and on Taiwan, 1943–1958," *Australian Journal of Chinese Affairs*, no. 24 (July 1990): 127.
28. Ibid., 128.
29. Ibid.
30. Ibid., 131–132.
31. Ibid.
32. Kim Woodard, *The International Energy Relations of China* (Stanford, CA: Stanford University Press, 1980), 52–53.
33. Ibid., 33.
34. Wright, *History of China*, 148, 150.

35. "Zhou Enlai Announces Eight Principles of Foreign Aid," *China Daily*, August 13, 2010, http://www.chinadaily.com.cn/china/2010-08/13/content_11149131.htm.

36. Kossi Ayenagbo et al., "Sino-Africa Economic and Trade Relations: Its Impact and Implications on the African Continent," *African Journal of Business Management* 6, no. 21 (May 30, 2012): 6421.

37. Weizao Teng, "Socialist Modernization and the Pattern of Foreign Trade," in *China's Search for Economic Growth: The Chinese Economy Since 1949*, ed. Dixin Xu et al. (Beijing, China: New World Press, 1982), 167–192.

38. *China Statistical Yearbook 1990 [Zhongguo Tongji Nianjian 1990]* (Beijing: China Statistical Publishing House, 1990).

Chapter 3

1. Lester Brown, "Who Will Feed China?" *World Watch* 7, no. 5 (September 1994).

2. For example, "China Lifts Price Controls on Grain, Meat and Eggs in Some Areas," *New York Times News Service,* November 29, 1992.

3. Elizabeth Economy, *The River Runs Black*, 2nd ed. (Ithaca, NY: Cornell University Press, 2010), 81.

4. U.S. Energy Information Administration (U.S. EIA), "China: Total Coal Consumption (Thousand Short Tons)," International Energy Statistics, http://www.eia.gov/cfapps/ipdbproject/iedindex3.cfm?tid=1&pid=1&aid=2&cid=CH,&syid=1980&eyid=2010&unit=TST; and U.S. EIA, "China: Total Petroleum Consumption (Thousand Barrels per Day)," International Energy Statistics, http://www.eia.gov/cfapps/ipdbproject/iedindex3.cfm?tid=5&pid=5&aid=2&cid=CH,&syid=1980&eyid=2010&unit=TBPD.

5. U.S. EIA, "International Energy Statistics: China, Dry Natural Gas Consumption (Billion Cubic Feet)," http://www.eia.gov/cfapps/ipdbproject/iedindex3.cfm?tid=3&pid=26&aid=2&cid=CH,&syid=1998&eyid=2011&unit=BCF.

6. World Steel Association, "Annual Crude Steel Production, 1980–2010," accessed March 2013, http://www.worldsteel.org/statistics/statistics-archive/annual-steel-archive.html; World Aluminium, "Primary Aluminium Production," International Aluminium Institute, March 20, 2013, http://www.world-aluminium.org/statistics/; and Zhongkui Wang, "Current Situation of China's Nonferrous Metals Industry and Development Trend," UNCTAD Multi-Year Expert Meeting on Commodities and Development, March 20, 2013, http://unctad.org/meetings/en/Presentation/SUC_MYEM2013_20032013_Zhongkui%20WANG.pdf.

7. Information Office of the State Council of the People's Republic of China, "China's Policy on Mineral Resources," White Paper, December 23, 2003.

8. Ibid.

9. U.S. EIA, "International Energy Statistics," accessed May 2013, http://www.eia.gov/cfapps/ipdbproject/IEDIndex3.cfm.

10. Jeffrey D. Wilson, *Governing Global Production: Resource Networks in the Asia-Pacific Steel Industry* (electronically published, Palgrave Macmillan, 2013).

11. "Thomson Reuters/Jefferies CRB Index," http://www.jefferies.com/Commodities/2cc/389.

12. U.S. EIA, "Petroleum & Other Liquids: Spot Prices (Crude Oil in Dollars per Barrel, Products in Dollars per Gallon)," release date February 27, 2013, http://www.eia.gov/dnav/pet/pet_pri_spt_s1_d.htm.

13. U.S. Geological Survey, "Copper," Mineral Commodity Summaries, January 2003, http://minerals.usgs.gov/minerals/pubs/commodity/copper/240303.pdf; and U.S. Geological Survey, "Copper," Mineral Commodity Summaries, January 2009, http://minerals.usgs.gov/minerals/pubs/commodity/copper/mcs-2009-coppe.pdf.

14. U.S. Department of Agriculture, "Economics, Statistics and Market Information System (ESMIS): National Agricultural Statistics Service," http://usda.mannlib.cornell.edu/MannUsda/viewDocumentInfo.do?documentID=1002. Wheat prices are more heterogeneous, so the multiple will depend on the type of wheat in question.

15. Jim Lennon, "Base Metals Outlook: Drivers on the Supply and Demand Side," February 2012, http://www.macquarie.com/dafiles/Internet/mgl/msg/iConference/documents/18_JimLennon_Presentation.pdf.

16. Based on Food and Agriculture Organization of the United Nations, "FAOSTAT," http://faostat3.fao.org/home/index.html; and U.S. EIA, "International Energy Statistics: Total Petroleum," http://www.eia.gov/cfapps/ipdbproject/iedindex3.cfm?tid=5&pid=5&aid=2&cid=regions,&syid=2007&eyid=2011&unit=TBPD.

17. For example, Dambisa Moyo, "The Resource Shortage Is Real," *Time*, June 8, 2012; and Jeremy Grantham, "Time to Wake Up: Days of Abundant Resources and Falling Prices Are Over Forever," GMO Quarterly Letter, April 2011, http://www.theravinaproject.org/JGLetterALL_1Q11.pdf.

18. BP, *Statistical Review of World Energy June 2012* (London: BP, 2012).

19. U.S. EIA, *International Energy Outlook 2000* (Washington, DC: U.S. Department of Energy, 2000).

20. Blake Clayton, *Panic: A Century of Oil Market Madness* (Oxford University Press, forthcoming).
21. See David G. Victor, David R. Hults, and Mark C. Thurber (eds.), *Oil and Governance: State-Owned Enterprises and the World Energy Supply* (Cambridge: Cambridge University Press, 2012). Even governments that allow private resource development can fall prey to the same dynamic if they depend on resource revenues for their budgets. Rising resource prices can reduce their need to open more land, or tempt them to raise taxes and other levies on production. These sorts of steps deter investment and curb the tendency of production to rise with price.
22. Dmitry Zhdannikov and Claire Milhench, "Oil Bull Goldman Sees End to Rising Prices," *Reuters,* October 18, 2012.
23. Kenneth B. Medlock III, "U.S. LNG Exports: Truth and Consequence," Rice University, August 10, 2012. "The average cost of shipping U.S. natural gas to Japan will be $9.05 from 2011 to 2020, assuming a U.S. price of $3.98, leaving a loss of 96 per million Btu taking into account the costs of transportation and liquefaction, the study shows." As reported in Matthew Brown, "U.S. LNG Profit Seen Elusive as Price Gap Closes: Energy Markets," *Bloomberg News,* January 11, 2013.
24. Metal Bulletin, "Metal Bulletin Copper High-Grade Cathode Spot Price," *Bloomberg,* accessed April 4, 2013.
25. Ross Garnaut, "The Contemporary China Resources Boom," *Australian Journal of Agricultural and Resource Economics* 56, no. 2 (2012). The capital cost of bringing the average new mine into production has reportedly more than doubled since 2000 (on a per-ton basis), with costs for marginal mines (which ultimately set prices) rising even more strongly.
26. For example, Ernst & Young, "Business Risks Facing Mining and Metals 2012–2013," accessed May 5, 2013, www.ey.com/Publication/vwLUAssets/Business-risk-facing -mining-and-metals-2012-2013/$FILE/Business-r isk-facing-mining-and-metals-2012-2013.pdf.
27. U.S. Geological Survey, "Historical Statistics for Mineral and Material Commodities," accessed April 3, 2013, http://minerals.usgs.gov/ds/2005/140/.
28. Stuart Burns, "Bauxite and Alumina Moving Rapidly to Spot Pricing," MetalMiner, August 16, 2010, http://agmetalminer.com/2010/08/16/bauxite-and-alumina-moving-rapidly-to-spot-pricing/.
29. For drivers of bauxite demand growth, see World Bank, "Prospects for Commodity Markets," Global Economic Prospects,

Commodity Annex, June 2012, http://siteresources.worldbank.org/INTPROSPECTS/Resources/334934-1304428586133/GEP2012b_Commoditiy_Appendix.pdf.

30. See Yongzhen Yu, *Identifying the Linkages Between Major Mining Commodity Prices and China's Economic Growth—Implications for Latin America*, IMF Working Paper WP/11/86, April 2011, http://www.imf.org/external/pubs/ft/wp/2011/wp1186.pdf; "New Shape for the Bauxite and Alumina Industry," *Reuters*, Roskill Information Services Press Release, January 21, 2013, http://www.reuters.com/article/2013/01/21/idUSnPreqy79pa+100+PRN20130121; and "China's Transformation of the Aluminum Industry," FNArena News, April 18, 2013, http://www.fnarena.com/index2.cfm?type=dsp_newsitem&n=0FF5247F-A8B1-B36B-29EA5C0B50749D0E.

31. Jenifer Piesse and Colin Thirtle, "Three Bubbles and a Panic: An Explanatory Review of Recent Food Commodity Price Events," *Food Policy* 34, no. 2 (2009).

32. "U.S. Department of Agriculture; World Bureau of Metal Statistics; British Petroleum; and IMF staff." As cited in Thomas Hebling, Valerie Mercer-Blackman, and Kevin Cheng, "Riding a Wave: Commodities Boom," *Finance & Development* 45, no. 1 (March 2008). See also Bryan Lohmar and Fred Gale, "Who Will China Feed?" *Amber Waves* 6, no. 3 (June 2008).

33. The U.S. Department of Agriculture, for example, sees Chinese demand for imported wheat as relatively stable over the next decade; juxtaposed with rising demand elsewhere, particularly in the Middle East and Africa, the result is a declining Chinese share in global trade. U.S. Department of Agriculture Economic Research Service, "USDA Wheat Baseline, 2012–21," November 20, 2012, accessed September 5, 2013, http://web.archive.org/web/20130223212408/http://@ers.usda.gov/topics/crops/wheat/usda-wheat-baseline,-2012-21.aspx. Only Chinese demand for oilseeds—primarily soybeans used as animal feed—occupies a large share of projected global growth in the FAO-OECD estimates, contributing about a quarter of the global increase through 2021. Food and Agriculture Organization of the United Nations, *OECD-FAO Agricultural Outlook*, 18th ed. (OECD Publishing and FAO, June 2012).

34. Information Office of the State Council of the People's Republic of China, "The Grain Issue in China," 1996.

35. Ibid.

36. "China Pledges More Efforts to Stabilize Prices," *ChinaView*, November 14, 2007, http://news.xinhuanet.com/english/2007-11/14/content_7074656.htm.

37. "Interview with Han Changfu, Minister of Agriculture," *Study Times*, June 1, 2011, http://www.rweek.cn/Weeklyx.asp?id=1490. In Chinese.

38. Ibid.

39. Information Office of the State Council of the People's Republic of China, "The Grain Issue in China," 1996.

40. National Bureau of Statistics of China, "China Statistical Yearbook 2011," http://www.stats.gov.cn/tjsj/ndsj/2011/indexeh.htm.

41. Soybeans are used largely as an animal feed, which partly shields final consumers from the price volatility that comes with exposure to global markets, potentially making import dependence more politically palatable to Chinese leaders.

42. All agricultural production shares a common set of scarce inputs; land drawn into soybean production, for example, is land that cannot be used to produce wheat, with the result of higher wheat prices even if China does not import any wheat. See C. Peter Timmer, *Causes of High Food Prices*, ADB Economics Working Paper Series no. 128 (Manila: Asian Development Bank, 2008). Fertilizer and machinery are also common inputs that help keep prices for various agricultural commodities moving together. Food prices also tend to move together because many agricultural commodities are substitutes; when the price of wheat rises, for example, many people shift consumption to corn, driving up its price too.

43. This is not to suggest that this outcome is likely; some analysts have actually argued that productivity gains herald decreasing land use for agriculture. See Jesse H. Ausubel, Iddo K. Wernick, and Paul E. Waggoner, "Peak Farmland and the Prospect for Land Sparing," *Population and Development Review* 38, supplement S1 (February 2013).

44. U.S. Bureau of Economic Analysis, "Table 1.1.10. Percentage Shares of Gross Domestic Product," National Income and Product Accounts Tables, last revised July 31, 2013, http://www.bea.gov/iTable/iTable.cfm?ReqID=9&step=1#reqid=9&step=3&isuri=1&903=14.

45. Eurasia Group, *China's Great Rebalancing Act* (New York: Eurasia Group, 2011), 2.

46. "Exports of Goods and Services (% of GDP)," World Bank, accessed August 2013, http://data.worldbank.org/indicator/NE.EXP.GNFS.ZS.

47. "China Exports Account for 11.1% of World Trade," *Xinhua*, December 27, 2012, http://english.peopledaily.com.cn/90778/8072157.html.

48. "Household Final Consumption Expenditure, etc. (% of GDP)," World Bank, accessed September 6, 2013, http://data.worldbank.org/indicator/NE.CON.PETC.ZS.

49. Ma Kai, "The 11th Five-Year Plan: Targets, Paths and Policy Orientation," Gov.cn, March 19, 2006, http://english.gov.cn/2006-03/23/content_234832.htm.

50. NPC & CPPCC National Committee Annual Sessions 2006, "Facts and Figures: China's Main Targets for 2006–2010," March 6, 2006, http://english.gov.cn/2006-03/06/content_219504.htm.

51. Calla Wiemer, "China's Worsening Imbalances," *Wall Street Journal*, April 11, 2012; Chetan Ahya, Derrick Y. Kam, and Jenny Zheng, "Asia Insight: Why China Needs Consumption and India Needs Investment,"Asia/Pacific, Morgan Stanley Research, October 28, 2011; Victoria Ruan, "S&P Sounds Alarm on China's Overinvestment," *South China Morning Post*, February 1, 2013; and "Free Exchange: Capital Controversy," *Economist*, April 14, 2012.

52. Steven S. Roach, *China's 12th Five-Year Plan: Strategies vs. Tactics* (New York: Morgan Stanley, 2011), 2.

53. Edward L. Morse, Heath R. Jansen, Daniel P. Ahn, Jon Bergtheil, Aakash Doshi, Viswanathrao Kintali, Seth Kleinman, Eric G. Lee, Ulhas Shenoy, Johann Steyn, David B. Wilson, and Anthony Yuen, "The New Abnormal: 2013 Commodities Outlook," *Commodities Strategy*, Citi Research, November 19, 2012, 9.

54. Yongzhen Yu, *Identifying the Linkages Between Major Mining Commodity Prices and China's Economic Growth-Implications for Latin America*, IMF Working Paper (Washington, DC: International Monetary Fund, 2011), 22.

55. Ibid.

56. Ibid., 23.

57. Richard Dobbs et al., *Resource Revolution: Meeting the World's Energy, Materials, Food, and Water Needs* (McKinsey Global Institute, November 2011); and authors' calculations.

58. Marina Fischer-Kowalski et al., *Decoupling Natural Resource Use and Environmental Impacts from Economic Growth*, report of the Working Group on Decoupling to the International Resource Panel (United Nations Environment Programme, 2011).

59. R. Glenn Hubbard and Robert J. Weiner, "Long Term Contracting and Multiple Price Systems," NBER Working Paper No. 3782 (1991).

60. They also control roughly 35 percent of global production.

61. Tarun Khanna, Aldo Musacchio, and Ricardo Reisen de Pinho, "Vale: Global Expansion in the Challenging World of Mining," Harvard Business School Case Study, October 14, 2010, 10.

62. Ibid.

63. Samir Singh, David Hoyt, and Hau Lee, "Rio Tinto Iron Ore: Challenges of Globalization in the Mining Industry," Stanford Graduate School of Business: Global Supply Chain Management Forum, July 3, 2007, https://gsbapps.stanford.edu/cases/documents/gs56riotinto070307.pdf.

64. Ibid., 9. In contrast with North America, where steel makers are largely integrated, most domestic Chinese ore was also sold on a spot basis.

65. "Chapter 2: Trade—Section 8: Non-Tariff Controls," *China Doing Business in China*, Economist Intelligence Unit, February 1, 2010, http://store.eiu.com/article.aspx?productid=1950000195&articl eid=1915242576; and Zhengzheng Gong, "Iron Ore Import Rules Tightened," *China Daily*, December 29, 2006, http://www.chinadaily.com.cn/bizchina/2006-12/29/content_770678.htm.

66. Wei Jiang, "China Accepts 19% Rise in Iron Ore Price," *China Daily*, June 21, 2006, http://www.chinadaily.com.cn/china/2006-06/21/content_622052.htm.

67. "FM: China to Handle Spy Case of Rio Tinto Employees 'According to the Law,'" *Xinhua*, July 9, 2009, http://news.xinhuanet.com/english/2009-07/09/content_11680535.htm.

68. "Watchdog on Secrets: Rio Caused 'Huge Loss,'" *Xinhua*, August 10, 2009, http://news.xinhuanet.com/english/2009-08/10/content_11857950.htm

69. In the months that followed, Chinese authorities began to walk back their accusations. In early August 2009, the charges were reduced to "mere" corporate espionage and bribery. The *Wall Street Journal* reported that "About a month after the Rio Tinto executives were detained, Beijing downgraded the case by appearing to drop the national espionage allegations and has ever since contended it was a nonpolitical, commercial criminal matter." The *Journal* later noted: "The motive behind the bribes for the salesmen isn't clear but analysts say prosecutors likely alleged that steelmakers offered cash in order to secure access to supplies of iron ore, a prized commodity that is subject to a chaotic trading environment in China." What actually happened remains unclear; those who know the most aren't the ones who are talking to journalists or scholars. See James T. Areddy, "Rio Tinto Trial Adjourns," *Wall Street Journal*, March 24, 2010.

70. Khanna et al., "Vale," 10.

71. Javier Blas, "Annual Iron Ore Contract System Collapses," *Financial Times*, March 30, 2010. Average spot market prices—first quarterly and then over shorter periods—have been used instead.

72. Ibid.

73. The large producers, once big defenders of the annual contract approach, have pushed steadily toward more flexible and transparent markets, with prices even under long-term contracts adjusting ever more frequently. Consumers, long used to relatively stable prices, have had second thoughts. Although derivatives markets for iron ore have begun to emerge, the process is exposing producers to high price volatility with only limited opportunity to protect themselves.

74. Jiangning Yan and Boling Zhang, "Death Knell for Benchmark Iron Ore Pricing," *Caixin*, April 9, 2010, http://english.caixin.com/2010-04-09/100133292.html.

75. Gustavo Bonato and Leila Coimbra, "UPDATE 3-Posco Wants Benchmark Iron Ore Prices, Vale Amenable," *Reuters*, June 21, 2012.

76. Burns, "Bauxite and Alumina Moving Rapidly to Spot Pricing."

77. Warner ten Kate, László Varró, and Anne-Sophie Corbeau, *Developing a Natural Gas Hub in Asia: Obstacles and Opportunities* (Paris: International Energy Agency, 2013).

78. "As Chairman D'Amato noted in his testimony, 'it is critical to persuade China to abandon this mercantilist spree to lock up attractive energy supplies wherever it can, and instead participate [with the International Energy Agency] to plan for sharing oil in the case of supply disruptions, and to participate in the open market buying of its supplies and begin relying on free markets to promote energy security for everyone.'" From U.S.-China Economic and Security Review Commission, *2005 Report to Congress*, 109th U.S. Congress, First Session, November 2005, 171.

79. Erica S. Downs, "The Fact and Fiction of Sino-African Energy Relations," *China Security* 3, no. 3 (2007); Downs, "Inside China, Inc: China Development Bank's Cross-Border Energy Deals," Washington, DC, Brookings Institution, March 2011; and Shaofeng Chen, "Has China's Foreign Energy Quest Enhanced Its Energy Security?" *China Quarterly* 207 (September 2011).

Chapter 4

1. Justin Scheck, Liam Moloney, and Alexis Flynn, "Eni, CNPC Ink Deal in Mozambique," *Wall Street Journal*, March 14, 2013.

2. "Rio Tinto Writes Down Its Mozambique Assets," *Zimbabwean*, January 17, 2013, http://www.thezimbabwean.co/news/africa/63196/rio-tinto-writes-down-its.html.

3. Stanley Reed, "Natural Gas Discovery Promises a Boon for Eni and Mozambique," *New York Times*, December 5, 2012.

4. Globalization Monitor, "Preliminary Report on China's Going Global Strategy: A Labour, Environment, and Hong Kong Perspective," Working Paper Series, February 2009, http://www.globalmon.org.hk/

en/wp-content/uploads/2009/03/china_going_global_strategy_final. pdf, 21–24.

5. Ibid., 15–16.

6. Peter J. Buckley, L. Jeremy Clegg, Adam R. Cross, Xin Liu, Hinrich Voss, and Ping Zheng, "The Determinants of Chinese Outward Foreign Direct Investment," *Journal of International Business Studies* 38 (July 1, 2007): 514.

7. "Cheng Ming (Hong Kong Monthly), 176, March 5, 1992." As cited in Suisheng Zhao, "Deng Xiaoping's Southern Tour: Elite Politics in Post-Tiananmen China," *Asian Survey* 33, no. 8 (August 1993): 742.

8. "Southern Tour Legacy," *Global Times*, accessed April 24, 2013, http://www.globaltimes.cn/SPECIALCOVERAGE/ Dengssoutherntour.aspx.

9. Zemin Jiang, "Accelerating the Reform, the Opening to the Outside World and the Drive for Modernization, so as to Achieve Greater Successes in Building Socialism with Chinese Characteristics," Jiang Zemin's Report to the 14th Party Congress, October 12, 1992.

10. Ibid.

11. Rongji Zhu, "Report on the Outline of the Tenth Five-Year Plan for National Economic and Social Development," Report to the Fourth Session of the Ninth National People's Congress, March 5, 2001.

12. Ibid.

13. Author interview with Chinese scholar and CSR consultant, Beijing, China, June 21, 2013.

14. Leslie Hook, "Sinopec Chief Tipped for Political Post," *Financial Times*, March 22, 2011.

15. Yuanyuan Ding, "The Party, the Oil Companies, and Energy Security: Who Determines Chinese Policy?" Georgia State University Department of Political Science, April 22, 2008.

16. Author interview with Chinese scholar and CSR consultant.

17. Barry Naughton, "SASAC and Rising Corporate Power in China," *China Leadership Monitor*, March 12, 2008, http://media.hoover.org/ sites/default/files/documents/CLM24BN.pdf.

18. "Hu Jintao: China Will Further Adhere to 'Bringing in and Going out' [Hu Jintao: Zhongguo Jiang Jin Yibu Jianchi 'Yin Jinlai He Zou Chuqu']," *Xinhua*, December 11, 2011, http://finance. qq.com/a/20111211/000657.htm.

19. "Full text of Chinese President Hu Jintao's speech at opening ceremony of Boao Forum," *Xinhua*, April 15, 2011, http://english.gov. cn/2011-04/15/content_1845382.htm.

20. "Xi Jinping Had Informal Discussions and Issued a Speech with Representatives of Chinese-backed Companies in Angola [Xi Jinping Yu Zhu Angela Zhongwi Qiye Daibiao Zuotan Bing Fabiao

Jianghua]," *Xinhua*, November 21, 2010, http://news.xinhuanet.com/politics/2010-11/21/c_12798135.htm.

21. "Xi Jinping: China's Development Will Bring Enormous Business Opportunities for Companies in Many Countries [Xi Jinping: Zhongguo Fazhan Jiang Gei Geguo Qiye Dailai Juda Shangji]," *Xinhua*, February 20, 2011, http://www.chinanews.com/gn/2012/02-20/3683583.shtml.

22. Jiangning Yan, "MCC Seeks Mineral Wealth Abroad [Zhongye Haiwai Zhao Kuang Lu]," *Century Weekly*, September 6, 2010, http://magazine.caixin.com/2010-09-04/100177070.html.

23. Deborah Brautigam, "Chinese Development Aid in Africa: What, Where, Why, and How Much?" in *Rising China: Global Challenges and Opportunities*, ed. Jane Golley and Ligang Song (Canberra: Australian National University E Press, June 2011), 204–205.

24. Erica S. Downs, "Chapter 4: Who's Afraid of China's Oil Companies," in *Energy Security: Economics, Politics, Strategies, and Implications* (Washington, DC: Brookings Institution Press, 2010).

25. Peter Cai, "Chinese Urged to Invest in Resources," *Sydney Morning Herald*, March 15, 2012, http://www.smh.com.au/business/chinese-urged-to-invest-in-resources-20120314-1v3mu.html.

26. "Global Investment Still Active in China's Mining Industry," *China Daily*, November 7, 2011, http://www.chinadaily.com.cn/bizchina/2011-11/07/content_14047390.htm.

27. Global Environmental Institute, *Environmental Policies on China's Investment Overseas* (Beijing: China Environmental Science Press, 2011), 42.

28. Johanna Jansson, Christopher Burke, and Wenran Jiang, "Chinese Companies in the Extractive Industries of Gabon & the DRC: Perceptions of Transparency," Centre for Chinese Studies at the University of Stellenbosch (August 2009), 12. The report is a research undertaking by the Centre for Chinese Studies, prepared for the Extractive Industries Transparecy Initiative (EITI) and the Revenue Watch Institute (RWI).

29. Global Environmental Institute, *Environmental Policies*, 38.

30. "China in Africa," IDE-JETRO, http://www.ide.go.jp/English/Data/Africa_file/Manualreport/cia_11.html.

31. William Laurance, "China's Appetite for Wood Takes a Heavy Toll on Forests," Yale Environment 360, November 17, 2011, http://e360.yale.edu/feature/chinas_appetite_for_wood_takes_a_heavy_toll_on_forests/2465/.

32. This description is from Kevin P. Gallagher, Amos Irwin, and Katherine Koleski, "The New Banks in Town: Chinese Finance in Latin America," Inter-American Dialogue Report, February 2012.

33. Ibid.

34. This description comes from Steve Coll, *Private Empire: ExxonMobil and American Power* (New York: Penguin Press, 2012).

35. China National Petroleum Corporation, "Annual Report 2011," http://www.cnpc.com.cn/resource/english/images1/pdf/11AnnualReportEn/0-CNPC%20Annual%20Report%202011.pdf?COLLCC=1054606136&,%202; and authors' calculations. The balance of production went to its joint venture partners and to host governments.

36. The figures for ExxonMobil include "domestic" production in the United States, while those for CNPC do not include production in China, but since China is largely closed to Western oil and gas companies, this is the right comparison when looking at the presence of both countries in international oil and gas production. ExxonMobil, "2011 Annual Report," http://www.annualreports.com/HostedData/AnnualReports/PDF/XOM2011.pdf.

37. "Sinopec Group Says Plans to Double Overseas Equity Oil Output," *Reuters*, January 4, 2012, http://www.reuters.com/article/2012/01/05/china-oil-sinopec-idUSL3E8C50HI20120105; and Sinopec Corp., "2011 Annual Report and Accounts," March 28, 2012, http://www.sinopecgroup.com/english/Pages/2011AnnualReport.pdf, 12.

38. CNOOC Limited, "Annual Report 2011," March 28, 2012, http://www.cnoocltd.com/encnoocltd/tzzgx/dqbd/nianbao/images/2012412936.pdf, 11.

39. Julie Jiang and Jonathan Sinton, *Overseas Investments by Chinese National Oil Companies: Assessing the Drivers and Impacts*, Information Paper (Paris: International Energy Agency, June 2011).

40. "GABON: Oil Pact with China Aims to Boost Falling Reserves," Integrated Regional Information Networks, February 5, 2004; and author interviews in Nairobi, Kenya, with investors and industry officials, February 2013.

41. Woodrow Wilson Center, "Stepping Lighter? Environmental and Social Impacts of China's Overseas Oil, Mineral, and Gas Investments," China Environmental Forum, January 13, 2012, http://www.wilsoncenter.org/event/stepping-lighter-environmental-and-social-impacts-china%E2%80%99s-overseas-oil-mineral-and-gas.

42. China Council for the Promotion of International Trade, "Survey on Current Conditions and Intention of Outbound Investment by Chinese Enterprises," April 2010, 21.

43. Ibid.

44. Dinny McMahon and David Wessel, "Corporate China Spreads Its Wings," *Wall Street Journal*, November 9, 2011.

45. Authors' calculations based on Heritage Investment Tracker.

46. "Yanzhou Coal Successfully Acquires Australian Mining Company [Yanzhou Meiye Zaici Chenggong Shougou Aodaliya Kuangye]," Department of Outward Investment and Economic Cooperation, December 23, 2011; and Luke Hurst and Bijun Wang, "Australia's Dumb Luck and Chinese Investment," East Asia Forum, April 1, 2012, http://www.eastasiaforum.org/2012/04/01/australias-dumb-l uck-and-chinese-investment/.

47. Authors' calculations based on Heritage Investment Tracker.

48. Barbara Kotschwar, Theodore H. Moran, and Julia Muir, "Chinese Investment in Latin American Resources: The Good, the Bad, and the Ugly," Peterson Institute for International Economics, Working Paper Series, February 2012, 3.

49. Sonali Paul, "China Mine Hunt Turns to Africa, S. America, Asia," Reuters, March 23, 2012; and Woodrow Wilson Center, "Stepping Lighter?"

50. "Chinese Companies Signed Investment Promotion and Protection Agreements with the Zambian Government [Zhongguo Qiye Yu Zanbiya Zhengfu Qianding Touzi Cujin Yu Baohu Xieyi]," Xinhua, July 23, 2009, http://news.xinhuanet.com/fortune/2009-07/23/ content_11761607.htm.

51. Charlie Zhu and Alison Lui, "China Shenhua Says Hopes to Restart Talks on Mongolia Mine," Mongolian Economy and Finance, March 26, 2012, http://mongoliaeconomy.blogspot.com/2012/03/ china-shenhua-says-hopes-to-restart.html; and Jonathan Millet, "Mongolia's Tavan Tolgoi Basin to Sell Fuel to Shenhua Group Corp," ForexMinute.com, October 30, 2013, http://www. forexminute.com/commodities-news/mongolias-tavan-tolgoi-basin-to-sell-fuel-to-shenhua-group-corp-19810.

52. Woodrow Wilson Center, "Stepping Lighter?"

53. "China Now No. 1 Investor in Burma," Mizzima News, January 18, 2012, http://www.mizzima.com/business/6436-china-now-n o-1-investor-in-burma.html.

54. Peter Drysdale, "Australia: Time to Adapt," East Asia Forum Quarterly 4, no. 2 (April–June 2012): 33.

55. Juan Andrés Camus et al., "Strictly Business? An Examination of China's Natural Resource Acquisition Strategy in Latin America," Stanford Institute for Economic Policy Research, SIEPR Policy Brief, April 2013, http://siepr.stanford.edu/?q=/system/files/shared/pubs/ papers/briefs/Policy_Brief_04_2013v4.pdf.

56. Jansson et al., "Chinese Companies."

57. Magnus Ericsson and Viktoriya Larsson, "E&MJ's Annual Survey of Global Mining Investment," Engineering & Mining Journal Website, January 22, 2012, accessed September 4, 2013.

58. Duncan Freeman, Jonathan Holslag, and Steffi Weil, "China's Foreign Farming Policy: Can Land Provide Security?" *Asia Paper* 3, no. 9 (2008).
59. Freeman et al., "China's Foreign Farming."
60. Beidahuang Group, "Unique Advantages of Beidahuang Group," 2007, accessed April 2013, http://www.chinabdh.com/english/index_3.htm.
61. Carin Smaller, Wei Qu, and Yalan Liu, "Farmland and Water: China Invests Abroad," IISD Report (2012), 5.
62. United Nations Conference on Trade and Development, *World Investment Report 2013* (Switzerland: United Nations, 2013).
63. Stephen Chen, "Party Cadre Zhu Zhangjin Pins Hopes of Food Security on Overseas Farms," *South China Morning Post*, March 24, 2013, http://www.scmp.com/news/china/article/1198218/party-ca dre-zhu-zhangjin-pins-hopes-food-security-overseas-farms.
64. Phillippe Asanzi, "Chinese Agricultural Investments in Africa—Interests and Challenges," *China Monitor*, March 2012, 7.
65. Chen, "Party Cadre."
66. Ibid.
67. It is, however, "traded" in an embedded form when it is used to produce foodstuffs (notably soybeans) that are later traded internationally.
68. Yan Feng and Daming He, "Transboundary Water Vulnerability and Its Drivers in China," *Journal of Geographical Sciences* 19, no. 2 (2009): 195.
69. Peter H. Gleick, "China and Water," in *The World's Water 2008–2009: The Biennial Report on Freshwater Resources*, ed. Peter H. Gleick et al. (Chicago: Island Press, 2008), 89.
70. Feng and He, "Transboundary Water," 195.
71. Ibid.
72. Ibid.

Chapter 5

1. Chuin-Wei Yap, "Mongolia Is Feeling Friendlier Toward Foreign Investors," *Wall Street Journal*, August 28, 2013; and Clara Ferreira-Marques, "UPDATE 2-Mongolia Woos Back Miners After Investment Slump," *Reuters*, April 17, 2013.
2. "Mongolia's Neighbors Vie for Maximum Role," *Associated Press*, January 2, 2013.
3. Charles Hutzler, "Mongolia Finds That China Can Be Too Close for Comfort," *Associated Press*, December 5, 2012.
4. Sant Maral Foundation, Politbarometer #10(43), April 2012, http://santmaral.mn/sites/default/files/SMPBE12.Apr__0.pdf.

5. Peter Ford, "Mongolia's Relationship Status with China? Complicated," *The Christian Science Monitor*, July 25, 2012, http://www.csmonitor.com/World/Asia-South-Central/2012/0725/Mongolia-s-relationship-status-with-China-Complicated.

6. Hutzler, "Mongolia Finds That China."

7. Fuli Song, Hong Zhang, and Jinghuai Wang, translated by Na Zhu, "Chinese Discrimination in Mongolia," *Nation* no. 583 (August 20, 2012): 12, accessed July 2013, http://www.eeo.com.cn/ens/2012/0823/232367.shtml.

8. By creating demand for skilled labor, multinationals also put pressure on host countries (those into which foreign investment flows) to invest in education and vocational training. See Organization for Economic Co-operation and Development, "Foreign Direct Investment for Development: Maximising Benefits, Minimising Costs" (OECD, 2002). Host countries may then develop the talent necessary to encourage further foreign investment.

9. Layna Mosley and Saika Uno, "Racing to the Bottom or Climbing to the Top? Economic Globalization and Collective Labor Rights," *Comparative Political Studies* 40, no. 8 (August 2007): 3.

10. Feng Helen Liang, "Does Foreign Direct Investment Harm the Host Country's Environment? Evidence from China," Haas School of Business at UC Berkeley, April 12, 2006.

11. Interestingly, an OECD study suggests that FDI has a larger positive impact on the host country's productivity when the technology gap between the host country and the foreign investor is small. Organization for Economic Co-operation and Development, "Foreign Direct Investment for Development: Maximising Benefits, Minimising Costs" (OECD, 2002).

12. Dambisa Moyo, "Beijing, a Boon for Africa," *New York Times*, June 27, 2012.

13. Paul Collier, *The Bottom Billion* (New York: Oxford University Press, 2007), 86.

14. Deborah Brautigam, *The Dragon's Gift* (New York: Oxford University Press, 2009), 21.

15. Abdoulaye Wade, "Time for the West to Practise What It Preaches," *Financial Times*, January 23, 2008.

16. Mike Cohen, "China's EXIM Lend More to Sub-Sahara Africa Than World Bank, Fitch Says," *Bloomberg*, December 28, 2011.

17. Xiaojuan Wang, "Thorns in the African Dream," China Dialogue, January 2, 2012, www.chinadialogue.net/article/show/single/en/4748-thorns-in-the-African-dream-1.

18. Juan Andrés Camus et al., "Strictly Business? An Examination of China's Natural Resource Acquisition Strategy in Latin America," Stanford Institute for Economic Policy Research, SIEPR Policy Brief,

http://siepr.stanford.edu/?q=/system/files/shared/pubs/papers/briefs/
Policy_Brief_04_2013v4.pdf.

19. Author interview, Lusaka, Zambia, January 2013.

20. Author interview with senior oil official, Maputo, Mozambique, January 2013.

21. Esther Tanquintic-Misa, "UPDATE: Mining Rights to Gabon's Belinga Iron Ore Deposit in BHP Billiton's Hands Soon," *International Business Times*, January 31, 2012, http://au.ibtimes.com/articles/290110/20120131/australia-gabon-africa-china-iron-ore-bhp.htm#.UYk-bVeFN8F.

22. Howard W. French, "China in Africa: All Trade, With No Political Baggage," *New York Times*, August 8, 2004, www.nytimes.com/2004/08/08/international/asia/08china.html.

23. Ian Bremmer, "New Strings Attached in the China-Africa Relationship," *Globe and Mail*, April 3, 2013.

24. Macky Sall, "Africa's Turn," *Foreign Affairs* (September/October 2013), www.foreignaffairs.com/discussions/interviews/africas-turn?page=show.

25. Author interview with Dipak Patel, Lusaka, Zambia, January 2013.

26. Doug Tsuroka, "China's Trade Embargo on Rare Earth Exports to Japan a First," Investors.com, September 23, 2010, blogs.investors.com/click/index.php/home/60-tech/2015-chinas-trade-embargo-on-rare-earth-exports-to-japan-a-first.

27. Hutzler, "Mongolia Finds That China."

28. Jing Vivian Zhan, "Natural Resources and Corruption: Empirical Evidence from China," paper prepared for APSA 2011 Annual Meeting, September 1–4, 2011, Seattle, WA.

29. Ibid., 9–10.

30. Ivar Kolstad and Arne Wiig, "What Determines Chinese Outward FDI?" CMI Working Paper, 2009, http://www.cmi.no/publications/publication/?3332=what-determines-chinese-outward-fdi.

31. Charles Wallace, "China, Not U.S., Likely to Benefit from Afghanistan's Mineral Riches," *Daily Finance*, June 15, 2010, www.dailyfinance.com/2010/06/14/china-us-afghanistan-mineral-mining/.

32. James Yeager, "The Aynak Copper Tender: Implications for Afghanistan and the West," 2009, 19, 45, http://www.scribd.com/doc/22004530/The-Aynak-Copper-Tender-Implications-for-Afghanistan-and-the-West.

33. Author interview with senior oil official, Maputo, Mozambique, January 2013.

34. Author interviews with Brazilian Ministry of Foreign Affairs officials, Brasilia, March 27, 2013.

35. Bijian Zheng, "China's 'Peaceful Rise' to Great-Power Status," *Foreign Affairs* (September/October 2005), 22.
36. Ibid., 20.
37. Lamido Sanusi, "Africa Must Get Real About Chinese Ties," *Financial Times*, March 11, 2013.
38. Dun Chen and Jialei Zhou, "Social Responsibility: A Problem Chinese Enterprises Overseas Must Confront [Shehui Zeren: Zhongguo Qiye 'Zou Chuqu' Bixu Yingdui De Wenti]," *China Economy and Trade*, May 23, 2012.
39. Bo Ma and Chunlin Xin, "A Study of CSR Development in China [Woguo Qiye Shehui Zeren Fazhan Yanjiu]," *Chemical Enterprise Management*, July 2012, 81.
40. Chen and Zhou, "Social Responsibility."
41. "Zhonghui Mining Optimistic of Finalizing the Ichimpe Mine," SteelGuru.com, June 8, 2011, http://www.steelguru.com/metals_news/Zhonghui_Mining_optimistic_of_finalizing_the_Ichimpe_mine/208824.html.
42. "Zhonghui Mining Calls for Support for Ichimpe Copper and Cobalt Mine in Zambia," SteelGuru.com, May 28, 2011, http://www.steelguru.com/metals_news/Zhonghui_Mining_calls_for_support_ffor_Ichimpe_copper_and_cobalt_mine_in_Zambia/207298.html.
43. Author interview, Lusaka, Zambia, January 2013.
44. "Base Metals Highlights: Top Stories of the Day," 4-traders.com, May 30, 2012, http://www.4-traders.com/news/BASE-METALS-HIGHLIGHTS-Top-Stories-Of-The-Day--14349610/.
45. "Environmental Policy," Export-Import Bank of China, April 2007, http://pacificenvironment.org/downloads/Chexim%20environmental%20policy%20Chinese%20and%20English.pdf.
46. "Country Guidelines for Foreign Investment: Zambia [Duiwai Touzi Hezuo Guobie (Dichu) Zhinan: Zanbiya]," Department of Outward Investment and Economic Cooperation at China's Ministry of Finance, 2011.
47. Author interview, Lusaka, Zambia, 2013.
48. Ibid.
49. Joseph Nana Yaw Cobbina, "Illegal Chinese Miners Will Be Flushed out from Ghana," Sino-Africa, March 12, 2013, www.sinoafrica.org/en/node/2308.
50. Ibid.
51. Ibid.
52. Afua Hirsch, "Ghana Deports Thousands in Crackdown on Illegal Chinese Goldminers," *Guardian*, July 15, 2013.
53. "Chinese and Russian Companies 'Most Likely to Bribe,'" *BBC News*, November 1, 2011.

54. Author interview with extractive industry consultant, Maputo, Mozambique, January 2013.

55. "2010 Social Responsibility Report [2010 Nian Shehui Zeren Baogao]," China Metallurgical Group Corporation.

56. "Country Guidelines for Foreign Investment: Papua New Guinea [Duiwai Touzi Hezuo Guobie (Dichu) Zhinan: Babuya Xin Jineiya]," Department of Outward Investment and Economic Cooperation at China's Ministry of Finance, 2011.

57. "Landholders Vow to Stop Ramu Mine Production," PNG Mine Watch, December 12, 2011, www.Ramumine.wordpress. com/2011/12/12/landholders-vow-to-stop-ramu-mine-production/.

58. Ibid.

59. Rainforest Portal, "Action Alert: Resistance Growing to Ecologically Devastating Chinese Mining Invasion of Madang, Papua New Guinea," April 1, 2010, http://forests.org/shared/alerts/sendsm. aspx?id=png_ramu_mine_1_4_2010.

60. Ibid.; and Kevin Pamba, "New PNG Mine Project Stirs up Furore," *Asia Times Online*, August 27, 1999, www.atimes.com/oceania/ AH27Ah01.html.

61. Mohamed Hassan, "PNG's Ramu NiCo Mine: An Environmental Time Bomb?" Pacific Scoop, November 8, 2012, http://pacific.scoop. co.nz/2012/11/pngs-ramu-nico-mine-an-environmental-time-bomb/.

62. "Minister Orders MCC to Stop Work at Ramu Mine," PNG Mine Watch, April 5, 2012, http://ramumine.wordpress.com/2012/04/05/ minister-orders-mcc-to-stop-work-at-ramu-mine/.

63. Papua New Guinea National Court of Justice, "WS NO 1192 of 2010," 2011, http://ramumine.files.wordpress.com/2011/07/ medaing-v-mcc-the-state-iamo.pdf; and "Mine Tailings: A Christmas Present For Raikos People," PNG Mine Watch, December 24, 2011, http://ramumine.wordpress.com/2011/12/24/ mine-tailings-a-christmas-present-for-raikos-people/.

64. Carlos H. Conde, "Philippines Suspends Chinese-funded Projects in Wake of Scandal," *New York Times*, September 25, 2007.

65. J. M. Anthorpe, "China's Global Hunt for Food Security," *Vancouver Sun*, Feburary 3, 2010, http://www.canada.com/ vancouversun/news/editorial/story.html?id=335af985-b78f-4e7b-b 8ba-ae179890d64d.

66. Robin Paxton, "Kazakh Opposition Calls for Halt to China Expansion," *Reuters*, May 28, 2011.

67. Author interview with Ministry of Agriculture officials, Brasilia, Brazil, March 27, 2013.

68. Author discussions with business roundtable, Sao Paolo, Brazil, March 28, 2013.

69. "New Agricultural Agreement in Argentina: A Land Grabber's 'Instruction Manual,'" GRAIN.org, January 27, 2011, http://www.grain.org/article/entries/4139-new-agric ultural-agreement-in-argentina-a-land-grabber-s-instruction-manual.

70. Mia De Graaf, "Limiting Foreign Land Ownership: A Law in the Making," *Argentinian Independent*, September 28, 2010, http:// www.argentinaindependent.com/currentaffairs/newsfromargentina/ limiting-foreign-land-ownership-a-law-in-the-making/.

71. Shuping Niu, "China Overseas Food Push Not Realistic," *Reuters*, May 9, 2008, http://uk.reuters.com/article/2008/05/09/uk-china-f ood-overseas-interview-idUKPEK12378520080509.

72. Lu Chang, "A Lot on the Plate," *China Daily*, March 31, 2012, www. chinadaily.com.cn/china/2012-03/31/content_14956810_3.htm.

73. Michael Bristow, "China in Africa: Developing Ties," *BBC News*, November 29, 2007, http://news.bbc.co.uk/2/hi/africa/7118941. stm.

74. "Buying Farmland Abroad: Outsourcing's Third Wave," *Economist*, May 21, 2009; and Deborah Brautigam, "China in Africa: Seven Myths," Real Institutu Elcano, August 2, 2011, http://www.realinstitutoelcano. org/wps/portal/rielcano_eng/Content?WCM_GLOBAL_CONTEXT=/ elcano/elcano_in/zonas_in/ari23-2011.

75. Chen and Zhou, "Social Responsibility."

76. Smith, "Slave Labour?"

77. Johanna Jansson, Christopher Burke, and Wenran Jiang, "Chinese Companies in the Extractive Industries of Gabon & the DRC: Perceptions of Transparency," Centre for Chinese Studies, August 2009.

78. Qingfen Ding, "Companies Still Drawn to Peru, Despite Obstacles," *China Daily*, December 11, 2012, http://europe.chinadaily.com.cn/ business/2012-12/11/content_16004359.htm.

79. Simon Romero, "Tensions over Chinese Mining Venture in Peru," *New York Times*, August 14, 2010.

80. Lucien O. Chauvin, "Hierro Peru: China's Footprint in the Andes," China Dialogue, December 1, 2006, https://www.chinadialogue.net/ article/show/single/en/595-Hierro-Peru-China-s-footprint-in-the-Andes; and Kotschwar et al., "Do Chinese Mining Companies Exploit More?".

81. Amos Irwin and Kevin P. Gallagher, "Chinese Investment in Peru: A Comparative Analysis," Working Group on Development and Environment in the Americas, 34 (December 2012), 20.

82. Ibid., 21.

83. Kotschwar et al., "Do Chinese Mining Companies Exploit More?"; and David Caploe, "Peru Mine Conflict: Problem for China

Commodity Strategy," EconomyWatch.com, September 1, 2010, http://www.economywatch.com/economy-business-and-finance-news/peru-mine-conflict-problem-for-china-commodity-strategy-01-09.html.

84. Irwin and Gallagher, "Chinese Investment in Peru."

85. "Shougang Resumes Peru Iron Ore Mine Operations," *Bloomberg*, April 18, 2007, http://www.chinamining.org/Investment/2007-04-18/1176865882d4777.html.

86. Alex Emery, "Shougang's Peruvian Unit Declares Iron-Ore Force Majeure on Labor Strike," *Bloomberg*, July 5, 2010.

87. "Update 1-Shougang Hierro Peru Workers to Strike on Aug 31," *Reuters*, August 24, 2011; and Ryan Dube, "Peru Union Starts Strike at Shougang Iron Mine," *Wall Street Journal Market Watch*, October 9, 2012.

88. "China on Track to Invest US$5.24 Billion in Peru's Mining Sector," SinoLatinCapital.com, April 5, 2012, http://www.sinolatincapital.cn/show_newsletter_news.asp?id=903&n_id=.

89. "Latin America's Best Companies," LatinTrade.com, November 23, 2011, http://latintrade.com/2011/11/latin-america%E2%80%99s-best-companies.

90. "Country Guidelines for Foreign Investment: Peru [Duiwai Touzi Hezuo Guobie (Dichu) Zhinan: Bilu]," Department of Outward Investment and Economic Cooperation at China's Ministry of Finance, 2011.

91. Irwin and Gallagher, "Chinese Investment in Peru," 14.

92. Ibid., 12–13.

93. Author interview with civil society researcher, Lusaka, Zambia, January 2013.

94. Author interview with former nickel mine worker, Lusaka, January 2013.

95. Author interview with Joaquim Chissano, Maputo, Mozambique, January 2013.

96. Lucy Corkin, "China and Angola: Strategic Partnership or Marriage of Convenience?" *Angola Brief* 1, no. 1 (January 2011): 2.

97. Author interview with Chinese Ministry of Foreign Affairs officials, November 2012.

98. Author interview with transparency expert, Maputo, Mozambique, January 2013.

99. Smith, "Slave Labour?"

100. "Project Conflict Between China and Vietnam," Asia Economic Institute, http://www.asiaecon.org/special_articles/read_sp/12915.

101. Scott Pegg, "Social Responsibility and Resource Extraction: Are Chinese Oil Companies Different?" *Resources Policy* 37, no. 2 (June 2012): 164–165.

102. Deborah Brautigam and Xiaoyang Tang, "Economic Statecraft in China's New Overseas Special Economic Zones," IFPRI Discussion Paper, no. 01168 (March 2012): 8–9.

103. Ibid., 16.

104. Ana Cristina Alves, "Chinese Economic and Trade Co-operation Zones in Africa: Facing the Challenges," SAIIA Policy Briefing no. 51 (June 2012): 2–3.

105. Jin Zhu, "Program to Improve Africa's Agriculture," *China Daily*, November 13, 2012, http://usa.chinadaily.com.cn/world/2012-11/13/content_15923701.htm.

106. Linda Nordling, "Africa Analysis: Directing Technology Transfer from China," SciDev.net, February 8, 2012.

Chapter 6

1. "Issue 83: March 21, 2013," China Media Bulletin, March 21, 2013, http://www.freedomhouse.org/sites/default/files/83_032113.pdf.

2. "Social Security Top Concern Ahead of 'Two Sessions,'" *Xinhua*, February 20, 2013, http://english.people.com.cn/90882/8137040.html.

3. Ma and Xin, "A Study of CSR Development."

4. Stephan Rothlin, "Towards a Socially Responsible China: A Preliminary Investigation of the Implementation of the Global Compact," *Journal of International Business Ethics* 3, no. 1 (2010): 4–5.

5. United Nations, "United Nations Global Compact Annual Review 2010," http://www.unglobalcompact.org/docs/news_events/8.1/UN_Global_Compact_Annual_Review_2010.pdf.

6. Ma and Xin, "A Study of CSR Development."

7. Nathalie Bernasconi-Osterwalder, Lise Johnson, and Jianping Zhang, eds., *Chinese Outward Investment: An Emerging Policy Framework* (Winnipeg, Manitoba, Canada: International Institute for Sustainable Development, 2013), 168.

8. Li-Wen Lin, "Corporate Social Responsibility in China: Window Dressing or Structural Change," *Berkeley Journal of International Law* 28, no. 1 (2010): 77.

9. Michael A. Levine, "China's CSR Expectations Mature," *China Business Review*, November–December 2008, 51–52, www.secure-www.net/files/24063_levine2.pdf.

10. Peiyuan Guo, Dylan Meagher, Yanjing Wu, and Anna-Sterre Nette, "Transparency Matters: Disclosure of Payments to Governments by Chinese Extractive Companies," Global Witness and SynTao (January 2013): 14.

11. "Emerging Best Practices of Chinese Globalizers: The Corporate Global Citizenship Challenge," World Economic Forum and Boston Consulting Group, 2012, 20.

12. Jiufang Tang and Pengfei Li, "Corporate Social Responsibility and Firms Environmental Performance of Chinese Listed Companies," *International Journal of Computer Science Issues* 10, no. 1 (January 2013): 777.

13. Bernasconi-Osterwalder et al., *Chinese Outward Investment*, 172–174.

14. " 'Performance in 2010,' CDB 2010 CSR Report." As cited in note 50 in "China Development Bank's Overseas Investments: An Assessment of Environmental and Social Policies and Practices," Bank Track and Friends of the Earth, July 2012, http://www.foe.org/system/storage/93/2b/2/2245/China_Development_Banks_overseas_investments_-_An_assessment_of_environmental_and_social_policies_and_practices.pdf.

15. "The Export-Import Bank of China Company Profile Report," Hoovers, www.hoovers.com/company-information/cs/company-profile.The_Export-IMport_Bank_ of_china.4f1a9005b57ad9ca.html, 18.

16. Bernasconi-Osterwalder et al., *Chinese Outward Investment*, 176.

17. "The New Great Walls: A Guide to China's Overseas Dam Industry," International Rivers, November 2012, 29.

18. "China's Central SOEs Perform Well Abroad," *Xinhua*, February 22, 2011, http://www.china.org.cn/business/2011-02/22/content_21979349.htm.

19. Xiaosheng Mi, "Challenges and Solutions of Chinese-funded Enterprises in Africa [Zai Fei Zhongzi Qiye De Tiaozhan Ji Duice]," China.com.cn, June 7, 2012, http://www.china.com.cn/international/txt/2012-06/07/content_25592566.htm.

20. Zhong Sheng, "Chinese Firms Must Tread Lightly When Investing Overseas," *People's Daily Online*, September 6, 2011, http://english.peopledaily.com.cn/90780/7590088.html.

21. "Beijing New-century Academy on Transnational Corporations," China CSR Map, http://www.chinacsrmap.org/Org_Show_EN.asp?ID=754.

22. Author interview with Ministry of Commerce official, Beijing, June 21, 2013.

23. Bernasconi-Osterwalder et al., *Chinese Outward Investment*, 226.

24. "Administrative Regulations on Contracting Foreign Projects," Order of the State Council No. 527, July 21, 2008, http://www.cccc-3.com/en/jtxx_views.php?cid=70&id=703.

25. Peter Bosshard, "Chinese Loans Could Fuel Regional Conflict in East Africa," China Dialogue, January 14, 2013, www.chinadialogue.net/article/show/single/en/5601-chinese-loans-could-fuel-regional-conflict-in-east-africa.
26. Ibid.
27. Simon Zadek, Maya Forstater, and Kelly Yu, "Corporate Responsibility and Sustainable Economic Development in China: Implications for Business," U.S. Chamber of Commerce, March 2012.
28. The comparison included Chinalco, CNMC, Shougang, Shenhua Group, Minmetals, China Coal Energy, and China National Gold Group and compared them across fifteen variables: UN global compact membership, GRI membership, publication of a CSR report, listing on a stock exchange, ISO 26000 adherence, ISO 14000 adherence, CASS-CSR2.0 adherence, COD reduction, investment in workplace safety, fatality rate per million tons of raw coal production, number of employees killed, total social donation, investment in environmental protection, and SO2 reduction.
29. Approximately 150 Chinese companies use the international Global Reporting Initiative (GRI) guidelines for corporate social responsibility. The GRI, which was founded in the United States in 1997, promotes economic, environmental, and social sustainability and provides companies with comprehensive sustainability reporting guidance. Its office in Beijing is one of only five worldwide. The Global Reporting Initiative's detailed framework, which encourages greater organizational transparency and accountability and lays out performance indicators, may indicate why it is not more widely adopted in China. It is commonly implemented elsewhere, including in the United States. Carlos Noronha, Si Tou, M. I. Cynthia, and Jenny J. Guan, "Corporate Social Responsibility Reporting in China: An Overview and Comparison with Major Trends," *Corporate Social Responsibility and Environmental Management* 20, no. 1 (2013): 29–42.
30. Noronha et al., "Corporate Social Responsibility Reporting in China," 29–42.
31. "China Petroleum & Chemical-A (600028: Shanghai): Fu Chengyu," *Bloomberg Businessweek*, accessed September 5, 2013, http://investing.businessweek.com/research/stocks/people/person.asp?personId=83535916&ticker=600028:CH.
32. Rothlin, "Towards a Socially Responsible China," 7.
33. "What Is the EITI?" accessed April 24, 2013, http://eiti.org/eiti.
34. Ibid.

35. After becoming a candidate, a country has two years to be validated by an independent auditor. Once they have been validated, it is designated a "compliant" country. In addition to resource-rich companies that volunteer to become candidates, resource-importing countries and resource companies can sign up to be supporters. For more information, see "What Is the EITI?" http://eiti.org/eiti.

36. Francisco Paris, "China and the EITI," EITI Blog, February 19, 2010, accessed April 24, 2013, http://eiti.org/blog/china-and-eiti.

37. "Stakeholders: Countries," EITI Website, accessed April 24, 2013, http://eiti.org/supporters/countries.

38. Michelle Chan, "Crude Beginnings: The Environmental Footprint of China National Petroleum Corporation Around the World," Friends of the Earth, February 17, 2012, http://www.foe.org/news/archives/2012-02-crude-beginnings-the-environmental-footprint-of-chin.

39. Author e-mail interview with Erica Downs.

40. Guo et al., "Transparency Matters," 16.

41. Christopher Burke, Johanna Jansson, and Wenran Jiang, "The Extractive Industries Transparency Initiative (EITI) and China's Energy Policy Formulation Process," Centre for Chinese Studies, August 2009, 21.

42. "About RWI," Revenue Watch Institute, http://www.revenuewatch.org/about.

43. Burke et al., "The Extractive Industries."

44. "Zambia Extractive Industries Transparencies Initiative: Independent Reconciliation for Year End December 2008," PricewaterhouseCoopers, February 2011, 30.

45. Pegg, "Social Responsibility and Resource Extraction," 162.

46. Author e-mail interview with Cynthia Sanborn, April 16, 2013.

47. Caroline Stauffer, "Chinese Miner Builds High-altitude Experiment in Peru," *Reuters*, July 1, 2012.

48. Ibid.

49. Eric Ng, "Chinalco Mining Offers Investors Exposure to Peru," *South China Morning Post*, January 21, 2013.

50. Amos Irwin and Kevin P. Gallagher, "Chinese Investment in Peru: A Comparative Analysis," *Working Group on Development and Environment in the Americas*, no. 34 (December 2012): 26.

51. "Emerging Best Practices of Chinese Globalizers," 15.

52. Kotschwar et al., "Do Chinese Mining Companies Exploit More?"

53. "Second National Reconciliation Study of the Extractive Industries Transparency Initiative (EITI) in Peru (2008–2010)," Ernst & Young, December 13, 2011.

54. Dan Collyns, "Chinese Mining Firm to Raze Peruvian Peak for 35 Years of Mineral Wealth," *Guardian,* December 20, 2012.

55. Guo et al., "Transparency Matters," 28–29.

56. Zadek et al., "Corporate Responsibility and Sustainable Economic Development," 4.

57. Sheng, "Chinese Firms."

58. Ibid.

59. Ibid.

60. Mi, "Challenges."

61. Xiaogang Yu, Chen Yu, and Yang Yong, "Chinese NGOs Travel to Myanmar," *China Development Brief,* no. 53 (June 2012).

62. Andrew Higgins, "Abduction of Chinese Workers in Sudan Stirs Criticism in Beijing," *Washington Post,* February 1, 2012.

63. "How to Maintain Safety for Chinese Companies After They 'Go Out' [Zhongguo Qiye 'Zou Chuqu' Hou De Anquan Celue]," *Xinhua,* February 6, 2012, http://ccnews.people.com.cn/GB/17032262.html.

64. Leslie Hook, "Chinese Investors Retreat from Politically Risky Markets," China Dialogue, April 17, 2013, http://www.chinadialogue. net/article/show/single/en/5915-chinese-investors-retreat-from-politica lly-risky-markets.

Chapter 7

1. Michael J. De La Merced and Ian Austen, "Chinese Oil Company Bids $15 Billion for Canadian Producer," Deal Book, *New York Times,* July 23, 2012, http://dealbook.nytimes.com/2012/07/23/ cnooc-to-buy-nexen-for-15-billion/.

2. De La Merced and Austen, "Chinese Oil Company Bids $15 Billion for Canadian Producer."

3. This refers to the sum of proved and probable reserves.

4. *Nexen Annual Report: Our Plan for Delivering Value* (Calgary, Canada: Nexen, 2011), http://www.nexeninc.com/en/investors/~/ media/Files/AnnualReports/2011/Nexen_2011_AnnualReportFINAL. ashx. About half of its natural gas production came from Canada too.

5. "Opposition Motion: Proposed Takeover of Nexen by CNOOC (Part III)," *House of Commons Debates,* 41st Parl., 1st Sess., No. 157 (October 2, 2012) at 10719, accessed July 2013, http://envirohansard.ca/2012/10/ opposition-motion-proposed-takeover-of-nexen-by-cnooc-part-iii/.

6. United Nations, UN Commodity Trade Statistics Database (UN Comtrade), 2009, http://comtrade.un.org/db/.

7. Xueli Huang and Ian Austin, *Chinese Investment in Australia: Unique Insights from the Mining Industry* (New York: Palgrave Macmillan, 2011), 7.

8. Ellis Connolly and David Orsmond, *The Mining Industry: From Bust to Boom* (Sydney: Economic Analysis Department, Reserve Bank of Australia 2011), 15.

9. Michael Plumb, Christopher Kent, and James Bishop, "Implications for the Australian Economy of Strong Growth in Asia," Research Discussion Paper RDP2013-03, March 2013, www.rba.gov.au/publications/rdp/2013/2013-03.html.

10. William Pesek, "Australians Should Be Careful of Dutch Disease," *Bloomberg*, May 10, 2012, http://www.bloomberg.com/news/2012-05-10/australians-should-be-careful-of-dutch-disease.html.

11. This section draws from the Foreign Investment Review Board's annual reports from 2000 to 2012. They are accessible at http://www.firb.gov.au/content/publications.asp. Foreign Investment Review Board (FIRB), *Annual Report, 2008–09* (Canberra: Commonwealth of Australia, 2010); and Australian Bureau of Statistics, "5352.0— International Investment Position, Australia: Supplementary Statistics 2012," May 2, 2013, http://www.abs.gov.au/AUSSTATS/abs@.nsf/DetailsPage/5352.02012?OpenDocument.

12. Huang and Austin, *Chinese Investment.*

13. Ibid., 58.

14. Foreign Investment Review Board (FIRB), *Annual Report, 2010–11* (Canberra: Commonwealth of Australia, 2012). The Shell bid was rejected on the grounds that Woodside held a dominant position in Australia's North West Shelf gas field and that it was "in the national interest that [the gas] be developed and marketed in preference to competing products from anywhere else in the world," something the Australian government was not confident Shell would do, even with conditions on the deal stipulating timelines and benchmarks for prompt development. Becky Gaylord, "Australia Rejects a Shell Takeover Bid," *New York Times*, April 24, 2001.

15. Huang and Austin, *Chinese Investment*, 64.

16. Ultimately, despite several years of attempts, Sinosteel was unable to buy anywhere close to half of the company at the price it was willing to pay. Jonathan Standing, "Australia to Allow Sinosteel to Buy into Murchison," *Reuters*, September 21, 2008.

17. For more on the security risks associated with rare earths, see Levi, *The Power Surge.*

18. Dexter Roberts and Chi-Chu Tschang, "Why Chinalco's Buying into Rio Tinto," *Bloomberg Businessweek*, February 5, 2008, http://www.businessweek.com/stories/2008-02-05/why-chinalcos-buying-into-rio-tintobusinessweek-business-news-stock-market-and-financial-advice.

19. Jiangning Yan and Jianfei Zhao, "Waiting Game for Chinalco's Rio Tinto Deal," *Caijing*, February 27, 2009, http://english.caijing.com. cn/2009-02-27/110074764.html.

20. Dana Cimilluca, Shai Oster, and Amy Or, "Rio Tinto Scuttles Its Deal with Chinalco," *Wall Street Journal*, June 5, 2009.

21. Qiu Lin, "Closer Look: A Steel of a Deal," *Caixin Online*, August 5, 2011, http://english.caixin.com/2011-08-05/100288091.html.

22. Peter Drysdale, "Australia Needs to Get Its Act Together on China, and Fast," *East Asia Forum*, June 7, 2009, http://www.eastasiaforum. org/2009/06/07/australia-needs-to-get-its-act-together-on-china-and-fast/.

23. Huang and Austin, *Chinese Investment*.

24. Malcolm Turnbull, "Transcript of the Hon. Malcolm Turnbull MP Address to the Lowy Institute," Lowy Institute, May 1, 2009.

25. Garry White, "Rio Tinto Faces Political Headwinds in Australia," *The Telegraph*, March 18, 2009.

26. Peter Costello, "The View from the East Has a Very Different Hue," *Sydney Morning Herald*, July 15, 2009.

27. Linda Ensor, "SA-born Billiton Chief 'Sank China Deal,'" *Business Day*, February 15, 2011, http://www.bdlive.co.za/articles/2011/02/15/ sa-born-billiton-chief-sank-china-deal;jsessionid=12C06EC1B9CFA91 45E3D21A1B01CE6C8.present2.bdfm.

28. Graeme Wearden, "Rio Agrees Deal with Rival BHP and Tees up Rights Issue," *Guardian*, June 5, 2009, http://www.guardian.co.uk/ business/2009/jun/05/rio-tinto-bhp-billiton-iron-ore-deal.

29. Terry Macalister, "Rio's Deal with Chinalco Collapses," *Guardian*, June 4, 2009, http://www.guardian.co.uk/business/2009/jun/04/rio-ti nto-chinalco-investment.

30. Fergus Hanson, *The Lowy Institute Poll 2009: Australia and the World: Public Opinion and Foreign Policy* (Sydney, Australia: Lowy Institute for International Policy, 2009).

31. Ibid.

32. Ibid.

33. Andrew Shearer, *Sweet and Sour: Australian Public Attitudes Towards China* (Sydney, Australia: Lowy Institute for International Policy, 2010).

34. "China Global Investment Tracker Interactive Map," Heritage Foundation, http://www.heritage.org/research/projects/ china-global-investment-tracker-interactive-map.

35. "GDP by Sector of the Canadian Economy," Industry Canada, last modified June 27, 2013, https://www.ic.gc.ca/app/scr/sbms/sbb/cis/ gdp.html?code=11-91&lang=eng#fnb2.

36. "Trade Data Online," Industry Canada, accessed September 6, 2013, https://www.ic.gc.ca/eic/site/tdo-dcd.nsf/eng/Home.
37. Ibid.
38. Ibid.
39. Bo Kong, *China's International Petroleum Policy* (Santa Barbara, CA: Praeger Security International, 2010), 81.
40. Kong, *China's International Petroleum Policy*, 81; Sizhi Guo, *The Business Development of China's National Oil Companies: The Government to Business Relationship in China* (Houston, TX: James A. Baker III Insitute for Public Policy at Rice University, 2007), 18; World Bank Social and Economic Development Group, "Chapter 4: MENA's Investment Links with China and India," in *Strengthening MENA's Trade and Investments Links with China and India* (Washington, DC: World Bank, 2008), 58; and Dan Child, "Opportunities for Alberta's Oil and Gas Industry in China's Emerging Economy," December 15, 2004, 5, http://www.business .ualberta.ca/Centres/CABREE/Energy/~/media/business/Centres/ CABREE/Documents/Energy/Oil/DanChild.ashx.
41. Sizhi Guo, *The Recent Financial and Operational Situation Conditions of the Chinese Oil Majors* (Tokyo: Institute of Energy Economics, Japan, 2004), 11.
42. All figures in this paragraph are based on "China Global Investment Tracker Interactive Map," Heritage Foundation, http://www.heritage.org/research/projects/china-global-investment -tracker-interactive-map.
43. For example, Bob Weber, "Chinese Could Shift Energy Investments to Forestry, Mining: Ambassador," *Canadian Business*, February 11, 2013, http://www.canadianbusiness.com/business-news/chinese-co uld-shift-energy-investments-to-forestry-mining-ambassador/; and "Will China Invest in Canada's Lumber Industry," March 4, http:// www.cnfpi.com/en/newsds.asp?NID=2071.
44. "China Global Investment Tracker Interactive Map," Heritage Foundation.
45. "Canada's State of Trade: Trade and Investment Update 2012," Foreign Affairs and International Trade Canada, last modified April 30, 2013, http://www.international.gc.ca/economist-economiste/ performance/state-point/state_2012_point/2012_6. aspx?lang=eng&view=d#t6-2.
46. For 2013, investments are defined as significant if they exceed $344 million in a year for a given investor from a WTO country. There are technicalities, and a lower threshold for non-WTO investors, but these are not relevant to the case of China. Industry Canada, "An Overview of the Investment Canada Act (FAQs)," March

8, 2013, accessed September 5, 2013, http://www.ic.gc.ca/eic/site/
ica-lic.nsf/eng/h_lk00007.html.

47. Simone Collins, "Recent Decisions Under the Investment Canada
Act: Is Canada Changing Its Stance on Foreign Direct Investment?"
Northwestern Journal of International Law & Business 32, no. 1
(Fall 2011).

48. Nathan VanderKlippe, "Canadarm Heads South as MDA Sells Units
for $1.3 Billion," *Star Phoenix*, January 9, 2008, http://www2.canada.
com/saskatoonstarphoenix/technology/story.html?id=678e3848-b
81a-4562-bafd-1bdd504d59f9&k=10661.

49. Collins, "Recent Decisions," 154.

50. Ibid.

51. "BHP Billiton Launches Hostile Bid for Potash," *BBC News*, August
18, 2010, http://www.bbc.co.uk/news/business-11009145.

52. Joseph Chaney et al., "Sinochem Won't Bid for Potash Corp,
Sources Say," *Reuters*, October 15, 2010, http://www.reuters.com/
article/2010/10/15/us-potash-sinochem-idUSTRE69E0NL20101015.

53. U.S. Geological Survey, "2012 Potash Statistics," last modified
November 1, 2012, http://minerals.usgs.gov/ds/2005/140/
ds140-potas.pdf.

54. PotashCorp, *The Next Stage of Growth: 2010 Summary Accountability
Report,* accessed September 5, 2013, http://www.potashcorp.com/
annual_reports/2010/.

55. PotashCorp, "Understanding the Potash Business," 2010 Online
Annual Report, accessed September 5, 2013, http://www.potashcorp.
com/annual_reports/2010/md_and_a/potash/understanding/.

56. Michael Grant, Michael Burt, and Lin Ai, *Saskatchewan in the
Spotlight: Acquisition of Potash Corporation of Saskatchewan Inc.—Risks
and Opportunities* (Ottawa, Ontario: Conference Board, 2010).

57. Collins, "Recent Decisions."

58. Paul Vieira, "Canada Opposition Party Says Govt Must Reject
CNOOC/Nexen Deal," Rigzone, October 4, 2012, http://www.
rigzone.com/news/oil_gas/a/121146/Canada_Opposition_Party_Says_
Govt_Must_Reject_CNOOCNexen_Deal.

59. Terence Corcoran, "Fascism by Another Name," *Financial Post*,
October 25, 2012, http://opinion.financialpost.com/2012/10/25/
terence-corcoran-fascism-by-another-name/.

60. Steven Chase, "Nexen Deal Called Dangerous Precedent," *Globe and
Mail*, September 26, 2012, http://www.theglobeandmail.com/news/
national/nexen-deal-called-dangerous-precedent/article4568593/.

61. Justin Trudeau, "Why the CNOOC-Nexen Deal Is Good
for Canada," Canada.com, November 19, 2012, http://o.
canada.com/2012/11/19/justin-trudeau-why-the-cnooc-ne

xen-deal-is-good-for-canada/; and Nathan Vanderklippe, Shawn McCarthy, and Jacquie McNish, "Harper Draws a Line in the Oil Sands," *Globe and Mail*, December 10, 2012, http://www.cigionline. org/articles/2012/12/harper-draws-line-oil-sands.

62. Industry Canada, "Guidelines—Investment by State-Owned Enterprises—Net Benefit Assessment," last modified December 7, 2012, http://www.ic.gc.ca/eic/site/ica-lic.nsf/eng/lk00064.html.

63. Asia Pacific Foundation of Canada, *2012 National Opinion Poll: Canadian Views on Asia* (Vancouver, BC, 2012).

64. Ibid., 17.

65. Ibid.

66. Ibid.

67. Ibid., 30. In 2006, 64 percent of those polled agreed that Canada "would benefit from more Asian investment to Canada, including the energy sector." See Gregg, Kelly, Sullivan, & Woolstencroft, The Strategic Counsel, *A Report to The Asia Pacific Foundation of Canada and The Globe and Mail: Canadian Views on Asia*, August 28, 2006, http://www.advisor.ca/news/industry-news/ briefly-888-30687.

68. Asia Pacific Foundation of Canada, *2012 National Opinion Poll*, 15.

69. Garth Stevenson, "Foreign Direct Investment and the Provinces: A Study of Elite Attitudes," *Canadian Journal of Political Science/Revue canadienne de science politique* 7, no. 4 (1974): 630–631.

70. "Statement by the Prime Minister of Canada on Foreign Investment," Canada News Centre, Government of Canada, December 7, 2012, http://news.gc.ca/web/article-eng.do?nid=711679.

71. Author interviews with Canadian industry sources.

72. OECD, StatExtracts, "FDI Flows by Industry," accessed September 6, 2013, http://stats.oecd.org/Index.aspx?DatasetCode=FDI_FLOW_ PARTNER.

73. OECD, StatExtracts, "FDI Flows by Partner Country," accessed September 6, 2013, http://stats.oecd.org/Index.aspx?DatasetCode= FDI_FLOW_PARTNER. Authors' calculations.

74. The Rhodium Group, "China Investment Monitor: Tracking Chinese Direct Investment in the U.S.," http://rhg.com/interactive/ china-investment-monitor.

75. Excluding a $1 billion investment in a Texas-based pipe-making plant in 2009, total Chinese investment in basic materials over the past decade is less than $400 million. Rhodium Group, "China Investment Monitor"; and Deloitte China Services Group, "Chinese Investment in the U.S.: Quarterly Digest," http://www.deloitte.com/

assets/Dcom-UnitedStates/Local%20Assets/Documents/us_csg_
InboundDigestQ22009_033101.pdf.

76. Rhodium Group, "China Investment Monitor."

77. Ibid.

78. Dick K. Nanto et al., "China and the CNOOC Bid for Unocal: Issues for Congress," Congressional Research Service, September 15, 2005, 11.

79. Daniel H. Rosen and Thilo Hanemann, "An American Open Door? Maximizing the Benefits of Chinese Foreign Direct Investment," Asia Society, May 2011.

80. Nanto et al., "China and the CNOOC Bid," 1.

81. Brad Foss, "Unocal Says It Was Ready to Accept Higher CNOOC Offer," *Associated Press*, July 25, 2005; Ben White, "Unocal Reveals Portrait of Negotiations," *Washington Post*, July 26, 2005; and "China Withdraws Unocal Bid," *Associated Press*, August 3, 2005.

82. Foss, "Unocal Says It Was Ready."

83. As quoted in Peter S. Goodman, "China Tells Congress to Back off Businesses," *Washington Post*, July 5, 2005.

84. As quoted in Don Lee and Elizabeth Douglass, "Chinese Drop Takeover Bid for Unocal," *Los Angeles Times*, August 3, 2006.

85. As reported in Paritosh Bansal, Soyoung Kim, and Benjamin Lim, "Special Report: The U.S. and China Start an M&A Cold War," *Reuters*, April 16, 2011, http://in.reuters.com/article/2011/04/16/idINIndia-56278420110416?feedType=RSS&feedName=everything&virtualBrandChannel=11709.

86. Keith Bradsher and Michael J. De La Merced, "China Woos Overseas Companies, Looking for Deals," Deal Book, *New York Times*, http://dealbook.nytimes.com/2012/12/11/china-woos-overseas-companies-looking-for-deals/?_r=0.

87. Ryan Dezember, "China Goes Shopping for Shale in U.S., Canada," *Deal Journal*, May 11, 2012, http://blogs.wsj.com/deals/2012/05/11/china-goes-shopping-for-shale-in-u-s-canada/.

88. Ibid.

89. Tasman Metals Limited, "Tasman Provides First NI 43-101 Resource for Olserum Heavy Rare Earth Element Project, Sweden," press release, February 27, 2013, http://finance.yahoo.com/news/tasman-provides-first-ni-43-134500782.html; and Robert Sullivan, "TMR Report Ranks Top 5 Rare Earth Mines Outside of China," Rare Earth Investing News, August 22, 2011, http://rareearthinvestingnews.com/4695-tmr-report-ranks-top-5-rare-earth-mines-outside-of-china.html.

90. Lydia Mulvany, "Pentagon Challenges Chinese Monopoly on Rare Earths," *Bloomberg News*, November 7, 2012.

Chapter 8

1. For example, Michael T. Klare, *Resource Wars: The New Landscape of Global Conflict* (New York: Macmillan, 2002).
2. Ibid.
3. David G. Victor, "What Resource Wars?" *National Interest* no. 92 (November/December 2007): 48–55.
4. For example, if oil prices were to rise to $200 a barrel, the oil import bill would still be barely more than 5 percent of Chinese GDP. Similarly, iron ore imports totaled slightly less than $100 billion in 2012, about 1.4 percent of GDP; China could afford to handle a substantial price rise even from there. For the latter figure, see Leslie Hook, "China Iron Ore Imports Hit Fresh High," *Financial Times*, January 10, 2013.
5. International Crisis Group, "Stirring up the South China Sea (I)," *Asia Report* no. 223 (April 23, 2012): 1; and Sam Bateman and Ralf Emmers, eds., *Security and International Politics in the South China Sea: Towards a Co-operative Management Regime* (New York: Routledge, 2008), 80.
6. U.S. Geological Survey, "Assessment of Undiscovered Oil and Gas Resources of Southeast Asia, 2010," World Petroleum Resources Assessment Project, 2010, http://pubs.usgs.gov/fs/2010/3015/pdf/FS10-3015.pdf.
7. "An Estimate of Undiscovered Conventional Oil and Gas Resources of the World, 2012," World Petroleum Resources Project, 2012, http://pubs.usgs.gov/fs/2012/3042/fs2012-3042.pdf.
8. International Crisis Group, "Stirring up the South China Sea (I)," 25.
9. U.S. EIA, "South China Sea," Analysis Briefs, last updated February 7, 2013, http://web.archive.org/web/20121207073513/http://www.eia.gov/countries/regions-topics.cfm?fips=SCS.
10. As described in Leslie Hook, "Gas Finds Give Impetus to China Sea Claim," *Financial Times*, November 9, 2012.
11. International Crisis Group, "Stirring up the South China Sea (I)," 25.
12. CNOOC Ltd., "Annual Report," 2011, http://www.cnoocltd.com/encnoocltd/tzzgx/dqbd/nianbao/images/2012412936.pdf, 3.
13. U.S. EIA, "East China Sea," Analysis Briefs, last updated September 25, 2012, http://www.eia.gov/countries/analysisbriefs/east_china_sea/east_china_sea.pdf.
14. Ibid.
15. Ibid.
16. Leszek Buszynski, "The South China Sea: Oil, Maritime Claims, and U.S.-China Strategic Rivalry," *Washington Quarterly* 35, no. 2 (2012): 140.

17. Grace Oh, "S. Korea Submits Formal Claim on East China Sea Shelf to U.N.," *Yonhap News Agency*, December 27, 2012, http://english. yonhapnews.co.kr/national/2012/12/27/43/0301000000AEN201 21227001100315F.HTML; and Ben Dolven, Shirley A. Kan, and Mark E. Manyin, *Maritime Territorial Disputes in East Asia: Issues for Congress*, Congressional Research Service, January 30, 2013.

18. Han-Yi Shaw, "The Inconvenient Truth Behind the Diaoyu Senkaku Islands," On the Ground, *New York Times*, April 19, 2012, http://kristof.blogs.nytimes.com/2012/09/19/the-inconvenient-tr uth-behind-the-diaoyusenkaku-islands/.

19. Aibing Guo and Rakteem Katakey, "Disputed Islands with 45 Years of Oil Split China, Japan," *Bloomberg Businessweek*, October 12, 2012, http://www.businessweek.com/news/2012-10-10/ disputed-islands-with-45-years-of-oil-split-china-japan.

20. Kevin Voigt, "Dangerous Waters: Behind the Islands Dispute," *CNN*, September 24, 2012, http://www.cnn.com/2012/09/24/world/ asia/china-japan-dispute-explainer; and Tania Branigan and Justin McCurry, "Japan Releases Chinese Fishing Boat Captain," *Guardian,* September 24, 2010.

21. Chinese Foreign Ministry spokesperson Jiang Yu, as quoted in "China FM Summons Japanese Ambassador over Japan's Seizure of Chinese Fishing Boat," *Xinhua,* September 10, 2010, http://news.xinhuanet. com/english2010/china/2010-09/10/c_13489262.htm

22. Martin Fackler and Ian Johnson, "Arrest in Disputed Seas Riles China and Japan," *New York Times,* September 19, 2010. From the Japanese Foreign Ministry: "The Ministry of Foreign Affairs of China announced that they 'would take strong counter measures' against Japan on its website. Xinhua News Agency reported the temporal suspension of mutual visits by ministerial level officials and above and the cancellation of aviation talks between Japan and China. The same announcement was made by a spokesperson of the Ministry of Foreign Affairs of China by September 20." See Ministry of Foreign Affairs of Japan, "Major Exchanges Between Japan and the People's Republic of China Concerning the Collision Incident Between Japan Coast Guard Patrol Vessels and a Chinese Fishing Trawler in Japanese Territorial Waters off the Senkaku Islands," October 2010, accessed July 2013, http://www.mofa. go.jp/region/asia-paci/china/r-relations/major_e.html.

23. As described and quoted in Fackler and Johnson, "Arrest in Disputed Seas."

24. As reported in Jiao Wu, "Premier Wen Urges Japan to Release Captain," *China Daily,* September 22, 2010, http://www.chinadaily. com.cn/china/2010-09/22/content_11337158.htm.

25. Keith Bradsher, "Amid Tension, China Blocks Vital Exports to Japan," *New York Times,* September 22, 2010.
26. Branigan and McCurry, "Japan Releases Chinese Fishing Boat Captain"; "Japan to Free Illegally Detained Chinese Boat Captain," *Xinhua,* September 24, 2010, http://news.xinhuanet.com/english2010/china/2010-09/24/c_13527494.htm; and "China to Bring Back Trawler Captain by Chartered Flight: FM Spokesperson," *People's Daily Online,* September 25, 2010, http://english.people.com.cn/90001/90776/90883/7149097.html.
27. Keith Bradsher, "China Restarts Rare Earth Shipments to Japan," *New York Times,* November 19, 2010.
28. As quoted and reported in "Senkaku Islands Dispute Escalates as China Sends out Patrol Ships," *Associated Press,* September 11, 2012.
29. As quoted in ibid.
30. As quoted in "China Issues White Paper on Diaoyu Dao, Asserting Indisputable Sovereignty," *Xinhua,* September 25, 2012, http://news.xinhuanet.com/english/china/2012-09/25/c_131872082.htm.
31. As described and reported in Chris Buckley, "China Denies Directing Radar at Japanese Naval Vessel and Copter," *New York Times,* February 8, 2013.
32. Ibid. Full remarks from U.S. Department of State, "Daily Press Briefing," August 28, 2012, http://www.state.gov/r/pa/prs/dpb/2012/08/196986.htm#JAPAN.
33. Quote from transcript, U.S. Department of State, "Daily Press Briefing."
34. John H. Noer, *Choke Points: Maritime Economic Concerns in Southeast Asia,* Institute for National Strategic Studies at the National Defense University (Washington, DC: National Defense University Press, 1996), 31.
35. Office of the Secretary of Defense, *Annual Report to Congress: Military and Security Developments Involving the People's Republic of China* (May 2012), 37; and "Territorial Claims in South China Sea," *New York Times,* May 31, 2012, http://www.nytimes.com/interactive/2012/05/31/world/asia/Territorial-Claims-in-South-China-Sea.html.
36. Nong Hong, *UNCLOS and Ocean Dispute Settlement: Law and Politics in the South China Sea* (New York: Routledge, 2012), 16.
37. Noer, *Choke Points.*
38. As quoted in Ronald O'Rourke, "Maritime Territorial and Exclusive Economic Zone (EEZ) Disputes Involving China: Issues for Congress," *Congressional Research Service,* October 22, 2012, 7.
39. Ibid.

40. Kirk Spitzer, "New Garrison, Old Troubles in the South China Sea," *Time*, July 26, 2012, http://nation.time.com/2012/07/26/new-garrison-old-troubles-in-the-south-china-seas/.

41. The term was not formally defined until 2009, when State Councilor Dai Bingguo stated it at the July 2009 U.S.-China Strategic and Economic Dialogue. "Closing Remarks for U.S.-China Security and Economic Dialogue," U.S. Department of State, July 28, 2009, http://www.state.gov/secretary/rm/2009a/july/126599.htm.

42. "China Officially Labels Senkakus a 'Core Interest,'" *Japan Times*, April 27, 2013.

43. As described in Jane Perlez, "Alarm as China Issues Rules for Disputed Area," *New York Times*, December 1, 2012.

44. Ibid. For an alternative expert interpretation, see M. Taylor Fravel, "Hainan's New Maritime Regulations: An Update," *Diplomat*, January 3, 2013.

45. O'Rourke, "Maritime Territorial and Exclusive Economic Zone," 4.

46. Jörn Dosch, "The Spratly Islands Dispute: Order-Building on China's Terms?" *Harvard International Review*, August 18, 2011, http://hir.harvard.edu/the-spratly-islands-dispute-or der-building-on-china-s-terms.

47. "The South China Sea: A Maritime Hotspot," German Marshall Fund of the United States, June 6, 2012, http://blog.gmfus.org/2012/06/06/the-south-china-sea-a-maritime-hotspot/.

48. Richard Bush, "Chinese and Japanese Geo-Strategic Interests in the East China Sea," in *Conference Report of CNA Maritime Asia Project Workshop One: The Yellow and East China Seas*, ed. Michael A. McDevitt and Catherine K. Lea (Center for Naval Analysis, May 2012).

49. Phillip C. Saunders, Christopher Yung, Michael Swaine, and Andrew Nein-Dzu Yang, eds., *The Chinese Navy: Expanding Capabilities, Evolving Roles*, Center for the Study of Chinese Military Affairs of the Institute for National Strategic Studies (Washington, DC: National Defense University Press, 2011), 61.

50. J. E. Peterson, "Sovereignty and Boundaries in the Gulf States," in *International Politics of the Persian Gulf*, ed. Mehran Kamrava (Syracuse, NY: Syracuse University Press, 2011), 40.

51. Azerbaijan and Kazakhstan have both come to their own bilateral agreements with Russia regarding their maritime boundaries. Bernard A. Gelb, "Caspian Oil and Gas: Production and Prospects," Congressional Research Service, updated September 8, 2006. Iran and Turkmenistan, however, have resisted agreement. And the UN Convention on the Law of the Sea, which many would like to use in East Asia, applies only to waters accessible to all nations, not to

the landlocked Caspian. See Ben N. Dunlap, "Divide and Conquer? The Russian Plan for Ownership of the Caspian Sea," *Boston College International & Comparative Law Review* 27, no. 1 (2004).

52. As described in "U.N. to Consider Validity of China's Diaoyu Islands Claim," *Sina English*, January 25, 2013, http://english.sina.com/world/2013/0124/553404.html. According to the UN Committee on the Limits of the Continental Shelf, "The term 'continental shelf' is used by geologists generally to mean that part of the continental margin which is between the shoreline and the shelf break or, where there is no noticeable slope, between the shoreline and the point where the depth of the superjacent water is approximately between 100 and 200 metres. However, this term is used in article 76 as a juridical term. According to the Convention, the continental shelf of a coastal State comprises the submerged prolongation of the land territory of the coastal State—the seabed and subsoil of the submarine areas that extend beyond its territorial sea to the outer edge of the continental margin, or to a distance of 200 nautical miles where the outer edge of the continental margin does not extend up to that distance. The continental margin consists of the seabed and subsoil of the shelf, the slope and the rise. It does not include the deep ocean floor with its oceanic ridges or the subsoil thereof." See *United Nations Oceans and Law of the Sea*, "Commission on the Limits of the Continental Shelf (CLCS): The Continental Shelf," http://www.un.org/Depts/los/clcs_new/continental_shelf_description.htm#definition.

53. Guo and Katakey, "Disputed Islands."

54. As described in "U.N. to Consider Validity."

55. Office of the Secretary of Defense, *Annual Report to Congress* (May 2012), 37.

56. Ibid.

57. "Statement by Secretary of Foreign Affairs Albert del Rosario on the UNCLOS Arbitral Proceedings Against China to Achieve a Peaceful and Durable Solution to the Dispute in the WPS," http://www.gov.ph/2013/01/22/statement-the-secretary-of-foreign-affairs-on-the-unclos-arbitral-proceedings-against-china-january-22-2013/; and Pia Lee-Brago, "China Rejects UN Arbitration on West Phl Sea," *Philippine Star*, February 20, 2013, http://webcache.googleusercontent.com/search?q=cache:2o6SHHRXJwsJ:www.philstar.com/headlines/2013/02/20/910910/china-rejects-un-arbitration-west-phl-sea+&cd=1&hl=en&ct=clnk&gl=us&client=firefox-a, accessed September 6, 2013.

58. BP, *BP Statistical Review of World Energy 2012* (London: BP, June 2012), 20; and authors' calculations.

59. Ibid.; and authors' calculations.

60. Daniel Yergin, *The Quest: Energy, Security, and the Remaking of the Modern World* (New York: Penguin Group, 2011), 47.

61. Ibid.

62. "Statement of Steven R. Mann, Principal Deputy Assistant Secretary of State for South and Central Asian Affairs Before the House Committee on International Relations, Subcommittee on the Middle East and Central Asia, July 25, 2006 (henceforth Mann, Testimony)." As referenced in Stephen Blank, "U.S. Interests in Central Asia and the Challenges to Them," Strategic Studies Institute, U.S. Army War College, March 2007, 3.

63. Edward C. Chow and Leigh E. Hendrix, "Central Asia's Pipelines: Field of Dreams and Reality," National Bureau of Asian Research, September 2010, 34.

64. Ramakant Dwivedi, "China's Central Asia Policy in Recent Times," *China and Eurasia Forum Quarterly* 4, no. 4 (2006): 142.

65. For concerns about spillover, see M. Taylor Fravel, *Strong Borders, Secure Nation: Cooperation and Conflict in China's Territorial Disputes* (Princeton, NJ: Princeton University Press, 2008), 160.

66. Niklas Swanstrom, "China and Central Asia: A New Great Game or Traditional Vassal Relations?" *Journal of Contemporary China* 14, no. 45 (November 2005): 571–572.

67. "Shanghai Cooperation Organisation Charter," *Xinhua*, June 12, 2006, accessed September 5, 2013, http://web.archive.org/web/20120414193018/http://www.chinadaily.com.cn/china/2006-06/12/content_614628.htm.

68. Fravel, *Strong Borders, Secure Nation.*

69. Ibid.

70. "China Global Investment Tracker," Heritage Foundation, http://www.heritage.org/research/projects/china-global- investment-tracker-interactive-map.

71. "Update 2-CNPC, KazMunaiGas Buy MangistauMunaiGas for $2.6 bln," *Reuters*, November 25, 2009.

72. Julie Jiang and Jonathan Sinton, *Overseas Investments by Chinese National Oil Companies: Assessing the Drivers and Impacts*, Information Paper (Paris: International Energy Agency, June 2011), 18.

73. Jiang and Sinton, *Overseas Investments*, 18.

74. Interview with industry expert, Washington, DC, October 22, 2010; and "Majors Play Waiting Game in Turkmenistan," *Petroleum Intelligence Weekly*, December 7, 2009. As attributed in Erica Downs, *Inside China, Inc: China Development Bank's Cross-Border Energy Deals*, John L. Thornton China Center Monograph Series, no. 3 (Washington, DC: Brookings Institution, 2011), 53.

75. U.S. EIA, "China," Country Analysis Briefs, last updated September 4, 2012, http://www.eia.gov/countries/cab.cfm?fips=CH; and Marat Gurt, "China Asserts Clout in Central Asia with Huge Turkmen Gas Project, *Reuters*, September 4, 2013.

76. Erica Downs, "Inside China, Inc: China Development Bank's Cross-Border Energy Deals," presentation at the Woodrow Wilson Center, January 13, 2012, http://www.wilsoncenter.org/sites/default/files/Inside%20China%20Inc-Erica%20Downs.pdf, 13.

77. Vladimir Socor, "Beijing Proposes Turkmenistan-China Gas Pipeline Through Northern Afghanistan," *Eurasia Daily Monitor* 4, June 19, 2012, http://www.jamestown.org/single/?no_cache=1&tx_ttnews%5Btt_news%5D=39510.

78. U.S. EIA, "Kazakhstan," Country Analysis Briefs, last updated September 18, 2012, http://www.eia.gov/countries/analysisbriefs/Kazakhstan/kazakhstan.pdf; and BP, *Statistical Review of World Energy 2012* (London: BP, 2012), www.bp.com/statisticalreview.

79. Adam Blinick, "The Kazakh-China Oil Pipeline: 'A Sign of the Times,'" Working Paper No. 21, Center on China's Transnational Relations, the Hong Kong University of Science and Technology, Working Paper No. 21 (2006); and "Background Information," Kazakhstan-China Pipeline LLC, accessed August 2, 2013, http://www.kcp.kz/en/information/.

80. "Kazakhstan-China Oil Pipeline Opens to Commercial Operation," *Xinhua*, July 21, 2006, http://www.chinadaily.com.cn/china/2006-07/12/content_639147.htm; and Maria Golovnina, "Kazakhstan, China Agree on Pipeline from Caspian," *Reuters*, August 18, 2007, http://uk.reuters.com/article/2007/08/18/kazakhstan-china-idUKL1872705320070818.

81. U.S. EIA, "Kazakhstan."

82. U.S. EIA, "China"; and U.S. EIA, "Kazakhstan."

83. U.S. EIA, "China."

84. Ibid.

85. Downs, *Inside China, Inc*, 1–2.

86. John Roberts, "China, Turkmenistan Ink Loans-for-gas Deals; China to Lend $4 Billion to Ashgabat, to Get 40 Bcm/year of Gas," Platts Oilgram News, June 26, 2009. As cited in Downs, "Inside China, Inc." (2011), 53. Chinese companies have completed other natural gas deals in connection with the CAGP. In 2011, CNPC and Uzebekistan completed an agreement for delivery of more than 1 bcf per day through a line that connects with the CAGP, and in 2010 Kazakhstan and China agreed to form a joint venture to construct another pipeline to join to the CAGP, which will add another 360 bcf per day from Kazakhstan to the CAGP. U.S. EIA, "China."

87. Stephen Blank, "China's Water Policies in Central Asia and Leadership Potential," CACI Analyst, *Central Asia-Caucasus Institute*, November 26, 2009, http://cacianalyst.org/?q=node/5223.

88. Jeremy Allouche, "The Governance of Central Asian Waters: National Interests Versus Regional Cooperation," *Disarmament Forum*, 52.

89. UN Development Programme in Kazakhstan, *Water Resources of Kazakhstan in the New Millennium*, UNDPKAZ 07 (Almaty: LEM Printhouse, 2004), 41; "Aral Sea 'One of the Planet's Worst Environmental Disasters,'" *Telegraph*, April 5, 2010; Blank, "China's Water Policies"; and Eric Hagt, "China's Water Policies: Implications for Xinjiang and Kazakhstan," CACI Analyst, Central Asia-Caucasus Institute, July 30, 2003, http://www.cacianalyst.org/publications/analytical-articles/item/8255-analytical-articles-caci-analyst-2003-7-30-art-8255.html.

90. Sebastien Peyrouse, "Flowing Downstream: The Sino-Kazakh Water Dispute," *Jamestown Foundation China Brief* 7, no. 10 (May 16, 2007); and Allouche, "Governance of Central Asian Waters," 52.

91. "Conflict of Interest Has Created Water Crisis," European Dialogue, April 13, 2011, http://eurodialogue.org/conflict-of-interests-has-created-water-crisis.

92. "Kazakhstan and China Discuss Construction of Waterworks Facilities at Transborder Rivers," *Oslo Times*, January 18, 2013, http://theoslotimes.com/index.php?option=com_content&view=article&id=8414:Kazakhstan-and-china-discuss-construction-of-waterworks-facilities-at-transborder-rivers.

93. Aygun Badalova, "Kazakhstan, China to Build Waterworks Facilities on Trans-border Rivers," Trend News Agency, January 22, 2013, http://en.trend.az/regions/casia/kazakhstan/2110713.html; and "Kazakhstan-Chinese Water Control Structure Opened on Khorgos River," BK News, July 5, 2013, http://www.bnews.kz/en/news/post/147600/.

94. Elizabeth Economy, "Prepared Statement of Dr. Elizabeth Economy: Testimony Before the U.S.-China Economic and Security Review Commission," Hearing: China's Global Quest for Resources and Implications for the United States, January 26, 2012, 37.

95. Marko Keskinen, Katri Mehtonen, and Olli Varis, "Transboundary Cooperation vs. Internal Ambitions: The Role of China and Cambodia in the Mekong Region," in *International Water Security: Domestic Threats and Opportunities,* ed. Nevelina I. Pachova, Mikiyasu Nakayama, and Libor Jansky (Tokyo: United Nations University Press, 2008), 82.

96. "Kristensen, J. 2001A. Food Security and Development in the Lower Mekong River Basin: A Challenge for the Mekong River Commission.

Paper delivered at the Asia and Pacific Forum on Poverty: Reforming Policies and Institutions for Poverty Reduction, Manila, 5–9 February 2001." As referenced in Jeffrey W. Jacobs, "The Mekong River Commission: Transboundary Water Resources Planning and Regional Security," *Geographical Journal* 168, no. 4 (December 2002): 356; and Evelyn Goh, "China in the Mekong River Basin: The Regional Security Implications of Resource Development on the Lancang Jiang," Institute of Defence and Strategic Studies, Working Paper No. 69, July 2004, 1.

97. Ellen Bruzelius Backer, "The Mekong River Commission: Does It Work, and How Does the Mekong Basin's Geography Influence Its Effectiveness?" *Südostasien aktuell* 4/2007, 2007, 37–38.

98. Matthew Garcia, "Chinese Dam Building Tests Southeast Asian Resilience," *Atlantic Sentinel*, March 10, 2012, http://atlanticsentinel. com/2012/03/chinese-dam-building-tests-southeast-asian-resilience/.

99. Goh, "China in the Mekong River Basin"; Fred Pearce, "The Damming of the Mekong: Major Blow to an Epic River," Yale Environment 360 Report, June 16, 2009, http://e360.yale.edu/ feature/the_damming_of_the_mekong_major_blow_to_an_epic_ river/2162/; and "China becomes hydro superpower," *Xinhua*, August 26, 2010, http://www.chinadaily.com.cn/business/2010-08/26/ content_11204360.htm.

100. Pearce, "Damming of the Mekong"; and Yoolim Lee, "China Hydropower Dams in Mekong River Give Shocks to 60 Million," *Bloomberg*, October 26, 2010, http://www.bloomberg. com/news/2010-10-26/china-hydropower-dams-in-mekong-ri ver-give-shocks-to-60-million.html.

101. Pearce, "Damming of the Mekong."

102. Keskinen et al., "Transboundary Cooperation," in *International Water Security*, ed. Pachova et al., 82–83.

103. "Kummu and Varis 2007; Kummu et al. 2007." As referenced in Keskinen et al., "Transboundary Cooperation," in *International Water Security*, ed. Pachova et al., 82.

104. As reported in Pearce, "Damming of the Mekong."

105. "MRC http://www.lars2.org/Proceedings/vol1/Mekong_River_system. pdf." As referenced in Philip Hirsch and Kurt M. Jensen, "National Interests and Transboundary Water Governance in the Mekong," University of Sydney, May 2006, 16.

106. Calum MacLeod, "China's New Dam Seen as a Water Hog," *USA Today*, April 22, 2010, http://usatoday30.usatoday.com/news/world/ environment/2010-04-21-china-dam_N.htm.

107. Ibid.

108. Yonglin Tang, "Lancang River Will Test China's River Diplomacy [Lancang Jiang Kaoyan Zhungguo Heliu Waijiao]," *Southern Weekend*, April 1, 2010, http://www.infzm.com/content/43354.
109. Ibid.
110. MacLeod, "China's New Dam."
111. Banyan, "Drought, Floods and China's Dam-building Plans in Yunnan: Dammed If You Do," *Economist*, July 4, 2010, www.economist.com/blogs/banyan/2010/07/drought_floods_and_chinas_dam-building_plans_yunnan.
112. Mekong River Commission for Sustainable Development, "Mekong Prime Ministers Agree to Prioritise Climate Change as Summit Ends," press release, April 5, 2010, http://www.mrcmekong.org/news-and-events/news/mekong-prime-ministers-agree-to-prioritise-climate-change-as-summit-ends/.
113. Isabel Hilton, "Diverting the Brahmaputra—Much Ado About Nothing?" China Water Risk, February 9, 2012, http://chinawaterrisk.org/opinions/diverting-the-brahmaputra-much-ado-about-nothing/.
114. "Horgan, J., 1996. Peaceful Nuclear Explosions: China's interest in this technology may scuttle a test-ban treaty. Scientific American, 274(6): 14–15"; and "Cathcart, R. B., 1999. Tibetan power: A unique hydro-electric macroproject servicing India and China. Current Science, 77(7): 854–855." As referenced in Muhammad M. Rahaman and Olli Varis, "Integrated Water Management of the Brahmaputra Basin: Perspectives and Hope for Regional Development," *Natural Resources Forum Special Issue: Integrated Water Resources Management in Water-Stressed Countries* 33, no. 1 (February 2009): 72.
115. Chellaney, *Water*, 132.
116. Ibid.
117. Jonathan Watts, "Chinese Engineers Propose World's Biggest Hydro-electric Project in Tibet," *Guardian*, May 24, 2010, http://www.guardian.co.uk/environment/2010/may/24/chinese-hydroengineers-propose-tibet-dam; and U.S. EIA, "International Energy Statistics," http://www.eia.gov/cfapps/ipdbproject/iedindex3.cfm?tid=90&pid=44&aid=8.
118. Chellaney, *Water*, 139.
119. Ibid., 154.
120. Ananth Krishnan, "Brahmaputra Waters Will Not Be Diverted, Indicates China," *Hindu*, June 14, 2011, www.thehindu.com/news/international/article2103736.ece.
121. Indrani Bagchi, "Relief for India as China Says No Brahmaputra Diversion," *Times of India*, October 14, 2011, http://articles.timesofindia.indiatimes.com/2011-10-14/india/30278545_1_brahmaputra-yarlung-tsangpo-india-and-china.

122. Robert G. Wirsing, Christopher Jasparro, and Daniel C. Stoll, *International Conflict over Water Resources in Himalayan Asia: Conflict and Cooperation over Asia's Water Resources* (New York, Palgrave Macmillan, 2013), 123.

123. Hilton, "Diverting the Brahmaputra."

124. Brahma Chellaney, "The Sino-Indian Water Divide," *Project Syndicate*, August 3, 2009, http://www.project-syndicate.org/commentary/the-s ino-indian-water-divide.

125. "In the Fight for China's Water Resources, Who Will the Next Country Be? [Zhengduo Zhongguo Shui Ziyuan, Xia Yige Guojia Hui Shi Shei?]" ChinaIISS.com, March 28, 2013, http://grass.chinaiiss. com/html/20103/28/wa2ca8.html.

126. Wang Yan, "The River Wild," *NewsChina Magazine*, January 2012, http://www.newschinamag.com/magazine/the-river-wild.

127. Phunchok Stobdan, "IDSA Comment: China Should Not Use Water as a Threat Multiplier," Institute for Defence Studies and Analyses, October 23, 2009, http://www.idsa.in/idsastrategiccomments/ Chinashouldnotusewaterasathreatmultiplier_PStobdan_231009.

128. "Abu Dhabi Host the 4th Dialogue on Southern Asia Water Cooperation," AMEinfo.com, October 24, 2009, http://www. ameinfo.com/213463.html.

129. Ananth Krishnan, "China Gives Go-ahead for Three New Brahmaputra Dams," *The Hindu*, January 30, 2013.

130. "PM Allays Fears on China Dams," *Assam Tribune*, March 7, 2013, http://www.assamtribune.com/scripts/detailsnew.asp?id=mar0713/ at05.

Chapter 9

1. Josh Chin, "China Vows to Protect Chinese in Libya," *Wall Street Journal*, February 25, 2011.

2. Gabe Collins and Andrew Erickson, "China Dispatches Warship to Protect Libya Evacuation Mission: Marks the PRC's First Use of Frontline Military Assets to Protect an Evacuation Mission," China SignPost, No. 25, February 24, 2011, http://www. chinasignpost.com/2011/02/china-dispatches-warship-to-protect-li bya-evacuation-mission-marks-the-prc%E2%80%99s-first-use- of-frontline-military-assets-to-protect-an-evacuation-mission/.

3. Julie Jiang and Jonathan Sinton, *Overseas Investments by Chinese National Oil Companies: Assessing the Drivers and Impacts*, Information Paper (Paris: International Energy Agency, June 2011), 8.

4. U.S. EIA, "World Oil Transit Chokepoints," Analysis Briefs, last updated August 22, 2012.

5. Ibid.

6. It might seem as though ships from the southern part of South America would do better to travel around the southern tip of South America and onward through the Pacific. But sea currents move in the opposite direction, and the passage below South America is particularly treacherous.

7. Office of the Secretary of Defense, *Annual Report to Congress: Military and Security Developments Involving the People's Republic of China* (2011).

8. Ibid., 24.

9. " '近岸' can also be translated as 'in-shore.' '近海' is sometimes translated as 'off-shore.' But 'off-shore' is too vague to reflect the relative distance that the Chinese term intends to express. To the extent the Eurocentric terms of Near East, Middle East, and Far East are translated as 近东, 中东, and 远东, it is appropriate to translate the Sinocentric terms of '近海,' '中海,' and '远海' as 'near seas,' 'middle seas,' and 'far seas' to reflect the relative distance from China's shores." As described in note 6 in Nan Li, "The Evolution of China's Naval Strategy and Capabilities: From 'Near Coast' and 'Near Seas' to 'Far Seas,'" in *The Chinese Navy*, ed. Saunders et al., 135.

10. As quoted in Nan Li, "The Evolution of China's Naval Strategy and Capabilities: From 'Near Coast' and 'Near Seas' to 'Far Seas,'" in *The Chinese Navy*, ed. Saunders et al., 129.

11. "Jiang and Hu cited in Tang and Wu, 'A Study of China's Sea Defense Strategy,' 93; Jiang cited in Wang Zhigang, 'Haijun shi hanwei guojia liyi tuozhan de zhongyao liliang' [Navy Is an Important Force in Defending the Extension and Development of National Interests], *Guofang daxue xuebao (Journal of NDU)*, no. 10 (2005), 24; and in Chen Xuesong, Du Kai, 'Zhongguo de haiquan yu haijun fazhan jianshe' [China's Sea Power Consciousness and Navy Development and Construction], *Military History*, 4 (2008), 72." As cited in note 67 in Nan Li, "The Evolution of China's Naval Strategy and Capabilities: From 'Near Coast' and 'Near Seas' to 'Far Seas,'" in *The Chinese Navy*, ed. Saunders et al., 139.

12. David Lai, "Chinese Military Going Global," *China Security* 5, no. 1 (Winter 2009): 4.

13. "On the PLA's Historical Mission in the New Stage of the New Century," *Jiefangjun Bao* (PLA newspaper), January 9, 2006. As described in note 3 in Lai, "Chinese Military Going Global," 4.

14. John Garnaut, "Xi's War Drums," *Foreign Policy* (May/June 2013).

15. Office of the Secretary of Defense, *Annual Report to Congress* (2011).

16. Ibid.

17. Ibid.

18. Andrew Erickson and Lyle Goldstein, "Gunboats for China's New 'Grand Canals'?" *Naval War College Review* 62, no. 2 (Spring 2009).

19. Teddy Ng, "Xi Jinping Calls on Navy to Be Prepared for Struggle," *South China Morning Post*, April 12, 2013.

20. Erickson and Goldstein, "Gunboats," 60.

21. Ibid., 64.

22. Collins and Erickson, "China Dispatches Warship"; and Gabe Collins and Andrew Erickson, "The PLA Air Force's First Overseas Operational Deployment: Analysis of China's Decision to Deploy IL-76 Transport Aircraft to Libya," China SignPost, March 1, 2011, http://www.chinasignpost.com/2011/03/ the-pla-air-force%E2%80%99s-first-overseas-operational -deployment-analysis-of-china%E2%80%99s-decision-to-de ploy-il-76-transport-aircraft-to-libya/.

23. "PLA Navy Escort Mission in the Gulf of Aden," SinoDefence.com, May 1, 2009, http://www.sinodefence.com/special/operations/ anti-piracy.asp.

24. Cong Wang, "China to Send Navy to Fight Somali Pirates," *Xinhua*, http://news.xinhuanet.com/english/2008-12/18/content_10525310. htm.

25. Ministry of Foreign Affairs of the People's Republic of China, "Foreign Ministry Spokesperson Liu Jianchao's Regular Press Conference on December 18, 2008," http://www.fmprc.gov.cn/eng/ xwfw/s2510/t526955.htm.

26. Ibid.

27. "PLA Navy Escort Mission."

28. China Military Online, "14th and 15th Chinese Naval Escort Taskforces Complete Mission Handover," *People's Daily Online*, August 26, 2013, http://english.people.com.cn/90786/8377070.html.

29. Kamlesh K. Agnihotri, "Four Years of Anti-Piracy Mission: Chinese Navy's Showcase Achievement," National Maritime Foundation, January 22, 2013, http://www.maritimeindia.org/four-years-anti- piracy-mission-chinese-navy%E2%80%99s-showcase-achievement. html.

30. Daozu Bao, "Pirate Attacks Prompt Tighter Security," *China Daily*, November 26, 2010, http://english.sina.com/ china/2010/1125/349691.html.

31. In June 2008, the UN Security Council adopted a resolution that called on countries to use " 'all necessary means' to repress acts of piracy and armed robbery at sea." See Department of Public Information, "Security Council Condemns Acts of Piracy, Armed Robbery off Somalia's Coast, Authorizes for Six Month 'All

Necessary Means' to Repress Such Acts: Resolution 1816 (2008) Adopted Unanimously with Somalia's Consent; Measures Do Not Affect Rights, Obligations Under Law of Sea Convention," UN Security Council, June 2, 2008; and UN Security Council, "Security Council Resolution 1816 (2008) on Acts of Piracy and Armed Robbery Against Vessels in Territorial Waters and the High Seas off the Coast of Somalia," S/RES/1816 (2008), June 2, 2008, http://www.unhcr.org/refworld/docid/48464c622.html. In October 2008, the UNSC passed another resolution that urged "States that have the capacity to do so to cooperate with the [Transitional Federal Government] in the fight against piracy and armed robbery at sea in conformity with the provisions of resolution 1816 (2008)" and followed it up with another resolution in early December 2008 that called upon "states and regional organizations that have the capacity to do so, to take part actively in the fight against piracy and armed robbery at sea off the coast of Somalia...by deploying naval vessels and military aircraft." See UN Security Council, "Security Council Resolution 1838 (2009) on Acts of Piracy and Armed Robbery Against Vessels in Territorial Waters and the High Seas off the Coast of Somalia," S/RES/1838 (2008), October 7, 2008, http://www.unhcr.org/refworld/docid/48ef651f2.html; and UN Security Council, "Security Council Resolution 1846 (2008) on Repressing Acts of Piracy and Armed Robbery at Sea off the Coast of Somalia," S/RES/1846 (2008), December 2, 2008, http://www. unhcr.org/refworld/docid/493e3f852.html. The UNSC repeated this call to action later on December 16, 2008. See UN Security Council, "Security Council Resolution 1851 (2008) on Fight Against Piracy and Armed Robbery at Sea off the Coast of Somalia," S/RES/1851 (2008), December 16, 2008, http://www.unhcr.org/ refworld/docid/4952044e2.html. By the time China deployed, many other countries, among them Denmark, the United States, the United Kingdom, Malaysia, Russia, and India as well as EU member states (Finland and France) and NATO forces, were already active in counter-piracy operations in the region. See Commodore Per Bigum Christensen, "Task Force 150 Anti-piracy Operations," presentation, Combined Maritime Forces, January 25, 2009, http:// www.doc-txt.com/Pirates.ppt; Admiral Danish Fleet, "Task Force 150 / 151," Navy, accessed on March 1, 2013, http://forsvaret.dk/ SOK/eng/International/TF150/Pages/default.aspx; and Combined Maritime Forces Public Affairs, "New Counter-Piracy Task Force Established," U.S. Navy NNS090108-01, January 8, 2009, http:// www.navy.mil/submit/display.asp?story_id=41687.

32. "Combined Task Force (CTF) 151," Combined Maritime Forces, accessed September 5, 2013, http://web.archive.org/web/20121022004947/http://www.cusnc.navy.mil/cmf/151/.

33. "CMF Hosts 21st SHADE Meeting," Combined Maritime Forces, September 27, 2011, http://combinedmaritimeforces.com/2011/09/27/cmf-hosts-21st-shade-meeting/.

34. Daniel J. Kostecka, "Places and Bases: The Chinese Navy's Emerging Support Network in the Indian Ocean," *Naval War College Review* 64, no. 1 (Winter 2011).

35. C. Raja Mohan, *Samudra Manthan: Sino-Indian Rivalry in the Indo-Pacific* (Washington, DC: Carnegie Endowment for International Peace, 2012), 127.

36. Declan Walsh, "Chinese Company Will Run Strategic Pakistani Port," *New York Times*, January 31, 2013.

37. As reported in Farhan Bokhari and Kathrin Hille, "Pakistan Turns to China for Naval Base," *Financial Times*, May 22, 2011. See also Gideon Rachman, "A Chinese Base in Pakistan?" The World, *Financial Times,* May 23, 2011, http://blogs.ft.com/the-world/2011/05/a-chinese-base-in-pakistan/.

38. The authors thank Erica Downs for this observation.

39. "Hoffman, 2010, p. 54." As cited in Ryan Henry et al., *Promoting International Energy Security: Volume 3, Sea-Lanes to Asia*, RAND Project Air Force (Santa Monica, CA: Rand Corporation, 2012), 23.

40. "The term 'place' as opposed to a 'base' was used by Adm. Thomas B. Fargo, then commander, U.S. Pacific Command, during March 31, 2004, testimony before the House Armed Services Committee, available at www.pacom.mil/." As cited in Kostecka, "Places and Bases."

41. Dingli Shen, "Don't Shun the Idea of Setting up Overseas Military Bases," China.org.cn, January 8, 2010, http://www.china.org.cn/opinion/2010-01/28/content_19324522.htm.

42. Kostecka, "Places and Bases," 72.

43. Ibid.

44. The first stage was completed in 2009 and runs west to east from Taishet (in East Siberia) to Skovorodino, roughly forty miles from the Chinese border, but still in Russian territory. This part of the pipeline has a capacity of 600,000 barrels a day. In 2009, China agreed to finance Russian construction of a thirty-eight-mile overland spur to China. Under the deal, backed by $25 billion in Chinese loans, Russia agreed to sell China 300,000 barrels of oil a day through the pipeline for twenty years. CNPC and the Russian company Rosneft then signed a twenty-year contract for the delivery of 300,000 barrels per day to China, starting in 2011. See Platts, "Russian Crude Oil Exports to the Pacific Basin—an ESPO Update," Special Report, February 2011.

45. Sudha Ramachandran, "China Secures Myanmar Energy Route," *Asia Times Online*, April 3, 2009, http://www.atimes.com/atimes/South_Asia/KD03Df03.html.

46. "Burma-China Gas Pipeline Ready in May," *Irrawaddy*, January 22, 2013, http://www.irrawaddy.org/archives/24800.

47. Andrew S. Erickson and Gabriel B. Collins, "China's Oil Security Pipe Dream: The Reality, and Strategic Consequences, of Seaborne Imports," *Naval War College Review* 63, no. 2 (Spring 2010); and May Thingyan Hein, "Myanmar-China Pipeline Leaves Trail of Worries, Complaints," *Business Recorder*, January 21, 2013, http://www.brecorder.com/index.php?option=com_news&view=single&id=1146110.

48. Boyuan Chen, "Myanmar Pipeline Project Gives China Pause for Thought," China.org.cn, June 21, 2013, www.china.org.cn/business/2013-06/21/content_29188744.htm.

49. Ibid.

50. European Council on Foreign Relations and Asia Centre, "China's Sea Power, Reaching out to the Blue Waters," *China Analysis*, March 2011, http://www.ecfr.eu/page/-/China%20Analysis%200311.pdf.

51. Bo Kong, *China's International Petroleum Policy* (Santa Barbara, CA: Praeger Security International, 2010), 130.

52. Ibid.

53. Sui Southern Gas Co. Ltd., "Karakoram Oil Pipeline: Gawadur to Khunjraab Pass to China," presentation, http://www.ssgc.com.pk/ssgc/media_center/presentations/pdf/karakorum.pdf.

54. Olivier Degomme and Debarati Guha-Sapir, "Patterns of Mortality Rates in Darfur Conflict," *Lancet* 375, no. 9711 (January 23, 2010).

55. International Crisis Group, "Darfur: The Failure to Protect," *Africa Report* no. 89, March 8, 2005, http://www.crisisgroup.org/en/regions/africa/horn-of-africa/sudan/089-darfur-the-failure-to-protect.aspx; and Alex de Waal, "Darfur and the Failure of the Responsibility to Protect," *International Affairs* 83, no. 6 (November 2007).

56. International Crisis Group, "Darfur's New Security Reality," Africa Report no. 134, November 26, 2007; and de Waal, "Darfur and the Failure." Most sources suggest Khartoum lacked the capacity to disarm the militias anyway.

57. China National Petroleum Corporation, "CNPC in Sudan," 2011, http://www.cnpc.com.cn/en/cnpcworldwide/sudan/PageAssets/Images/CNPC-in-Sudan.pdf?COLLCC=35518968&.

58. Julie Jiang and Jonathan Sinton, *Overseas Investments by Chinese National Oil Companies: Assessing the Drivers and Impacts*, Information Paper (Paris: International Energy Agency, June 2011), 14.

59. Ibid., 17.

60. Daniel Large, "China's Sudan Engagement: Changing Northern and Southern Political Trajectories in Peace and War," *China Quarterly*, no. 199 (September 2009).

61. "9 Chinese Oil Workers Are Kidnapped in Sudan," *Reuters,* October 19, 2008.

62. U.S. EIA, "Total Oil Supply (Thousand Barrels Per Day)," *International Energy Statistics*, March 1, 2013, http://www.eia.gov/cfapps/ipdbproject/iedindex3.cfm?tid=5&pid=53&aid=1&cid=regions&syid=2004&eyid=2011&unit=TBPD.

63. Human Security Baseline Assessment, "Arms, Oil, and Darfur: The Evolution of Relations Between China and Sudan," *Sudan Issue Brief: Small Arms Survey* (7), July 2007, http://www.smallarmssurveysudan.org/fileadmin/docs/issue-briefs/HSBA-IB-07-Arms.pdf.

64. "Li Anshan, 'China and Africa: policy and challenges,' China Security, Vol. 3 No. 3 (2007), p. 77." As cited in Large, "China's Sudan Engagement," 619.

65. Gaafar Karrar Ahmed, "The Chinese Stance on the Darfur Conflict," SAIIA China in Africa Project, Occasional Paper No. 67, September 2010, 6–7.

66. Ibid.; and Human Security Baseline Assessment, "Arms, Oil, and Darfur."

67. Human Security Baseline Assessment, "Arms, Oil, and Darfur," 7.

68. Ibid.; and Human Security Baseline Assessment, "United Nations Resolutions on Sudan," Sudan Documents, http://www.smallarmssurveysudan.org/documents/united-nations-resolutions-on-sudansouth-sudan.html.

69. Ahmed, "The Chinese Stance," 8–10; and Human Security Baseline Assessment, "Arms, Oil, and Darfur," 8.

70. For views on China's abstentions, see Ahmed, "The Chinese Stance"; International Crisis Group, "China's Growing Role in UN Peacekeeping," Asia Report no. 166, April 17, 2009, http://www.crisisgroup.org/~/media/Files/asia/north-east-asia/166_chinas_growing_role_in_un_peacekeeping.ashx; and John Prendergast and David Sullivan, "Irresolution: The U.N. Security Council on Darfur," ENOUGH Strategy Paper 33, July 2008, http://www.enoughproject.org/files/unsc_%20july_%2024-2_0.pdf.

71. For example, see Stephanie Kleine-Ahlbrandt and Andrew Small, "China's New Dictatorship Diplomacy," *Foreign Affairs* 87, no. 1 (January/February 2008); and Nicholas D. Kristof, "China's Genocide Olympics," *New York Times,* January 24, 2008.

72. Amnesty International, *Sudan: No End to Violence in Darfur* (London: Amnesty International Publications, 2012); United Nations Security Council, "Report of the Panel of Experts Established Pursuant to Resolution 1591 (2005) Concerning the Sudan. S/2009/562 of 29 October 2009," 2009, http://www.smallarmssurveysudan.org/fileadmin/docs/documents/HSBA-Sec-Gen-2009-562.pdf; and Human Security Baseline Assessment, "Arms, Oil, and Darfur."

73. Hilary Andersson, "China 'Is Fuelling War in Darfur,'" *BBC News* July 13, 2008; and Stockholm International Peace Research Institute, "SIPRI Arms Transfers Database," http://www.sipri.org/databases/armstransfers.

74. David Albright and Andrea Stricker, "Iran's Nuclear Program," in *The Iran Primer: Power, Politics, and U.S. Policy*, ed. Robin Wright (Washington, DC: United States Institute for Peace Press, 2010).

75. U.S. EIA, "Iran," Country Analysis Briefs, last updated March 28, 2013, http://www.eia.gov/countries/cab.cfm?fips=IR.

76. Xiaocong Wang, "China's CNPC Performs Balancing Act in Iran," *Caixin Online*, September 26, 2012, http://articles.marketwatch.com/2012-09-26/industries/34084845_1_cnpc-south-pars-project-south-azadegan.

77. "Work Starts at 2 of Iran's Oil Fields to Produce 700,000 bpd," *Tehran Times*, July 8, 2012, http://tehrantimes.com/economy-and-business/99442-chinese-company-invests-20b-in-iranian-oil-fields; and Erica Downs, "Getting China to Turn on Iran," *National Interest*, July 19, 2012, http://nationalinterest.org/commentary/getting-china-turn-iran-7215?page=1.

78. Aizhu Chen and Chris Buckley, "Exclusive: China Curbs Iran Energy Work," *Reuters*, September 2, 2011.

79. U.S. EIA, "Iran."

80. Ibid.; and "Iran Warns of Cancelling $5 Billion China Gas Deal," *Nation*, December 25, 2012, http://www.nation.com.pk/pakistan-news-newspaper-daily-english-online/international/25-Dec-2012/iran-warns-of-cancelling-5-billion-china-gas-deal.

81. Sanchez Wang, "Iran, China Sign $5 Billion Contract on South Pars Gas Field," *Bloomberg*, June 9, 2009, http://www.bloomberg.com/apps/news?pid=newsarchive&sid=aWVnwjppjOXI.

82. Zahra Hosseinian, "Iran Warns China over South Pars Gas Deal-report," *Reuters*, June 17, 2011.

83. "China Pulls out of South Pars Project," *Upstream*, July 30, 2012, http://www.upstreamonline.com/live/article1261785.ece.

84. Wang, "China's CNPC Performs Balancing Act."

85. As quoted in S. Isayev, "CNPC Reveals Reason for Withdrawing from Iran's South Pars Project," TREND News Agency, *McClatchy Tribune Business News*, September 28, 2012. Accessed via Nexis.
86. Wang, "China's CNPC Performs Balancing Act."
87. As quoted in Chen Aizhu, "Exclusive: China Slows Iran Oil Work as U.S. Energy Ties Warm," *Reuters*, October 28, 2010.
88. Michael C. Davis, "The Reluctant Intervenor: The UN Security Council, China's Worldview, and Humanitarian Intervention," in *International Intervention in the Post-Cold War World*, ed. Michael C. Davis, Wolfgang Dietrich, Bettina Scholdan, and Dieter Sepp, (New York: Sharpe, 2004).
89. Matthew Kroenig, *Exporting the Bomb: Technology Transfer and the Spread of Nuclear Weapons* (Ithaca, NY: Cornell University Press, 2010); and John W. Garver, "Is China Playing a Dual Game in Iran?" *Washington Quarterly* 34, no. 1 (Winter 2011).
90. The credibility of such a prospect depends on how large the country in question is and on the length of the notional refusal to buy minerals; for at least short periods, China could substitute minerals from stockpiles for otherwise necessary imports.
91. Author interview with senior oil official, Maputo, Mozambique, January 2013.
92. Author interview with industry experts, Doha, Qatar, November 2012.
93. Author interview with industry experts, Kuwait, November 2012.

Chapter 10
1. U.S. Geological Survey, "Iron Ore," *Mineral Commodity Summaries*, January 2013, http://minerals.usgs.gov/minerals/pubs/commodity/iron_ore/mcs-2013-feore.pdf.
2. Michael Levi, *The Power Surge: Energy, Opportunity, and the Battle for America's Future* (New York: Oxford University Press, 2013).
3. Ibid.
4. The United States is taking action to become EITI-compliant, as of 2013. In 2011, the United States pledged to implement EITI.
5. Michael Levi, *A Strategy for U.S. Natural Gas Exports*, Hamilton Project, Discussion Paper 2012-4 (Washington, DC: Brookings Institution, June 2012).

MAPS

MAP 1. China and the Surrounding Region.
Source: Adapted from "Blank Maps: World Map Gallery Vol. 2," Alternate History Wiki, http://wiki.alternatehistory.com/doku.php/blank_map_directory/world_2, Accessed August 2013.

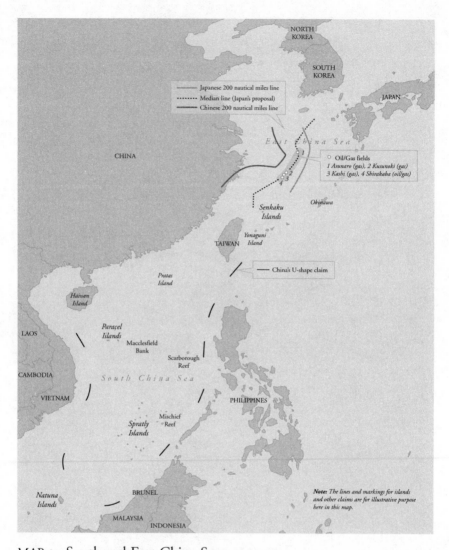

MAP 2. South and East China Seas.
Source: China and Japan Territorial Claims, in Ben Dolven, Shirley A. Kan, and
Mark E. Manyin, "Maritime Territorial Disputes in East Asia: Issues for Congress,"
Congressional Research Service, January 30, 2013, p. 14.

GLOSSARY OF CHINESE ENTITIES

Aluminum Corporation of China (Chinalco): A state-owned holding company that is one of the top aluminum and alumina producers in the world and the parent company of the New York Stock Exchange–listed Chalco.

Aluminum Corporation of China Limited (Chalco): China's largest alumina and aluminum producer; state-owned Aluminum Corporation of China (Chinalco) is its controlling shareholder. Chalco is listed on the New York, Hong Kong, and Shanghai stock exchanges.

Bank of China: The Bank of China is one of the four main Chinese state-owned commercial banks.

Baosteel (Shanghai Baosteel Group): Baosteel is a large state-owned holding group that primarily operates in iron and steel. Baosteel's subsidiary Baoshan Iron and Steel Company Limited is listed on the Shanghai and Shenzhen stock exchanges.

Beidahuang Group: Beidahuang Group is the largest state-owned agricultural enterprise in China.

Chalco: See Aluminum Corporation of China Limited.

China Banking Regulatory Commission (CBRC): Under the direction of the State Council, the CBRC supervises the banking sector and establishes rules and regulations for banking institutions.

China Development Bank (CDB): A state-owned bank under the jurisdiction of the State Council that is used to finance China's economic priorities and infrastructure.

China Investment Corporation (CIC): A state-owned investment institution, this sovereign wealth fund manages a substantial part of China's foreign exchange reserves.

China Metallurgical Group Corporation (MCC): A large state-owned holding group specializing in natural resources development and metallurgical engineering. Its subsidiary Metallurgical Corporation of China Limited is listed on the Shanghai and Hong Kong stock exchanges.

China National Agricultural Development Group Corporation (CNADC): A state-owned agricultural enterprise under direct governance of the State-owned Assets Supervision and Administration Commission.

China National Machinery and Equipment Import and Export Corporation (CMEC, or China Machinery Engineering Corporation): Founded in 1978 as a state-owned enterprise, CMEC was a large engineering and trade company and was renamed the China Machinery Engineering Corporation. CMEC is a subsidiary of the China National Machinery Industry Corporation and went public in 2012 on the Hong Kong Stock Exchange.

China National Offshore Oil Corporation (CNOOC): CNOOC is a state-owned enterprise and one of the three largest oil and gas companies in China. Its subsidiary CNOOC Limited is listed on the Hong Kong Stock Exchange and is China's largest producer of offshore crude oil and natural gas.

China National Petroleum Corporation (CNPC): One of the three largest oil and gas companies in China, CNPC is a state-owned enterprise. Its subsidiary PetroChina Company Limited, a joint stock company and one of the world's largest oil and gas producers and distributors, is listed on the Hong Kong, New York, and Shanghai stock exchanges.

China Nonferrous Metals Mining (Group) Company Limited: This state-owned company is active in nonferrous metal mineral resources, construction, and engineering. Its subsidiary, China Nonferrous Metals Corporation Limited, is listed on the Hong Kong Stock Exchange.

China Petroleum and Chemical Corporation (Sinopec Limited): Sinopec Limited is a petroleum and petrochemical company listed on the London, New York, Hong Kong, and Shanghai stock exchanges. Its parent company, China Petrochemical Corporation, or Sinopec Group, is China's largest oil and gas producer.

China State Farm Agribusiness Corporation (CSFAC): One of the largest state-owned agricultural enterprises, CSFAC began operating as a subsidiary of China National Agricultural Development Group Corporation in 2009. CSFAC is active in outward agriculture investment and is closely associated with the Ministry of Agriculture.

Chinalco: See Aluminum Corporation of China.

Chinese Academy of Social Sciences (CASS): An academic research institution of social sciences that provides research and policy support to the Central Committee and the State Council of the Chinese Communist Party.

CITIC Energy: A Hong Kong–based subsidiary of the CITIC Group that focuses on energy.

CITIC Group: Originally established in 1979 as the China International Trust and Investment Corporation, the CITIC Group is a large, diversified, state-owned investment company with more than forty-four subsidiaries.

Communist Party of China (CCP): The founding party of the People's Republic of China, the CCP has been the ruling political party since the country's establishment in 1949.

Department of Foreign Aid: Under the auspices of the Ministry of Commerce, the Department of Foreign Aid organizes China's grant programs, zero-interest aid loans, youth volunteer programs, and technical assistance.

Department of Outward Investment and Economic Cooperation: This department operates under the auspices of China's Ministry of Commerce. The department's main function is to organize and coordinate the implementation of China's "going global" strategy; this includes guiding and regulating overseas investment, promoting economic and labor service cooperation, formulating annual inspections of investment activity, and protecting the rights of overseas workers.

Export-Import Bank of China (EXIM Bank): A state-owned bank under the leadership of the State Council that provides financing through concessional and commercial loans, as well as export credits, to support foreign trade, investment, and the export of Chinese products and services.

Industrial and Commercial Bank of China (ICBC): The largest of China's four state-owned banks, the Industrial and Commercial Bank of China is also the largest bank in the world as of July 2013.

Jiangxi Copper Corporation: This state-owned enterprise is China's largest copper producer. Its subsidiary Jiangxi Copper Company Limited is listed on the Shanghai and Hong Kong stock exchanges.

Maritime Customs Service: The Chinese Maritime Customs Service (the Imperial Maritime Customs Service prior to 1912) was a governmental tax collection agency and information service prior to 1949. In 1949 it was renamed General Administration of Customs in mainland China.

Ministry of Commerce (MOFCOM): China's Ministry of Commerce is responsible for formulating foreign trade policy, import and export regulations, consumer protection, foreign direct investments, market competition, and negotiating trade agreements. Formerly the Ministry of Foreign Trade and Economic Cooperation (MOFTEC), the ministry was reorganized and renamed in 2003. MOFCOM operates under the State Council.

Ministry of Environmental Protection: The Ministry of Environmental Protection, under the direction of the State Council, is tasked with developing and organizing the implementation of national policies and plans for environmental protection, drafting laws and regulations, and formulating administrative rules and regulations. It was previously the State Environmental Protection Administration (until 2008), and before that it was the National Environmental Protection Agency (until 1998).

Ministry of Foreign Affairs (MOFA): China's Ministry of Foreign Affairs is responsible for helping formulate, coordinate, and implement the PRC's foreign policy. The MOFA operates under the State Council.

Ministry of Land and Resources (MLR): The Ministry of Land and Resources operates under the State Council and was formed in 1998 when the Ministry of Geology and Mining, State Administration of National Land, State Administration of National Oceans, and State Bureau of Surveying and Mapping were merged. The MLR is responsible for the regulation, organization, exploitation, and preservation of natural resources, such as land, mines, and oceans.

Ministry of Metallurgical Industry: Now defunct, China's Ministry of Metallurgical Industry once controlled several construction companies and scientific institutions, as well as the mining conglomerate now known as China Metallurgical Group Corporation (MCC).

Ministry of Water Resources (MWR): China's Ministry of Water Resources is one of several departments under the State Council of China responsible for the administration of China's water resources. The MWR's duties include the protection and allocation of water resources, drafting legislation to protect water sources, flood and drought control, water conservation, water infrastructures, irrigation, and the management of crimes and foreign affairs related to water issues.

National Defense Planning Commission: See National Resources Commission.

National Development and Reform Commission (NDRC): Named the State Development Planning Commission until 2003, the NDRC, also referred to as the State Development and Reform Commission, is a macroeconomic management agency under the direction of the State Council. Its main function is "to formulate and implement strategies of national economic and social development."

National Environmental Protection Agency: See Ministry of Environmental Protection.

National People's Congress (NPC): The NPC is China's primary legislative body and the highest organ of state power in China. It convenes annually, together with the People's Political Consultative Conference; its main functions include the "formulation of laws, [delegation of] authority, policy formulation, and supervision of other governing organs."

National Resources Commission (NRC): Originally established in 1932 by the Nationalist government as the National Defense Planning Commission, the NRC's mission was to develop and manage all of China's basic industries, mines, and other enterprises. The NRC was abolished in 1952.

Nationalist Party (Kuomintang, or KMT): Founded by Sun Yat-sen, the Chinese Nationalist Party was the dominant governing party of China during the period 1928 to 1949. Led by Chiang Kai-shek, the KMT established the Republic of China on the island of Taiwan following the Chinese Civil War.

NORINCO (China North Industries Corporation): A state-owned enterprise involved in defense technologies manufacturing as well as domestic construction projects.

Organization Department of the Communist Party of China: Under the direction of the Communist Party's Central Committee, the Organization Department controls the personnel assignments for the Chinese Communist party.

PetroChina Company Limited: PetroChina Company Limited is China's biggest oil producer, and its stock is traded in New York, Hong Kong, and Shanghai. It is the listed arm of the state-owned China National Petroleum Corporation (CNPC).

People's Liberation Army (PLA): The PLA is the military arm of China's Communist Party and the armed forces of the People's Republic of China. The PLA operates under the command of the Central Military Commission of the Communist Party and is the world's largest military force by number of personnel.

People's Liberation Army Air Force (PLAAF): The aerial warfare branch of the People's Liberation Army, the PLAAF is under the command of the Central Military Commission of the Communist Party.

People's Liberation Army Navy (PLAN): The PLAN is the naval warfare branch of the People's Liberation Army. Like the PLAAF and PLA, it operates under the command of the Central Military Commission of the Communist Party.

Shenhua Group Corporation: The state-owned Shenhua Group Corporation is the largest coal-producing company in the world; one of its main subsidiaries, China Shenhua Energy Company, is listed on the Shanghai and Hong Kong stock exchanges.

Shougang Group: State-owned Shougang Group (also called Shougang Company Limited) is one of China's largest steel companies. It has subsidiaries listed in the Shenzhen and Hong Kong stock exchanges.

Sinochem Corporation: Sinochem Corporation is a Chinese holding group whose subsidiaries primarily engage in the production and trading of chemicals, exploration and production of oil, and operation of China's state fertilizer monopoly. In 2009, Sinochem Corporation was converted to a joint-stock company, while the holding group was renamed Sinochem Group.

Sinohydro Group: Sinohydro is a Chinese state-owned hydropower engineering and construction company. Its main subsidiary, Sinohydro Group Limited, is listed on the Shanghai Stock Exchange.

Sinosteel Corporation: Sinosteel Corporation is a raw material processing company and China's second-largest importer of iron ore. Sinosteel is a state-owned enterprise with eighty-six subsidiaries.

Standing Committee of the National People's Congress: The Standing Committee of the NPC is a committee of approximately 175 members of the NPC that has constitutional authority to modify legislation within limits set by the NPC.

State Council: The State Council is China's chief administrative authority. It is chaired by the premier, currently Li Keqiang, and includes the heads of ministries and commissions. The State Council is responsible for carrying out the principles and policies of the Communist Party and implementing the regulations and laws adopted by the National People's Congress.

State Electric Power Corporation: The State Electric Power Corporation is responsible for the management of China's grid and power plants. It is divided into five power generation companies and two distribution companies.

State Oceanic Administration: The State Oceanic Administration is a Chinese administrative agency responsible for the supervision and management of sea areas under the jurisdiction of the People's Republic of China, safeguarding national maritime rights and interests, and organizing scientific and technical research in China's waters. It operates under the Ministry of Land and Resources.

State-owned Assets Supervision and Administration Commission (SASAC): SASAC, under the direction of the State Council, was established in 2003 and is either the owner or the controlling shareholder of China's 112 (as of December 2013) most powerful state-owned enterprises. SASAC has the power to appoint top executives, authorize mergers or sales, and draft laws related to SOEs.

Wuhan Iron and Steel (Group) Corporation (WISCO): The Wuhan Iron and Steel Corporation, a state-owned enterprise, is one of China's largest steelmakers. Its subsidiary Wuhan Iron and Steel Company Limited is listed on the Shanghai Stock Exchange.

Yanzhou Coal Mining Company Limited: Yanzhou Coal Mining's main operations include underground coal mining, preparation and processing, sales, and railway transportation of coal. It is a subsidiary of the Yankuang Group Corporation Limited and is listed on the New York, Hong Kong, and Shanghai stock exchanges.

Zhenhua Oil Company Limited: Zhenhua Oil Company Limited is a state-owned oil firm that is a wholly owned subsidiary of China North Industry Corporation (NORINCO). Zhenhua is small compared to the three major Chinese oil companies.

Zhonghui Mining Group of China: Zhonghui Mining Group is the largest privately owned Chinese company operating and investing in sub-Saharan Africa.

Zijin Mining Group Company Limited: Zijin Mining Group Company Limited is a leading Chinese gold, copper, and nonferrous metals producer and refiner. It is a subsidiary of Zijin Mining Group and is listed on the Hong Kong and Shanghai stock exchanges.

INDEX